Producing Workers

Critical Histories

David Ludden, Series Editor

A complete list of books in the series
is available from the publisher.

Producing Workers

The Politics of Gender, Class, and
Culture in the Calcutta Jute Mills

Leela Fernandes

PENN

University of Pennsylvania Press

Philadelphia

10 9 8 7 6 5 4 3 2 1

Published by
University of Pennsylvania Press
Philadelphia, Pennsylvania 19104-6097

Library of Congress Cataloging-in-Publication Data
Fernandes, Leela.
    Producing workers : the politics of gender, class, and culture in
the Calcutta jute mills / Leela Fernandes.
        p.   cm. — (Critical histories)
    Based on the author's Ph.D. thesis, University of Chicago.
    Includes bibliographical references and index.
    ISBN 0-8122-3372-7 (cloth : alk. paper). — ISBN 0-8122-1597-4
(paper : alk. paper)
    1. Jute industry workers—India—Calcutta.   2. Women—Employment—
India—Calcutta.   3. Discrimination in employment—India—Calcutta.
I. Title.   II. Series.
HD8039.J82I4835   1997
331.2′047713′0954147—dc21   96-6524
                                                              CIP

For Enrica
and Herman Fernandes

Despite our desperate, eternal attempt to separate, contain and mend, categories always leak.

—*Trinh T. Minh-ha*

The superstructures of civil society are like the trench systems of modern warfare.
—*Antonio Gramsci*

I think my problem and "our" problem is how to have simultaneously an account of radical historical contingency for all knowledge claims and knowing subjects, a critical practice for recognizing our own "semiotic technologies" for making meaning and a no-nonsense commitment to faithful accounts of a "real" world, one that can be partially shared and friendly to earth-wide projects of finite freedom, adequate material abundance, modest meaning in suffering and limited happiness.

—*Donna Haraway*

Contents

Illustrations

Preface

This book is about the politics of categories, the political processes that produce our classifications of social and cultural identities, meanings, and practices. In recent years, the politicization of cultural identities such as religion, ethnicity, gender, and race have come to play a central role in shaping relations between nation-states and processes of state and nation building. Affiliations based on religion and ethnicity continue to interact with and contest secular identities of class and citizenship. Meanwhile, in both social movements and theoretical representations, there has been a growing recognition that universalistic categories such as "woman" and "worker" are contingent on multiple social locations, whether of ethnicity, class, race, or gender. Persistent issues of difference raise unsettling questions about the ways identities overlap and group interests are represented. Categories of action and analysis have thus become critical sites of political conflict and contestation.

My concern in this book is with the question of how we can conceptualize the intersections between such categories and identities. In this ethnographic study of working-class politics in the Calcutta jute mills, I argue that the boundaries of a particular category are produced in relation to other social categories or identities. I examine the ways boundaries between class, gender, and community are the products of political processes that unfold through institutional, discursive, and everyday social and cultural practices. Unions, managers, and workers attempt to preserve particular hegemonic representations of class, gender, and community even as such representations are interrupted by moments of contestation. I analyze this dialectic of hegemony and resistance in various sites, such as the labor market, the family, and community organizations.

Throughout this book, I move away from the "either/or" logic that has produced a series of oppositions—for instance, between class and community, capitalist and precapitalist, modern and traditional, and "East" and "West." Such binaries have often obscured the dynamism of working-class politics in India by continually measuring Indian workers against an idealized version of the actions of English or European workers. In this endeavor, my focus on the politics of gender plays a central role, since, as a long tradition of feminist research has shown, gender and women cannot easily be added to preexisting frameworks without unsettling their foundations. Thus, gender cannot be limited either to a "capitalist" or "precapitalist" terrain; meanwhile, the marginalization of women workers is a phenomenon that has crossed the borders between "East" and "West."

In the analysis that follows, I draw on varied disciplinary approaches, presenting a contemporary social history of the Calcutta jute mills both through the *longue durée* of the period from the 1950s to the present and through an analysis of what Anthony Giddens has called the temporality of everyday experience (1981: 19). I employ methods of participant observation, and in my representation of this research I draw on recent anthropological work that analyzes the politics of fieldwork. Finally, I argue for an approach to the study of politics that not only specifies which variable can explain a particular form of collective action but also recognizes that politics is about the negotiations of power over the boundaries between categories. For, as we will see in this book, the production of such boundaries has political and material effects for different groups of workers and shapes and circumscribes the political participation of workers. The interdisciplinary approach I have used will no doubt deviate in some way from the standards of what counts as "history," "ethnography," or a "science of politics," for it is often at the moment of transgression that we confront the materiality of boundaries, whether of categories or of disciplines. Nevertheless, I hope this book will contribute to the production of an analytical space that confronts the very real political implications of the categories we construct and deploy in both theory and everyday practice.

The research and writing that have gone into this project have benefited from the encouragement and critical feedback of a number of people. I began research for the book for my Ph.D. dissertation in political science at the University of Chicago. During this process, my dissertation committee, including Susanne Rudolph (chair), David Laitin, Lloyd Rudolph, and Bill Sewell provided tremendous intellectual support. The book has substantially benefited from their ability consistently to provide engaged feedback and guidance while allowing me to develop my own questions and arguments.

The fieldwork for the book, which I conducted in 1990–1991, could not have been completed without the generosity of many people. Piya Chatterjee shared her home and her family during my initial months in

Calcutta. Thanks also go to Blossom and Vijay Sampat for their hospitality during trips to Bombay. Mr. R. P. Chatterjee introduced me to the industry, shared his knowledge, and provided immense help. Mr. C. N. Chakrabarty, secretary general of the Indian Jute Mills Association, provided access to his organization's resources and source materials. In addition, thanks go to the following people for helping me with sources: Timir Basu, Gautam Bhadra, Rakahari Chatterji, Gautam and Manju Chattopadhyay, and Ranajit Das Gupta. Several leading trade union officials (who must remain anonymous) also helped with sources and shared their experiences and knowledge. Finally, my greatest debt is to the workers, union leaders, and managers at the jute mill that was my primary site of ethnographic research.

A MacArthur scholarship from the Council for Advanced Studies on Peace and International Cooperation at the University of Chicago enabled me to complete the first year of fieldwork in 1990–1991. The Committee on Southern Asian Studies at the University of Chicago provided funding for the second year of fieldwork as well as for a year of writing in Chicago.

After Chicago, the manuscript benefited from criticism and support from a number of people. Thanks in particular go to David Ludden for his early interest in the manuscript and the sharp questions that helped me rethink and reframe my arguments. His faith in this project helped me to gather the energy to keep working. I am delighted that the book is part of his new series.

During two years of teaching at Oberlin, Sonia Kruks and Paula Richman provided personal and professional support. Since then, Rutgers University has provided a dynamic intellectual environment for the production of the final version of my manuscript. A postdoctoral fellowship at the Center for the Critical Analysis of Contemporary Culture (CCACC) at Rutgers provided the time, space, and resources that allowed me to finish the book. Thanks go to all the fellows in the CCACC seminar whose lively weekly engagement helped me to think through my arguments: Barbara Balliet, Elaine Chang, Sue Cobble, Cyndi Daniels, Judy Gerson, John Gillis, Janet Golden, Ruthie Gilmore, Atina Grossmann, Radha Hegde, Carol Helstosky, Nicky Isaacson, Ynestra King, Vince Lankewish, Adriana Ortiz-Ortega, Loretta Sernekos, Caridad Souza, Meredith Turshen, and Carolyn Williams.

Various chapters have benefited from close readings by Amrita Basu, Dipesh Chakrabarty, Michael Dawson, Jane Junn, Roz Petchesky, and Brinda Rao. Two anonymous reviewers also provided extensive and helpful suggestions for revision that have substantially improved the book. Parts of the book also profited from presentations at the South Asia

Seminar at the University of Pennsylvania and a workshop on labor history at the Department of History, Calcutta University (co-organized by Erasmus University).

A portion of Chapter 3 appeared in revised form as "Contesting Class: Gender, Community and the Politics of Labor in a Calcutta Jute Mill," *Bulletin of Concerned Asian Scholars*, 26 (1994). Thanks go to editors Bill and Nancy Doub for permission to reprint the material. Thanks also to Mike Siegal in the Geography Department at Rutgers for preparing the illustrations for the book. Finally, I am grateful to my editor at the University of Pennsylvania Press, Patricia Smith, for her enthusiasm for and support of the book.

Throughout the exhausting process of revision, friends and family members provided personal support and necessary distractions. When I was exhausted, Susanne Rudolph's belief in this project at critical points kept me working. Ruthie Gilmore, Sanjay Gupta, Prema Kurien, Ellie Marks, Asha Rani, Brinda Rao, Amrita Shodhan, and Caridad Souza have provided personal support and fun times. Thanks go to my sister and brother-in-law, Pearl and Milbhor D'Silva, and to Karl, Natalie, and Christopher for spoiling me during numerous vacations in England. Finally, my parents, Herman and Enrica Fernandes, have always provided encouragement for my education and choices in life. This book is dedicated to their labor.

Abbreviations

AITUC	All-India Trade Union Congress
BJP	Bharatiya Janata Party
BCMS	Bengal Chatkal Mazdoor Sangh (Bengal Jute Workers Union)
BMS	Bharatiya Mazdoor Sangh (Indian Workers Union)
CITU	Center of Indian Trade Unions
CPI	Communist Party of India
CPI(M)	Communist Party of India (Marxist)
ESI	Employees State Insurance
FB	Forward Bloc
FB(M)	Forward Bloc (Marxist)
HMS	Hind Mazdoor Sangh (Indian Workers Union)
IJMA	Indian Jute Mills Association
INTUC	Indian National Trade Union Congress
NUJW	National Union of Jute Workers
PF	Provident Fund
UTUC	United Trade Union Congress

Chapter 1
Introduction

On November 9, 1991, the workers of the weaving department of a jute mill in Calcutta participated in a wildcat strike to protest the suspension of four workers, including the general secretary of one of the leading trade unions in the factory. Management had suspended the workers in retaliation for a conflict between the workers and supervisors earlier that day. The conflict had begun as a quarrel between two workers on the shop floor. A weaver was waiting for his machine to be fixed by a mechanic. The mechanic did not arrive on time, and the weaver was angry at being unable to work; since his was a piece-rated occupation, the delay had resulted in a loss of wages for the weaver. When the *mistri* (mechanic) finally arrived, an argument started; the mechanic injured the weaver with his hammer, and in the ensuing fight the mechanic was also injured. At this point the general manager and personnel manager happened to be in the department, and they took the two to the dispensary. The general manager tried to resolve the conflict, and he made the two workers shake hands.

On the same day, the weaver, accompanied by three other workers from his caste group, went to the weaving department in the mill and confronted the assistant manager. The general secretary of the leading trade union, who was also present at the scene, was angry that the quarrel had been patched up by management without his consultation. At this point a large crowd had gathered, and the general manager tried to defuse the situation. In the midst of the argument, one of the four workers pushed the assistant manager, who fell against a machine. Management, in retaliation, gave orders that the four workers were not to be allowed inside the factory. Since two of the workers were temporary workers, their names were simply struck off the employment list. The other two workers were suspended from work.

In response, the general secretary of the union led a deputation of about fifteen or twenty workers to the labor office and told the labor officer that if management did not withdraw the charge sheets in twenty-four hours, the union would take further action. Meanwhile, the union leader also filed a police report against the mechanic. Management wanted the mechanic to file a report, but he refused because he was receiving threats in the labor lines. The mechanic did not have access to adequate protection, since his caste group was much smaller and since in such cases police protection is usually insufficient. According to one labor officer, the mechanic was being hunted by the weaver's caste members and was therefore in hiding. At this point the union held firm, and speeches were given at a gate meeting. The first speech, delivered by the union's general secretary, was a direct attack on management for charge sheeting the workers. The leader argued that the management was persecuting workers who had worked in the mill for thirty years. He contended that the union did not want violence but that they would not accept injustice. He denied that there had been any assault on management during the conflict. On the following morning the leaders of the union walked into the weaving department and called for a wildcat strike. Although the weavers struck for one hour, the leaders were unable to mobilize workers from other departments, and the strike unraveled without any effective challenge to management.

The narrative of the events leading up to the strike weaves together a complex configuration of interests and identities based on class and caste. On one level, the issues represent a clearly defined workplace conflict. According to some workers, the union leaders were angry because the management resolved the conflict without adequately addressing the mechanic's negligence. Workers and unions in the factory continually complain that their work is made difficult because machines are old and supervisors are lax in securing repairs. The incident also involved a conflict over the symbolic exercise of authority in the factory. Several workers and labor officers indicated that the union leader was angry because he was not consulted before the manager made the two workers shake hands. The fact that the manager made them shake hands represented a direct symbolic attack on the leader's position of power in the factory.

A second political strand in the conflict requires that we shift from the conventional boundaries of workplace conflicts to the internal identities and interests within the jute workers' communities. The weaver who was involved in the conflict was from the *goala* (buffalo herder) caste, which enjoyed a high degree of political power in the workers' communities. The two main unions had thus been involved in a competition to win the support of workers from the goala caste. The goala caste members had largely been under the leadership of one union, but a fraction of the caste had shifted allegiance to the union leader involved in the conflict. It was this fraction that had become involved in the conflict. If the general secretary of the union was able to successfully defend the weaver and the three other workers, he would potentially increase his support of the caste members. The mechanic, however, was from the relatively weaker *lohar* (metal worker) caste. The incident points to the significance of caste allegiance in trade-union mobilization within the factory.

A third strand of conflict emerged in the subsequent union-management confrontation. One of the workers charge sheeted was the assistant secretary of the union in question. Given his prominent position, the union could not back down without significantly undermining its political position in the mill. Moreover, some managers privately admitted that they were trying to use the incident to undermine the union. One high-level manager went so far as to clearly state that they wanted to "break" the general secretary of the union. At this stage, the conflict took the form of a traditional class-based opposition between the union and management, one in which the union leaders were placed in a vulnerable position.

Viewed within the larger social milieu of the factory, the interplay between these strands becomes evident. Although the strike was contained within a single department (the weaving section of the mill), the entire factory became a stage for a fierce ideological battle to define the meaning and history of the conflict. On one level, this battle was carried out by management, the union, and workers not involved in the original conflict. While management engaged in the reconstruction of the conflict through notices posted in the factory, the union held gate meetings in which it denied allegations that members had assaulted the assistant manager. Several versions of the events spread through the mill. During the brief course of the conflict, the ideological contest far surpassed the specific characteristics of the conflict. The strike's leader became a symbol of a standard of justice and equality that workers were denied within the factory. The strike itself, meanwhile, became a symbol of protest against what workers termed the management's *jungli raj* (uncivilized kingdom).

The incident reveals the manner in which worker resistance, such as a strike, may arise out of conflicts and social hierarchies between groups of workers. In this case the caste allegiance of the weaver shaped the union's participation and occurred at the expense of the mechanic. However, once the conflict involved a union-management confrontation, it acquired a different meaning for the participants and the workers in general. The wildcat strike rested on a link between the workers' caste positions and union mobilization. However, the meaning of the strike was not limited to this caste relationship. To many workers not involved in the initial conflict, the strike represented a challenge to an unfair system of authority, that is, within the capitalist system in the factory.

In short, there was continual slippage between the politics of caste and class through this sequence of events.

This case, in which a dispute among workers was transformed into a confrontation between unions and managers, is an example of an important category of conflicts that take place in the jute mills. A particular group or community of workers may bring to management a grievance against another worker. If management does not take action, the community may then mobilize in protest. For example, in one case a woman worker was sexually assaulted by another worker in the factory. The woman worker's community leaders brought the grievance to management and demanded that the male worker in question be fired: the assault represented an attack on the *izzat* (honor) of the woman and her community. Management, under pressure from this community of workers, fired the male worker. The worker's union then organized a wildcat strike. The strike was unsuccessful, and the worker was not reinstated.[1] Regardless of the final outcome of the strike, the central point for our purposes is that in this context a gendered conflict based on cultural meanings of honor[2] was transformed into a union-management confrontation.

Such incidents of labor conflicts in the Calcutta jute mills bring to the fore the issue of overlapping and conflicting identities. How do we explain the meaning of such cases? One possible and often used explanation is that the case reflects the persistence of primordial, precapitalist relations in a largely "traditional" society. A second explanation is that affiliations of caste serve as resources that are used and manipulated by workers, unions, and managers. Both explanations rest on an assumption that there exist pre-given boundaries between social categories such as caste, class, and gender. The central questions in this context ask which categories are central at particular historical moments and in specific political contexts and how they interact with each other.

I focus here on a third interpretation of overlapping identities, one that analyzes the ways boundaries between social categories and identities are constructed. As Stuart Hall has suggested, social categories are not natural, transhistorical entities but are created and marked by the production of "political, symbolic and positional boundaries" (Hall, 1992a: 30). In the case I narrated earlier, for example, unions produced a form of working-class politics that was constructed through caste politics. The boundaries of class interests thus became contingent on caste hierarchies through a specifically political process that involved the participation of workers, unions, and managers in the factory. The wildcat strike represented the culmination of a political struggle in which unions were contributing to the creation of a class identity that was marked by a particular form of caste hierarchy. My argument is, first, that such cases of social and political conflict in the factory can be understood in terms of a process through which the boundaries between categories are created and contested through a set of political processes; and, second, that the boundaries of a particular category are both constructed through and challenged by other social identities.[3] For example, in the case of the conflict arising out of the assault on the woman worker, class is constructed through the politics of gender and community. Politics in this context is not merely about mobilization around particular predefined identities but involves continual contests of power over the relationship between such identities. The "purity" or distinctiveness of a category or identity, then, is not a given but an effect of power, where, as Stuart Hall has put it, particular social actors attempt to "police the boundaries" (1992a: 30) of the category; in this process such "purity" usually signifies a particular hegemonic representation of the relationship between the category in question (for instance, class) and other forms of difference (for instance, gender or caste).

My argument builds on research concerning the significance of the intersections between identities such as gender, race, and class (Sacks, 1990). In the field of feminist studies, for example, recent research has deconstructed the transhistorical, universalistic conception of "woman" as an "always already constituted category" (Butler, 1990; Mohanty, 1991) and demonstrated that explanations of women's practices and attitudes must be contextualized in relation to differences based on race, class, and national origin. Feminist scholars have argued that the limited participation of African-American women in the mainstream American women's movement is a consequence of the movement's focus on narrow definitions of gender oppression which do not address differences of race and class (Giddings, 1984; hooks, 1984). The point is not just that black and white women may have different interests but that a movement that focuses solely on gender oppression may in fact be transforming "woman" into an exclusionary racialized category; gender in this context becomes defined through the boundaries of race. As Jacquelyn Hall has argued, the mobilization of African-American women in feminist campaigns against rape depends on the ability of women's organizations to confront the historical phenomenon of lynching, the corresponding (mis)construction of African-American men as rapists, and the use of an ideology of the protection of white women in order to justify the lynching of black men (Hall, 1983). An analysis of African-American women's participation in the women's movement requires a shift from a focus on the level of gender consciousness of African-American women to an understanding of the complex historical relationship between race and gender in the United States. An understanding of the construction of gender through historical and social conceptions of race thus produces a new understanding of political participation in the American women's movement.[4]

Such theoretical developments have opened up the space for analyzing specific political outcomes as products of intersections between class, gender, and community or "interlocking systems of oppression" (Collins, 1990). What is at stake here is the longstanding notion that there are discrete boundaries that can demarcate categories such as gender, class, ethnicity or, at a broader level, realms such as culture, politics, and economy. The question at hand is how to further a conceptualization of such forms of "intersectionality" (Crenshaw, 1992: 404) and move beyond an "interaction" or "interplay" between discrete identities, terms that continue to suggest static distinctions between categories of social analysis.[5]

A study of the contemporary history of the Calcutta jute workers reveals that the political boundaries that delineate relationships between gender, community, and class are constructed and reproduced through the production of such spheres as the labor market, the working-class family, and community organizations. These boundaries are the product of hegemonic practices and discourses that build on and reproduce distinctions and hierarchies among workers. The labor market, a sphere often associated with the politics of class, is constructed through conceptions and hierarchies of gender and community. Meanwhile, particular models of the working-class family are created and enforced by practices and discourses shared by managers, trade unions, and workers' community organizations and do not exist as transhistorical signifiers of patriarchy and gender oppression. In this situation, contemporary labor politics is not merely the product of the links or interplay between the distinct spheres of work and family, class and community, or capitalism and patriarchy. Rather, the definition of the lines that demarcate each sphere involves continual negotiations of power through institutional, discursive, and everyday social practices (Acker, 1988; Mies, 1986; Glenn, 1992).

Exclusionary representations of class, gender, and community, which produce hierarchies between particular groups of workers, in effect signify the "trench systems of modern warfare" (Gramsci, 1971: 235) that preserve relations of domination and subordination. I suggest that hegemony is in fact centrally about the ways in which we produce boundaries between social identities within various arenas in civil society. For instance, when trade unions in India construct the boundaries of class identity and politics through gender hierarchies, they are transformed into a site for the reproduction of a particular structure of gender oppression. Or, to return to the example of rape and racial violence in the United States, when women's organizations or media representations of violence against women fail to interrogate historical constructions and present gender as a racialized category, they facilitate the production of racial hierarchies. In other words, the relationship between culture, or the "superstructures of civil society" (Gramsci, 235), and hegemony cannot stop at "the question of which aspect of one's cultural identity becomes the basis for collective political action" (Laitin, 1986: 97) but must also ask how the boundaries of this identity are produced by and in relationship to other social identities in the particular context in question.

By placing the process of the social construction of categories within a theory of hegemony, I conceptualize this process not as random or continually changing but as fundamentally linked to forms of available resources that Bourdieu has classified as economic, cultural, symbolic, and social "capital"[6] (1985: 724); the project of boundary formation thus rests on both discursive and structural conditions.[7] I attempt to integrate the discursive and structural dimensions of categories throughout my analysis in the book by specifically analyzing categories in both temporal and spatial terms (Giddens, 1981). I address the ways social location is contingent on "spatial practices" (de Certeau, 1988: 96) on the shop floor, in the labor lines, and during the enactment of religious ritual practices, which position workers through the creation of particular distinctions of class, gender, and community. Meanwhile, I analyze the production of such distinctions as a dynamic process that can be grasped by recognizing "the temporality of immediate experience" (Giddens, 1981: 19). Through this history of the everyday, I examine the ways in which practices of managers, union leaders, and workers produce such boundaries, and I address the differential material effects for different groups of workers.

These boundaries produce hierarchies and exclusions that in turn provide spaces for contestation. For instance, exclusionary trade-union practices that have rested on gendered conceptions of working-class interests have in the past provoked independent mobilization by women workers in the jute mills. Meanwhile, while the central trade unions manufacture and build on caste and ethnic hierarchies, marginalized workers have responded by participating in alternative community organizations and on occasion creating smaller, ethnically based unions. The activities of these alternative organizations then provide the basis for alternative conceptions of class. In this context, the construction of the category of class becomes a dynamic political process that produces both hegemony and resistance.

Rethinking Boundaries: Class, Gender, Community

Although I argue for a reconsideration of the ways in which we create categorical distinctions between gender, class, and community, I do not suggest that these categories are identical and interchangeable. The point is that rigid demarcation has often led to competition or firm oppositions between such categories through what Patricia Hill Collins has termed "either/or thinking." For instance, analyses of labor politics have often viewed differences of race or gender as divisive of class unity. Meanwhile, recent feminist work has criticized the way in which the desire for unity among women has allowed differences of race and class to be viewed as obstacles that must be overcome.[8] When such concepts are treated as fixed and unitary, intersections between these categories become exceptional cases that must be explained—or explained away.

The conceptualization of class and its juxtaposition to cultural identities of religion, ethnicity, or gender must be contextualized within the longstanding assumptions of both the Marxian and Weberian theoretical traditions. Although these two traditions, which shape most studies of working-class politics, are often seen as competing or conflicting approaches, they in fact rest on certain shared assumptions in their conceptions of class. Marx's conceptualization of class can be understood in terms of the two main dimensions of the "class-in-itself/class-for-itself" model. The first aspect of this model consists of the structural component, that is, the worker's relationship to the mode of production. The second dimension of Marx's formulation is represented by the development of class consciousness and political activity. The structural dimension of class was a necessary but not a sufficient condition for the formation of a class. For example, in his analysis of the peasantry, Marx argued:

In so far as millions of families live under economic conditions of existence that separate their mode of life, their interests, and their culture from those of other classes, and put them in hostile opposition to the latter, they form a class. In so far as there is merely a local interconnection among these small-holding peasants, and the identity of their interests begets no community, no national bond and no political organization among them, they do not form a class. They are consequently incapable of enforcing their class interests in their own name, whether through a parliament or through a convention.[9]

Aside from the disparaging nature of Marx's image of the peasantry, this analysis demonstrates the significance of the elements of consciousness and agency in Marx's conception of class. The development of class consciousness was not predetermined by the structural component, the "class-in-itself," but was fundamentally the product of a dynamic and ongoing political process (Fantasia, 1988).

The central limitation of Marx's conception, in my understanding, is not rigid economic determinism but the assumption that this political process inevitably leads to unity. According to Marx, the "interests and conditions of life within the ranks of the proletariat are more and more equalized in proportion as machinery obliterates all distinctions of labor,"[10] a process that transforms "class" into an unquestionably homogeneous category: "The unceasing improvement of machinery, ever more rapidly developing, makes their livelihood more and more precarious; the collisions between individual workmen and individual bourgeois take more and more the character of collisions between two classes. Thereupon the workers begin to form combinations (Trade Unions) against the bourgeois."[11] This political process centers on two related and simultaneous movements, the move toward unity through "combinations" among workers and the move toward opposition through "collisions" between workers and the bourgeoisie. One of the foundational elements of Marx's conception of class lies in the link between the opposition between classes and the unity within a class. In this conception, unity among workers is a precondition for the opposition between classes.[12] This unity forecloses the conceptual space for an understanding of differences that might exist within the working class or for the possibility of such differences forming a basis for an oppositional relationship between classes. In effect, the emphasis on unity presumes the unitary character of the working class.[13]

While Max Weber's approach appears on many levels in very different terms from Marx's formulation of the working class, both Weber and Marx share assumptions regarding the unitary nature of the category of class. Weber defined class as a purely economic category where "the factor that creates class is unambiguously economic interest, and indeed only those interests involved in the existence of the 'market.'"[14] In contrast to Marx's understanding, issues of consciousness and political activity are not germane to Weber's definition of class.[15] In Weber's conception, class is a measure of the economic standing of the individual and the corresponding influence on the individual's future life-chances. Class is thus a signifier of commonalities in the economic situation of individuals rather than a critical basis for political activity. Classes are therefore not communities; rather, community can be understood in terms of Weber's second ideal type, the status group.[16] In this approach, cultural and social characteristics fall outside the category of class. That is, the complex sociocultural meanings of honor or religious cosmologies that Weber discussed elsewhere in his work are distinguished and externalized from the concept of class.[17]

Differences notwithstanding, then, Marx and Weber both share the assumption that there exists a singular, homogeneous form of class interest and action. For Weber, it takes the form of a purely economic interest derived from the market situation. For Marx, it takes the form of a model of unified political action and the corresponding form of class consciousness. Both views implicitly separate cultural identities and difference from the notion of class. This separation is reproduced even in rich historical research on the cultural construction of class identity, perhaps best marked by E. P. Thompson's seminal work, *The Making of the English Working Class*. In Thompson's approach, class formation involves a dynamic process that builds on complex cultural traditions of workers, yet the "making" of the working class must culminate in a final product, one that acts or must act as a unified subject with common interests.[18]

Meanwhile, comparative studies have demonstrated that class formation in different nations may be characterized by variations in culture, identity, and politics and need not conform to a predefined ideal model of working-class behavior (Chakrabarty, 1989; Katznelson and Zolberg, 1986; Ong, 1988; Taussig, 1980). Feminist scholars, in particular, have contributed to these revisions, effectively showing that class can be conceptualized as a gendered category, one that rests on links between workplace and family, sexual divisions of labor, and constructions of masculinity and femininity (Barrett, 1988; Kessler-Harris, 1990; Scott, 1988; Milkman, 1987; Stansell, 1986; Zavella, 1987).

In my approach, class represents a social relationship constituted of three central tiers—structure, consciousness, and political activity.[19] Each of these tiers is constructed in turn through the categories of gender and community. Thus, "the working class" does not represent a singular unit but is constituted by status differences. In an attempt to bridge the formulations of both Marx and Weber, I integrate the Marxian conception of class with the Weberian notion of status. When I argue that class is "constituted" by status, I mean that, on one level, the meaning and boundaries of class vary according to the "elements" through which it is formed. On a second level, these varying meanings do not merely coexist in a pluralistic array but often compete or conflict with each other. Class is therefore both a constructed and a contested category—constructed and contested not merely by academics within the realm of theory but by workers themselves within the factory and working-class communities. My argument does not rest on a conception of class as a purely discursive formation. The boundaries that define class hierarchies are rigid and consequently serve as "structural" constraints on individual or collective action. However, such economic "structure" is not determinate, for, as I argue in Chapter 3, an analysis of the labor market reveals that the structure of the jute working class is produced by meanings of gender and community. In Chapter 3 I examine the gendered and community-based division of labor in the jute mill, in which the positioning of workers on the shop floor of the jute mill is shaped by notions of "appropriate" work for women workers and workers of particular ethnic groups. Hence, social locations based on both gender and community constitute the structural layer of class and do not merely circulate as external symbolic or ideological forces.

I use the term "community" here as a broad grouping that includes identities of religion, region, caste, and language. I do not hold, however, that these identities represent the primordial or natural antithesis to the construct of class. My approach thus departs from traditional approaches that rest on a juxtaposition between community and society (Tonnies, 1988: 223). The distinction has reappeared in various forms intended to demarcate separate and opposed spheres, whether in terms of rural and urban, religious and political, community and class, or, more generally, modern and traditional. Once these spheres are designated as distinct they are also often explicitly or implicitly linked by a teleology, in which the traditional would necessarily transform or evolve into the modern, particularly in regions categorized as belonging to the "Third World."[20] In recent years, this teleology has undergone significant reformulation and critical reappraisal[21] as it has become clear that "traditional" spheres, including cultural and religious practices, have yet to dissipate and have often provided critical bases of action. With scholars' increasing acceptance of the notion that the two spheres continue to coexist and interact, the direction of research has shifted to a need to specify and explain the nature of this coexistence and interaction.[22] However, the separation of the two realms has persisted.

My intention is to circumvent both the teleological perspective and the conception of the coexistence of the "modern" and the "traditional." I dispute the assumption that we must simply wait for workers to shed their "precapitalist" orientations and begin to behave as a unified working class, whether in resistance or in quiescence. It is unlikely that in time religious and caste consciousness will evolve into a sole preoccupation with "secular" workplace concerns. In Chapter 4 I examine the ways in which unions assert their legitimacy as leaders through religious ritual practices, a form of public political activity contingent upon the production of particular narratives of religious, class, and gender identity.

Finally, my approach to gender does not rest on biologically determined or natural differences between "men" and "women" (Butler, 1990; Scott, 1988). First, gender represents a type of "structuring" category, a form of "habitus" that produces and negotiates patterns within social and cultural life; in this sense, as I have noted earlier, gender represents a structural force and is not limited to a discursive or symbolic category.[23] In Chapter 5 I examine how a shared conception of gender structures both the public sphere of management authority and the subaltern public sphere of the jute workers. The second layer of my analysis builds on Joan Scott's conception of gender as a signifier of power relationships, specifically, in this case, relationships and distinctions of class (1988). Hierarchies between classes and identities within a class are constructed through gendered meanings. For example, the asymmetrical social relationship between workers and managers in the jute mills may be signified through the creation of a sociospatial distance between the managers' wives and the workers: managers' wives live within the factory compound but avoid being seen publicly in this space. Conceptions of gender that restrict the mobility of upper-class women thus also serve to reproduce class distinctions between management and workers. Meanwhile, the fact that sociospatial distance also characterizes the relationship between upper-class women and working-class women problematizes the category of "woman" and serves as a reminder that gender is marked by class boundaries.

The construction of gender is also contingent on the politics of community. For example, relationships between women workers are shaped by caste distinctions. Thus, a woman worker of a high caste will not eat in the house of a lower caste woman in the working-class residences. Women workers are further marginalized by the gender hierarchies in the workplace and trade unions, as well as in community organizations. As I argue in Chapter 6, the particular social location occupied by women workers provides the potential space for the development of critiques of existing social hierarchies in the industrial arena. Such critiques do not, however, arise naturally from women's experiences;[24] rather, their particular social location provides the space for "critical practices" (Hennessy, 1994) that challenge the production of hegemonic boundaries of class or community interests. Women workers in the jute mills demonstrate a critical consciousness of the limits of union activity, or, as I argue in Chapter 2, women workers have mobilized independently to confront management authority as well as the hegemony of unions.

The Politics of Categories: Toward a Comparative Perspective

What purpose, then, is served by an attempt to question boundaries, categories, and dichotomies? What are the consequences and relevance of muddying the theoretical waters of our social scientific categories and concepts? One of my aims is to further the development of a comparative analysis of social, historical, and political phenomena. I am not arguing that we should set aside questions of generality or comparativist methods and accumulate a series of disparate, "local" case studies. The point is to develop an analytical framework that can generate generalities without creating a hierarchy of cases, in which one context provides the basis for an ideal type and other contexts provide the field for the application and testing of this ideal type. The establishment of such a hierarchy in fact hinders the comparativist project by creating both methodological and theoretical biases. When categories of analysis are derived from particular contexts, general conclusions drawn from such analysis reflect the conclusions of these particular contexts and do not provide us with a *comparative* understanding of social and political phenomenon. This disjuncture is perhaps most evident when categories derived from a Western European context are transposed onto "Third World" cases. The use of an extended case study to question and rethink the theoretical boundaries and dichotomies at the basis of social science analysis is thus of fundamental significance to comparative analysis.

The historical and cultural specificities of postcoloniality which characterize the jute mills can deepen our understanding of the relationship between social categories. The significance of the "politics of categories" can be contextualized within a broader "critique of modernity" that has enabled analyses of the construction of knowledge and the political implications of theoretical representations. In particular, this critique has resulted in an interrogation of such binary oppositions as the "modern" and "traditional," and has pointed to the ways in which identities and categories are socially constructed. The differences associated with the context of Indian politics or labor politics in the jute mills can allow us to rethink these formulations rather than merely serve as a means of distinguishing Indian jute workers from American workers or Western workers. The task at hand, then, is not to identify caste as an affiliation peculiar to India (or the Calcutta jute mills) but to ask what the politics of gender, caste, and class can also teach us about the relationship between race, class, and gender in the United States or Britain (Beteille, 1991). This is a fundamentally historical and political undertaking, one that uses a contemporary postcolonial history to contribute to a reconceptualization of theoretical categories that have in fact been constructed through (often partial) representations of particular European historical contexts (Chatterji, 1993; Mitchell, 1988; Prakash, 1990; Said, 1978).

This study allows us to rethink specific political outcomes—such as, for example, the ways we analyze cases of contemporary labor politics in India or in an advanced industrial country like the United States. Let us consider first the case of labor politics in India. Studies of organized labor in India have concentrated on explaining their "exceptional" nature. Many studies, regardless of their ideological and theoretical positions, share the view that there is a universal form of labor organization and behavior: that is, the European industrial union, organized labor movements, and class parties. Where this form of organization is absent or weak, it becomes an exceptional phenomenon that must be explained, whether in terms of structural reasons, issues of consent and false consciousness, or a collective action problem. For instance, many studies have noted the absence of a unified national trade-union movement in India. On the one hand, trade-union organizations in India have been fragmented by their links to political parties; on the other hand, they have been overshadowed by a strong state and extensive state-sponsored welfare policies (Chatterji, 1980). Meanwhile, leftist political parties (most notably the various Communist parties) that have claimed to represent the interests of the working classes have only enjoyed limited regional success and have not significantly shaped the direction of national parliamentary politics in India.[25] The disunity or limited scope of "formal" labor organizations such as unions and political parties then serve as an unquestioned mark of the irrelevance of class in the schema of Indian politics. Such approaches rest on an assumption that equates class with specific forms of organization and ignores other channels for the expression of class politics, such as women's networks, community organizations, and other cultural modes of expression (Berger, 1989; Ong, 1988). The implicit separation between class and the politics of gender and community that lies at the basis of such approaches results in a predetermined understanding of labor politics in India.

The presumed separation between class and such cultural identities as community and gender has taken a specific form in the study of Indian politics: an assumption that natural boundaries separate capitalist and precapitalist traditions and behavior, with precapitalist traditions encompassing religious, ethnic, and caste communities. This assumption has resulted in several explanations of Indian labor politics. Approaches within the frameworks of both modernization and Marxist theory lead to the view that industrial workers in India may behave according to "precapitalist traditions" but that these workers will or should evolve into a secular, unified working class. For example, religious or caste divisions within the labor force are analyzed as divisive elements that will dissolve with the development of capitalism; the Indian working class will thus eventually resemble an idealized vision of a unitary working class.[26] In another variant, studies have assumed that industrial workers have been governed by precapitalist identities; the Indian worker is therefore "different" and cannot be understood in terms of class identities.[27] These approaches, while often starkly different in their approaches and conclusions, rest on a shared conception of the working class. This conception is caught within a framework that either implicitly or explicitly measures the behavior of the Indian working classes against an idealized image of the working class. In this framework, the Indian working class is either similar or different from the ideal type.[28] As Dipesh Chakrabarty has insightfully argued, the framework rests on the assumption that "workers all over the world, irrespective of their specific cultural pasts, experience 'capitalist production' in the same way" (1989: 223). On the one hand, the ideal type purports to represent the universal nature of working-class politics. On the other hand, studies that challenge or deviate from this type are characterized as "exceptional" cases.

Recent research in the field of labor history has attempted to confront the coexistence and interplay between capitalist identities of class and precapitalist identities and to address issues of difference within the working class (Chakrabarty, 1989; Das Gupta, 1994; Simeon, 1995; Sen, 1992).[29] In particular, Chakrabarty's interrogation of the subjectivity of the "working class" has significantly fueled a revision of the concept of class and the cultural assumptions inherent in universalistic categories such as "labor" and "capital." He nevertheless falls short in his attempt to rethink the nature of the relationship between class and other social categories such as ethnicity, gender, and religion. Aside from the fact that gender is clearly not present as a category of analysis in his argument, his approach continues to rest on a juxtaposition of class with ethnicity and religion. Thus, although Chakrabarty presents a powerful critique of the presumed "uniform, homogenized, extrahistorical subjectivity" of the working class, he implicitly reproduces these assumptions in his analysis by slipping into the notion that identities of religion, language, and ethnicity are "narrower" than the identity of the "worker" (1989: 194). Chakrabarty subsequently forecloses the possibility of a reconception of class produced through (rather than necessarily opposed to) the politics of community (or gender). This issue points to a deeper limitation of Chakrabarty's conception of culture, which rests on an assumed juxtaposition of the "notion of a pre-capitalist 'community'—distinguished by hierarchical, inegalitarian, and illiberal relationships—and the notion of individualism that has been with us since the rise of the bourgeois order in Europe, entailing ideas of citizenship, equal rights, equality before the law" (Chakrabarty, 1989: 219). Chakrabarty's point is to question the cultural assumptions inherent in Marx's thought and to rethink the concept in light of the politics of cultural identity in colonial India. However, his framework reproduces an uninterrogated opposition between India and the "Western" (Enlightenment) tradition. Although Chakrabarty analyzes the significance of cultural hierarchies within the jute working class through a rich and complex historical analysis, the cultural and colonial difference that marks working-class politics in India is presented in frozen opposition to an idealized European version.

A long tradition of feminist research on gender hierarchies has already called into question idealized notions of cultural traditions within the working classes in Europe and the United States (Acker, 1988; Barrett and Hamilton, 1986; Kuhn and Wolpe, 1978; Davis, 1983; Scott, 1988). The analysis of gender is of fundamental significance, for it takes us beyond the capitalist/precapitalist or First World/Third World divides that often shape the direction of social science theory and research. In this context, cultural hierarchies would not signify a motionless difference between Indian culture and Western "hegemonic bourgeois culture" (Chakrabarty, 1989: xi) but would be used to engage with the contested meanings of "citizenship" and "equality" that have arisen from debates over gender, ethnicity, and racial difference in the "West." To think about the construction of categories in this way gives us space for a comparative perspective that can move us away from easy oppositions between "East" and "West" without erasing important historical differences.

A genealogical approach that addresses the process of production of categories can enrich comparative historical and political research by contributing to the explanation of outcomes in different contexts. We must, however, move away from a juxtaposition of the "context of discovery," in terms of the construction of categories and identities, and the "context of justification," where we delineate specific causal mechanisms in order to provide explanations for particular outcomes (Connolly, 1992; Harding, 1987; Somers and Gibson, 1994). In the United States, for example, the apparent absence of class politics provides a strong parallel to the Indian case. There is a significant school of literature that both explains and criticizes the argument of exceptionalism in the U.S. context.[30] My theoretical argument, based on the Indian case, can contribute to the possibility of reinterpreting the category of class in this debate—for instance, in relationship to the politics of race (Roediger, 1991). Stereotypes of African-American women on welfare[31] point to the ways in which the boundaries of class politics in the United States cannot be fully understood without also focusing on discourses of race and gender, particularly when such racialized representations are reproduced by white, working-class communities. An understanding of class politics in the United States may necessitate a shift from the study of traditional organized labor unions to the politics of race and community (Anderson, 1990). Different forms of community organization within African-American communities, then, potentially serve as better markers of class resistance than more traditional workplace resistance.

Crossing Boundaries: From the Practice of Representation to the Politics of Methodology

The methodological and representational practices I have used are fundamentally linked to the theoretical arguments of this book and provide an additional lens for viewing the significance of the relations between social identities. I conducted research in Calcutta over an eighteen-month period. I interviewed jute workers, managers, and union leaders at the factory level, met with West Bengal and national trade union leaders, and visited various mills in Calcutta and in neighboring rural areas in West Bengal. The primary focus of my field research, however, was one jute mill in Calcutta. A study based in Calcutta seemed ideal, since West Bengal has witnessed a long history of militant labor activism. The jute labor force, in particular, represents one of the most politically organized labor forces in India. The postcolonial period has witnessed seven prolonged general strikes that have shut down the industry. Moreover, the work force, comprised largely of rural migrants from various states in India, has been characterized by regional, religious, and gender diversity.

The jute industry itself, first established in the nineteenth century by Scottish industrialists, is one of the oldest industries in India. The industry is concentrated around Calcutta, where a series of jute mills is spread over the banks of the Hooghly river in West Bengal (see Figure 1). In the early part of the nineteenth century, the production of jute sacking and cloth was performed by Bengal handloom weavers. Jute gained international significance when tensions between Russia and Britain induced industrialists in Dundee, Scotland, to find a substitute for Russian flax. Jute soon became a cheap, attractive resource for the Scottish industry. The Bengal handloom industry faced a rapid decline after 1830, when the expansion of the Scottish industry made it increasingly profitable to export raw jute to Dundee (Gadgil, 1971: 57). The decline of the indigenous Indian jute handloom industry was consolidated when Scottish entrepreneurs established jute mills in Bengal in the mid-nineteenth century. The first jute mill set up in Calcutta in 1855 marked the beginning of the history of the Bengal jute mills. As jute became an increasingly profitable investment, the industry expanded significantly: in 1882 there were twenty jute mills; by 1919 this number had risen to seventy-six operating mills (Gadgil, 1971: 59). The labor force for these factories was recruited from rural areas in northern and eastern India, primarily from the states of Bihar, Uttar Pradesh, and Orissa (see Figure 1).

In the early years of Indian independence, the jute industry remained a central component of the West Bengal and Indian economies. In the 1950s jute goods represented one of India's primary foreign exchange

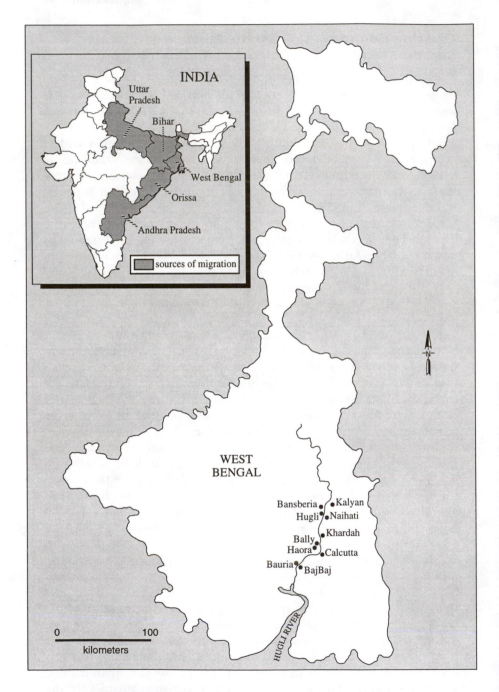

Figure 1. Jute Mill Areas in West Bengal

earners, comprising about 60 percent of all of India's dollar earnings.[32] This picture of the "golden fiber," however, has undergone stark revision in recent years. Competition from cheap paper and synthetic substitutes and from Bangladeshi jute products has plunged the industry into economic crisis, which has led to an exacerbation of labor-management conflict as management attempts simultaneously to reduce the labor force and increase labor productivity.

When I began my research, I was preoccupied with the effects of this crisis. I was particularly concerned with the fact that one of the primary consequences of labor force cutbacks was the displacement of women workers from the industry. The proportion of women employed in the jute mills had shrunk from approximately 20 percent in 1950 to less than 2 percent of the work force in the 1990s. I began my fieldwork in 1989 with a relatively modest question in mind: "Why did the economic crisis result in the differential displacement of women from the jute labor force?" I proceeded to focus my research on one jute factory in Calcutta. After receiving permission from factory management, which I gained through a personal contact[33] in the industry, I began to visit the mill on a daily basis for a period of eight hours. I began to conduct interviews with management, union leaders, and workers (both male and female). The most significant insight I gained in this process often resulted not from formal interviews but from participation in and observation of a wide array of incidents—informal conversations, spontaneous arguments between managers and union leaders, and religious rituals and festivals. The most significant aspect of the research lay not in the range of causal explanations I could obtain regarding the retrenchment of women workers but in an analysis of the political processes that unfolded on the shop floor and in workers' communities. The force of my argument thus does not rest on the economic position of the industry and the question of whether jute is a dying commodity. In fact, many of the patterns and processes of factory politics that build on and reconstitute gender or community have parallels in the most modern industries, whether they are multinationals in "Third World" areas or factories in advanced industrial countries (Fernandez-Kelly, 1983; Ong, 1992).

My starting point consisted of a recognition of the value of interpretative approaches. As Clifford Geertz incisively argues:

The methodological problem which the microscopic nature of ethnography presents is both real and critical. But it is not to be resolved by regarding a remote locality as the world in a teacup or as the sociological equivalent of a cloud chamber. It is to be resolved—or, anyway, decently kept at bay—by realizing that social actions are comments on more than themselves; that where an interpretation comes from does not determine where it can be impelled to go.

Small facts speak to large issues, winks to epistemology, or sheep raids to revolution, because they are made to. (1973: 23)[34]

Recent anthropological and feminist research has also brought to the forefront the limitations and "partial truths" produced by the methodologies we employ in the field.[35] The ethnographer has been displaced from the position of detached observer, and attention has increasingly been drawn to questions of the social identity and position of the researcher, the practices of ethnographic writing, and the politics of such representation (Behar and Gordon, 1995; Clifford and Marcus, 1986; Haraway, 1988). New self-reflexive methodologies have resulted in increasingly fluid boundaries separating methodology, theory, and representation. Such research has often focused on the politics of representation of ethnographic subjects. The situation in the field is, however, more complex, for there is often a reversal of the methodological problematic of the "self-other" relationship between the ethnographer and the research subject. In the factory, I found that workers and managers constructed me in a variety of ways as the "other."

During the initial period of my fieldwork, when I began to establish my presence in the factory, workers and managers were analyzing me. Management's permission to allow me to visit the factory was by no means unconditional: I had to confine myself to the factory area and not go to the workers' residences across the street; I was not to go onto the shop floor unless I was accompanied by a supervisor. Management provided me with office space for my personal use. These rules represented a dual process. On one level, they were clearly aimed at controlling my research and containing it within the sphere of management authority by specifying appropriate social locations. It was thus of central importance that I conduct my research in the factory compound and not in workers' residences, a space that management cannot supervise as effectively. On another level, management was attempting to construct a clearly defined class position for my presence in the mill. In a context where social divisions and hierarchies are symbolized even by the chair in which one sits (managers sit behind the desk, union leaders sit on regular chairs, workers stand or sit on wooden benches), a pretense of "classlessness" was, at best, irrelevant.

My social location was constructed through the politics of class, caste, and gender. The factory consisted of a labor force of approximately four thousand workers, of which less than two hundred were women. On the management side, there was only one female labor officer, who had recently been hired. The factory therefore represented a male domain. Although the management residences were in the mill compound, management wives and daughters generally did not enter either the management offices or the factory. The concept of an upper-class Indian woman walking around a factory and conversing with workers and union leaders went against the grain of the social and cultural norms that define caste, class, and gender. As the general manager said to me on my first day, "You can do it but it is not *appropriate* for you." With time I was eventually able to circumvent such strictures and to conduct interviews in both the factory and the labor lines—managers had to focus on maintaining production levels and could not spend their entire day watching over me. As I began to develop contacts with union leaders and workers, a few managers did resist speaking with me or providing information. This resistance was often subtle: the personnel manager, for example, would only agree to speak with me at 7 A.M. for no more than fifteen minutes at a time, and other supervisors would assure me that they would meet with me but would fail to keep appointments.

By analyzing these reactions to my own presence in the factory, I was able to deepen my understanding of the politics of class and gender. Consider the following example of an interaction early in my fieldwork. Management had specified that I should travel to the mill by taxi rather than by bus. In this way I would not have to stand outside the factory waiting for a bus. The well-intentioned purpose was to protect me from any undesirable incident, for the surrounding industrial area was considered "unsafe." This notion of protection also embodies, however, a much deeper ideology of protection that constricts the life of middle-class women. As I argue in Chapter 2, such norms have also been translated into the state "protective legislation" for women workers (including the prohibition against nightshift work for women and the provision of maternity benefits). Since the goal of my fieldwork was to traverse these protective boundaries, I would stop the taxi at the factory gate and then walk the length of the factory to the management building (instead of being driven to the door of the building). On the third day, the gate watchman (*durwan*) came up to me and exclaimed in frustration, "Why do you stop at the gate? Why can't you just take the taxi in?"

This incident brings together the central theoretical issues of this book. On one level, the watchman's response signifies the centrality of the spatial reproduction of class and status divisions. I would be breaking rigid class and status divisions by walking in the mill compound and sharing the same physical space with workers. However, the reason offered for preserving the spatial separation was presented in terms of my vulnerability as a woman. On the one hand, gender served as the means for the reproduction of a particular form of class hierarchy. On the other hand, this response also points to the reproduction of a form of gender hierarchy, where, as I indicated earlier, ideologies of protection may be used to circumscribe the movements of middle- and upper-class women.

Aside from these interpretations of the meanings of the watchman's response, the fact remains that my action was placing his job in jeopardy. If an "incident" were to occur, he risked being fired. The gateman's response must be understood in terms of his analysis of the hierarchical class relationship between his position and mine. If I had continued my act of walking in the factory with the aim of breaking class boundaries, I would in fact have been asserting my class position by superseding the gateman's authority. Needless to say, from then on I stayed inside the taxi.

An analysis of the interactive and oppositional relationship between my position as ethnographer and those of the workers and managers not only sheds light on issues of methodology but also represents a type of research finding. In this case, it demonstrates the interweaving of class and gender in everyday factory politics. Bourdieu has argued that "the presuppositions inherent in the position of an outside observer, who, in his preoccupation with *interpreting* practices, is inclined to introduce into the object the principles of his relation to the object, is attested by the special importance he assigns to communicative functions (whether in language, myth, or marriage)" (1977: 2). I suggest that a critical interrogation of such "presuppositions" can be conducted not just by a refinement of the researcher's approach, whether in terms of methodological practices or theoretical questions, but through an analysis of workers' and managers' reactions to my project. In effect, the response is based on an analysis of the ethnographer as an outsider and as a privileged "other." This otherness of the ethnographer does not contradict the fact that the researcher continues to occupy a position of power and privilege. (I must emphasize that the point is not to sympathize with a "helpless field researcher" in an alien context.) The researcher still chooses to enter, study, and leave the field and then acquires the authority to represent the experience.

The construction of the ethnographer's otherness is a continually shifting process, changing with time and context. Management's perceptions of my position and attempts to clearly designate my location in the mill were quite different from the perceptions of women workers. Union leaders, meanwhile, clearly understood that I was dependent on management for continued access to the mill. They would often provide me with information about where particular managers were in the factory in case I wanted to interview them or in case I needed to avoid them in order to speak with particular workers; at other times they would ask me if I knew where a particular manager was. In short, they incorporated me in a system of worker surveillance in which managers' movements are tracked in the mill. The union leaders, in particular, could relate to the way I was negotiating my location between managers and workers partly because in their own work their success depended on access to management. I often found myself waiting with union leaders in the management buildings, and I established connections with them in the process. Clearly, different groups in the mill constructed and interpreted my position in very different ways.

By categorizing the researcher as "other," I seek not to imply that I had a static or essentialized position in the factory but rather to find a means to reintroduce an additional narrative of the agency of the "subject," in this case of workers and managers. As Donna Haraway has argued, "coming to terms with the agency of the 'objects' studied is the only way to avoid gross error and false knowledge" (1988: 592). This was a crucial task in the process of conducting fieldwork, since this agency (workers' resistance, everyday practices, and identities of class, gender, and community) was one of my central subjects of study. I also want to make it clear, however, that I am not reverting to an argument that one should reproduce the workers' or managers' representation of his or her world as an authentic or "innocent" narrative without critical analysis; moreover, this agency does not transcend my own textual practices and strategies of representation. My goal is to link such modes of representation to the political dynamics of fieldwork by reintroducing a narrative of the workers' and managers' responses to and interpretations of my position as ethnographer.

Many conventional methods used to conduct field research exclude or silence resistance, particularly of subaltern subjects. The notion of the interview, for example, proved inadequate in many situations in my fieldwork. I often could not interview just one person, because other people would enter and a conversation would ensue. Such interventions often occurred even when I was interviewing management in their offices. During interviews with the personnel manager in the mill, for example, union leaders would often walk in and join our conversation.

There are two conventional options for interpreting this situation. First, the session could be dismissed (since a private, confidential interview was not conducted) and excluded from the ethnographic record or representation that is developed. A second, more insightful, option would be to analyze the cultural implications of the situation. The interview method assumes that there is a "private" space and that this space will be made available to the interviewer. Furthermore, the method contains the implicit cultural assumption that interaction can be defined in terms of individuals rather than groups.

I suggest that there is also a third possible interpretation of the inadequacy of the interview. The example I have described consists of the transformation of the interview into a *conversation*. This transformation signifies a shift in the structure and therefore the relationship of power that defines the interaction. The use of the interview represents an assumption of control. The act of another person—in this case, a union leader—walking in during an "interview" effectively dispels this control. This act represents an implicit rejection of the interviewer's authority over the dynamics of social interaction. The researcher trying to structure interviews is in a sense implicitly engaged in a political conflict as she tries to construct and impose a particular form of interaction from which to retrieve "information." I define the conflict as political because of the elements of power and hierarchy (whether of race, class, gender, or nationality) that characterize the relationship between researcher and subject. As Haraway has aptly noted, "accounts of a 'real' world do not, then, depend on a logic of 'discovery,' but on a power-charged social relation of 'conversation'" (1988: 593).

Consider the inadequacy of some of the more basic tools of the field-worker, such as the camera, the tape recorder, and, of course, the pencil and pen. In the jute mill where I conducted research, use of a tape recorder was out of the question. Labor-management conflict in the jute mill is highly volatile. Moreover, managers and workers alike face the continual underlying threat of suspension or dismissal. Any attempt to use a tape recorder would have produced unproductive conversations and interviews. Furthermore, the tape recorder becomes a symbol of power because it represents a particular level of privilege—not merely of money but of technology. These tools are inadequate not just because they create an additional divide between researcher and subject but because they create the impression that the ethnographer occupies a position external to (and above) the context in question. On many occasions I found it more useful to put down the pen and memorize the interview.

The separation between the academic and the field, however, does not preclude the naturalization of the researcher's position in the field. Workers and managers often created space for me in accordance with their codes of honor, courtesy, and kindness. Perhaps the best example of this accommodation occurred during the Id-ul fitr festival being held by Muslim workers in their quarters. During this event I was allowed in the mosque with approximately three hundred male workers. The Muslim community leaders broke crucial gender codes in their act of courtesy. By the end of the eighteen months I had been accepted as a routine fixture in the mill, and both workers and managers expressed surprise and disappointment at my departure.

This process of naturalization is always contingent on the particular position of the researcher. The fact that I was accepted does not mean that my class and gender position was in any way less important. On the contrary, the ethnographer is naturalized in terms of social location—that is, as a Western female or a Westernized male Indian, and so forth. The fact that I was constructed as "Indian," for example, must have facilitated the process of naturalization.[36] Although this is a significant point, the field method is still contingent on the construction of one's identity in terms of language, religion, gender, and class (Narayan, 1993). Such methodological interventions can be made to work in conjunction with the theoretical understanding of the intersections of class and gender in factory politics in contemporary India. I therefore insert my own position as ethnographer in the representation of the research in this study. This self-reflexive analysis of my methodological practices in the factory sheds light on the complex configurations of the politics of gender, community, and class in the Calcutta jute mills. On one level, responses of unions, managers, and workers to my position as female ethnographer demonstrate the gendered nature of class politics. On a second level, my analysis decenters the category of "woman" by refuting any claim to authenticity or access based on a self-conceived identity as an "Indian woman." This is perhaps best embodied in one woman worker's ironic analysis of my methods: "We are not educated like you. You can understand the world. We have to see to our compulsions [*majboori*] in our lives." My point is not that my interactions with women workers were only or primarily oppositional. For instance, many women I interviewed volunteered information about experiences of sexual harassment and specifically asked me to write down things they would say. However, calling attention to such resistance provides an effective means for avoiding an essentialized understanding of the category of "woman" or a universalistic conception of the system of "patriarchy." Self-reflexive methodologies can thus be transformed into textual strategies that do not claim to uncover a more authentic story but that can contribute to the reconfiguration of theoretical categories.

Outline of the Book

Chapter 2 provides a discussion of the common discourses of the state and trade unions: both entities conceive of labor as a monolithic category that transcends differences of gender and community, and this conception shapes the production of the legitimate boundaries of labor politics in the jute industry. Chapters 3, 4, and 5 examine the construction of class, community, and gender in the jute mills. Chapter 3 analyzes the effect of the politics of gender and community on the labor market and the structure of the jute labor force. Chapter 4 focuses on trade unions' use of religious rituals to reinforce their political legitimacy and to thereby create particular narratives of community identity, a process that occurs in a gendered public sphere and rests on the exclusion of women workers. Chapter 5 examines further the dynamics of this gendered public sphere. In particular, the chapter analyzes the enforcement of patriarchal models of the working-class family by unions and workers' community organizations. In Chapter 6, I examine particular life histories of women workers in the mill. The chapter explores the potential for the social location of women workers to serve as a source of resistance to the hegemonic practices of unions and community organizations. Finally, Chapter 7 considers the possibilities the genealogical approach of the study holds for recasting existing approaches to working-class politics.

The point of analyzing the constructed and contested nature of social classifications is not to question the analytical boundaries between such social categories as class, gender, and community. Clearly, such categories are of fundamental importance to my argument. The boundaries that define such categories as "worker," "family," or "woman" are real (and material), and often rigid. But the questions are: Who sets these boundaries? Who challenges their position and contests the spaces that lie within their borders? The answers are fundamentally political, and are continually produced and contested by workers, unions, and managers.

Chapter 2
Hegemonic Inventions of the "Working Class": The State, Unions, and Workers

The state and national trade unions in India have generated a set of shared discourses on the nature and interests of the industrial working classes. Such discourses have rested on a vision of the working class as a monolithic entity, where the identity of the worker is distinct from and superior to differences or hierarchies of gender, religion, language, or caste. In this vision, differences have either been suppressed or presented as "special" interests external to the primary general interests of the working class. The state, employers, and unions have then used this difference as the space for compromise, particularly during periods of crisis, conflict, or negotiation. For instance, political conflict generated by labor force cutbacks in the organized sector of the economy has often been resolved through the retrenchment of women workers. The result is a paradox wherein the national trade unions are transformed into organizations that defend the interests of particular sections of the work force while claiming to represent the interests of all workers—a claim contingent on the assumption that the issue of gender is external to the interests of the working class. The image of a unitary working class has played a significant role in producing forms of exclusionary trade union activity, thereby exacerbating the disjuncture between the national trade union organizations and the formation of an inclusive, mass-based labor movement.

State and union representations of the working class have not formed a coherent or "organized" system of ideas and beliefs; issues of culture and gender in fact often appear to linger on the margins of the formal ideologies and institutional arrangements in the Indian industrial arena. However, as I argue in this chapter, the construction of a monolithic working class is accomplished in various discursive sites—for example, in trade unions across the ideological spectrum and in particular arenas of state policy. Such discursive sites constitute the ideological trenches (Gramsci, 1971) that have facilitated the hegemonic incorporation of Indian trade unions, first by weakening the potential for the development of an independent national labor movement and then by allowing unions to serve as the sites for the production of social hierarchies and the exclusion of particular groups of workers.

Studies of Indian labor politics have explained the weakness of the Indian labor movement in terms of the particular historical and institutional characteristics of the system of industrial relations in India. Such studies document the debilitating effects of the legal and procedural issues regarding the recognition of trade unions, the links between unions and political parties, and the state-dominated system of compulsory adjudication on the development of a unified, independent national labor movement (Chatterji, 1980; Ramaswamy, 1984; Rudolph and Rudolph, 1989). Industrial workers in India have been represented by a politically fragmented trade union movement. Meanwhile, the realm of industrial relations has been dominated by a strong state that has claimed to represent the interests of labor. In this institutional context, Indian trade unions have been incorporated within a hegemonic bloc and have historically consented to the exercise of state power within the formal system of industrial relations in India (Chatterji, 1980; Rudolph and Rudolph, 1989). This framework has encompassed trade unions with sharply conflicting ideologies, including the liberal Congress Party union, the Communist trade unions, and unions affiliated with the right-wing Bharatiya Janata Party.

My present concern is with the ideology that has facilitated this direction of union activity and has allowed unions to act as the "trench systems of modern warfare" (Gramsci, 1971: 235) in the Indian industrial relations regime. My primary focus is not on the specific institutional constraints that have shaped contemporary labor politics or the differences in the formal ideological platforms of the unions and the political parties with which they are affiliated. The ideology that operates implicitly across the political spectrum of the central trade unions as well as within state policies can be understood in terms of union and state discourses that have centered on a conception of a monolithic working class even while reproducing inequalities between groups of workers. The national trade unions have indeed shared an exclusionary construction of the working class that has suppressed differences of gender and community and subsequently reproduced hierarchies that, as I will demonstrate in later chapters, play a central role in working-class politics at the local level of the shop floor and community. The result is a gulf between trade unions and marginalized sectors of the Indian labor force.

The Political Incorporation of Trade Unions

The political incorporation of Indian unions has centered on the development of particular links and dependencies among unions, political parties, and the state.[1] The central trade unions are formally bound by party policy and ideology, and they rely on political parties for legitimacy and support. Unions form an intrinsic part of the party machine apparatus, providing a base of support and mass mobilizational capacity for parties. In practice, the strength of a trade union is not merely dependent on its separate links with the state and a particular political party. Union strength is also dependent on the relationship *between* the political party and the state (in terms of both the central and state governments). A political party in power is in a position to favor its trade-union wing, which is then able to obtain advantages not only via its party but also through the government. The connection between the political system and the state-centered industrial-relations regime has been conducive to relationships of political patronage. The union-party-state nexus has been a defining characteristic of the industrial system, one that distinguishes Indian unionism from an ideal model of pluralism and places it closer to a model of societal corporatism (Schmitter, 1974). This nexus represents the crux of the political incorporation of national trade unions in India. Unions continue to represent a form of associational activity within the sphere of civil society, but an underlying continuum persists among union, political party, and state. The primary political purpose of a union has been to support the aspirations of its own political party rather than to challenge the system of industrial relations or to develop an organization independent from the political party. Although the aim of the union is to gain access to state power through its party, the result is the reinforcement of state power within the industrial realm.

The ability of unions to act as a bridge between the state and the industrial arena has been consolidated by the internal organizational structure of the unions. The national trade union federations have four levels of organization: first, the central leadership that represents the union at the national level; second, the state committees of the union; third, various industrywide federations at both the national and the state level; and, fourth, the actual plant-level units of organization.

The formal union structure follows a hierarchical model, and the various levels are linked through committees and dual representation. A leader may be involved in organizational activity at a certain level but may have formal or informal ties with one or more of the other levels. Such ties are strengthened by the fact that organizational offices of industrywide unions and the state committee are often housed in the same building or in the same room. However, the degrees of autonomy vary greatly. In some cases, for example, shop-floor units may barely reflect the formal policies of their industry, regional, or national units. The quality of leadership, organizational resources, nature of vested interests, patronage politics, conflicts between central and local leaders, and regional variations in interests are factors that determine the degree of autonomy between the various levels of organization.

There is a direct link between the central union leadership and its affiliated political party. This relationship is characterized by a "revolving door" phenomenon among the party and trade union leadership. High-level union representatives at the national and state levels are "professional" leaders rather than worker leaders, and trade-union leadership often serves as a vehicle for entry into high-level party and electoral participation. To some extent this professionalization of union leadership must be qualified by generational factors. Older leaders who participated in the early trade union movement during the colonial and the early independence years often view trade unionism primarily as a social and political movement. The new generation of leaders, on the other hand, often regards unionism in terms of political careerism (Ramaswamy, 1983: 80).

On a formal ideological and institutional level, the central industrial trade unions have tended to consent to incorporation within the state-oriented system of industrial relations, as revealed by an analysis of three of the central national unions: the Indian National Trade Union Congress (INTUC), the Bharatiya Mazdoor Sangh (BMS), and the Center for Indian Trade Unions (CITU). The Indian National Trade Union Congress, one of the prominent national labor federations, has enjoyed the advantages of its affiliation to the Congress Party, the dominant political party in the post-independence period. State policy in India has been strongly interwoven with the ideology and policy of the Congress Party. The position of the INTUC thus reflects the clearest hegemonic link to the state. As a wing of the ruling party, the INTUC has supported the development of the state-centered industrial-relations regime in the period following Indian independence. In return, it has enjoyed legitimacy and access to state power.

The stated aim of the INTUC was "to establish an order of society which is free from hindrance in the way of an all-round development of its individual members which fosters the growth of human personality in all its aspects, and goes to the utmost limit in progressively eliminating social, political, or economic exploitation and inequality."[2] The INTUC adopted a strategy of liberal reformism and corresponding ideological notions of individuality and equality. The approach favored collaboration with management and focused on the goals of national economic development rather than on class conflict. In this process the INTUC displaced questions of class in favor of a nationalist-oriented ideology. As one INTUC trade-union representative argued: "The INTUC is nationally directed. It is the tricolor union. Other trade unions are destructive. We believe in a constructive approach to trade union activity."[3]

The ideological orientation of the INTUC is underlined by the methods of action it has formally favored. According to the INTUC constitution, the just resolution of industrial conflict is constituted by "the redressal of grievances, without stoppage of work, by means of negotiation and conciliation and failing these by arbitration or adjudication."[4] In effect, a direct correspondence exists between the formal industrial regime and the INTUC's organization.

Recent political events—specifically, the rise of the Bharatiya Janata Party (BJP)—pose a growing challenge to the Congress's conception of nationalism. The BJP has attempted to replace the secular nationalism that has formally governed the Congress Party with a religious nationalism in which "India" is defined as a Hindu nation.[5] The position of the Bharatiya Mazdoor Sangha, the trade union affiliated with the BJP, reflects this ideological approach. According to D. B. Thengadi, one of the founders and leaders of the BMS:

Ideologically, the Bharatiya Mazdoor Sangh is the only organization that seeks to represent . . . "India" in the labor field today. It is wedded to no "ism." It is determined to eradicate economic inequality. But it is not "Leftist." It rejects the "class conflict" concept of Communism. But it is not "Rightist." Not mere "equality" but "oneness" is its motto. It is "Bharatiya" in the very sense of the term.[6]

This "oneness" is embodied in the concept of the nation. Once again the interests of the nation and the interests of labor are assumed to be compatible if not identical: "the whole nation is one unit. All the nationals are only so many limbs of the same body. Their interests cannot, therefore, be mutually conflicting. Naturally and necessarily they are complementary. Whosoever fails to realize this fact betrays lack of patriotism."[7] Thus the BJP and the Congress unions coincide in their belief in the predominance of nationalism over class.

The Communist union completes the range of the ideological spectrum in the formal political arena in India. The formal ideological approach of the Center of Indian Trade Unions (CITU) to labor organization has been guided by a Marxian model of class conflict. The CITU was formed in 1970 when it split from the All-India Trade Union Congress (AITUC). This schism was the result of the 1964 division of the Indian Communist movement into the "rightist" Communist Party of India (CPI) and the Communist Party of India (Marxist) (CPI[M]). The rupture in the Communist trade-union movement followed a political conflict between the two parties in which the CPI(M) accused the CPI leadership in the trade union of pursuing a class collaborationist policy. Activity of the CITU has generally been governed by a high degree of militancy and an emphasis on conflict between labor and industry. The CPI(M)-led union has thus represented the strongest alternative to the hegemonic pact with the state.

Both the CPI(M) and the CITU have opposed Congress rule and the existing framework of the Indian industrial regime. On the political front, they have consistently opposed the Congress Party through electoral means and have condemned the "anti–working class" policies of the various Congress regimes. On the industrial side, the CITU has adamantly supported measures such as the secret ballot that would initiate changes in the industrial regime. Furthermore, the CITU has attempted to combat fragmentation in the labor movement through alliances with other left-oriented trade unions.

Despite its formal support of militant unionism, however, the CITU has also tended to rely on the nexus between the political system and the industrial relations regime. In the CITU's interpretation of Marxism, the capture of state power is of critical significance for the interests of workers. According to the constitution of the CITU, "the exploitation of the working class can be ended only by socializing all means of production, distribution, and exchange and establishing a Socialist State."[8] This has led the CITU to focus on strengthening and consolidating its position in states in which the CPI(M) has held political power. According to the all-India vice-president of the CITU:

Though an all-India organization was formed, it was clear at the time of formation that the influence of CITU was limited to a few States only. From the report of the Credential Committee, it was seen that 1,759 unions having a membership of 8,04,637 joined CITU. West Bengal alone accounted for more than one half of the membership, its share being 960 unions with 4,70,702 members. Next came Kerala having 1,52,058 members in 424 union. Bombay, once the pride of the red flag, had only 20 unions with 19,766 members. Tamil Nadu had only 122 unions with 57,100 members. The other states' membership is not worth mentioning. There has not been any radical change in this respect after 15 years.[9]

Hence, the two states with the largest CITU strongholds, West Bengal and Kerala, have both been under Left Front governments for extended periods in post-independence India.

In practice, the CITU has thus implicitly accepted the rules of the game in which trade unions base their strength largely on the power of their affiliated political parties. Witness the role of the CITU in West Bengal: during the second period of Left Front rule in West Bengal, the government retained the pro-working-class rhetoric of its party ideology. After an initial period of government-supported labor militancy in 1967–1969, the Left Front government has in fact drastically changed its earlier approach to industrial relations.[10] The first labor minister in the newly formed government in 1977 claimed:

The Left Front Government of West Bengal is committed as a matter of policy to seeing that injustice done to workers and employees during the Emergency is revised and remedied. . . . The present Left Front government will give all-out support to the workers' legitimate demands and struggles. . . . This Government will ensure freedom of trade union functioning for everybody—irrespective of political affiliation and ideology—and will not allow the police and antisocial elements to interfere in trade union struggles.[11]

Despite the Left Front's increasingly strong electoral performance, it reverted to a labor policy that conformed closely to the national industrial-relations system. Since 1977 the CPI(M)-led government has reversed its policy of encouraging militant worker protest, and the majority of days lost in industrial conflict have been due to lockouts (98.7 percent) rather than worker strikes (1.3 percent).[12] The government has condemned management for instituting lockouts and has clearly stated:

We do not agree that the principal reasons for lockouts have been indiscipline and violence. . . . The employers have in fact resorted to lockouts on a larger scale with a view to pressuring their workers to accept wage cuts, increased workload and other terms dictated by them. We feel that in the face of this onslaught the trade unions have shown commendable restraint.[13]

However, no action has been taken on this issue. The government has not pressured management to reopen locked-out mills or declared specific lockouts illegal. Biren Roy, a longtime union activist and leader of the CITU, has criticized the Left Front government for failing to take initiatives to support alternative means, such as workers' cooperatives, to salvage locked-out companies.[14]

The shift in the approach of the CPI(M)-led Left Front government has arisen from its drive to win back capital for the ailing economy of West Bengal. West Bengal Chief Minister Jyoti Basu has spearheaded this gradual transition from a state-socialist economy to a market-oriented economy, a shift that has continued in the 1990s with the attempt to increase foreign investment in West Bengal. The West Bengal government's policies thus have been in line with India's move toward economic liberalization. This movement has been accompanied by a shift in the CPI(M)'s perception of the role of trade unions. Support for militant trade-union action has been replaced by a desire for stable industrial relations and restraint on the part of unions. As early as 1979, the government argued that "the sense of moderation and the high degree of maturity displayed by the organized trade union movement in keeping the situation in the field of industrial relations on an even keel in this state is noteworthy. This also indicates the success of the State Labor Policy."[15] The view that "moderation" is a sign of a "mature" trade union marks a significant contrast to the CPI(M)'s condemnations of the "class collaborationist" policies pursued by other unions in the 1960s. The CPI(M), in its endeavor to preserve industrial production, has even confronted its Left Front allies. For example, in one situation the Communist Party of India (CPI) and its trade union, the All-India Trade Union Congress (AITUC), adopted an industrial protest program that would involve stoppage of road transport (*rasta roko*) and rail transport (*rail roko*). This idea was vociferously opposed by both the CPI(M) and CITU. According to one report, the secretary of the West Bengal State Committee of the CPI(M) threatened the AITUC with severe police action. The threat of force in this situation is particularly significant since it is directed toward a party that is a member of the government coalition in West Bengal. Furthermore, the use of police was advocated not by the government but by a CPI(M) party leader. There has thus been an erosion of the lines between government, the CPI(M), and the industrial arena in West Bengal that resembles the erosion of the formal industrial system in the national context.

The effectiveness of the CPI(M)'s policy of moderation in the trade-union field has rested to a large extent on cooperation from its trade-union wing, the CITU. Although the CITU has been one of the more militant unions on a national level, its role in West Bengal has conformed to its party's focus on regulation and restraint. During the national conference of the CITU in 1990, one of the central issues addressed was the need for trade unions to introduce "work culture" into their policies. In order to combat industrial sickness, workers were urged simultaneously to improve productivity and to refrain from stopping production. The new intention of the CITU has been to complete the transition away from the mobilizational politics that marked the 1960s.[16] The contradictory nature of the CITU's position is exemplified by its response to India's move toward economic liberalization in the 1990s, specifically in relation to the role of foreign capital. While the CITU vociferously opposed such policies at the national level, particularly during the initial phase of liberalization in the early 1990s, it has been silent on Jyoti Basu's own pursuit of foreign capital in West Bengal.

In fact, the CPI(M) has relied on its trade union to preserve industrial order, and the CITU in return has acquired a position of power in the trade-union field in West Bengal. The state government has cooperated with the CITU on two levels. First, the CITU has enjoyed a great deal of leverage in tripartite bargaining and conciliation procedures. Smaller or weaker unions thus benefit by allying with the CITU, which in turn consolidates CITU's strength. Second, the CITU, as an affiliate of the ruling party, does not face the threat of police action or intimidation. Thus when CITU has opted to strike, it has operated in an atmosphere relatively free from intimidation and coercion.[17] The privileged position of the CITU and its relationship with the ruling CPI(M) in West Bengal reflects the political dependency of unionism in the Indian system of industrial relations.

Within the broad contours of this dependency, trade unions have not merely been passive vehicles manipulated by the state. The industrial unions have mobilized workers at various levels, from shop-floor resistance to industrywide general strikes. For instance, the early 1990s witnessed increased cooperation among various, primarily left-oriented, unions in opposition to Congress government policies aimed at privatization and economic restructuring. However, in light of political, party-based differences, the Congress and BJP unions refused to participate in these protest activities. The central trade unions have subsequently failed to sustain a prolonged, effective national campaign in opposition to such policies. Thus, while economic liberalization in India signals a shift from a state-dominated to private sector–oriented economy, the union-party-state nexus continues to permeate the political dynamics of this transition.

Furthermore, despite activities that momentarily challenge their hegemonic incorporation, the unions have represented a limited base of workers, primarily in the organized sector and among white-collar workers.[18] They have tended to correspond to a model of business unionism. As Touraine has argued, "Trade unionism was, at a given time, a social movement; it is now a political force that is necessarily subordinated to political parties and to governments because it tends to defend specific interests, much as most of the American unions always have been doing" (1986: 173). The central trade unions have viewed the focus on monetary issues as a sufficient condition for the mobilization of workers and for the creation of a unified labor organization. This view is linked to a deeper assumption that workers can be reduced to a homogeneous group with shared economic interests.

Discourses on Labor: Producing the Trenches of Hegemony

Union and state discourses that suppress cultural differences between workers operate as a form of ideology that has circumscribed the direction of union practices and the representation of workers' interests. This exclusionary conception of the working class has enabled the effective integration of Indian industrial unions into a hegemonic bloc and has allowed unions to act as the representatives of the interests of all workers without expanding their membership base beyond particular groups of organized workers. More specifically, the juxtaposition of the general interests of workers and the differences of community and gender in the approaches of trade unions has established a hierarchical edifice of power within union agendas and activities. Particular discursive formulations of the relationship between cultural difference, on the one hand, and the interests of workers, on the other, constitute an ideology that delimits union activity and subsequently results in differential material and political effects for workers.

Trade unions in India have been grounded in a belief in the "secular" nature of the working class. The formal ideologies of unions have rested on an assumption of the separation between religion and politics. According to one prominent trade-union leader, the late B. T. Ranadive, "Those who pray in the Church or Mosque, Temples and Synagogue along with those who have nowhere to pray, all are affected by the curse of unemployment accompanied by poverty. The religious faith of the Muslims, the Hindus, the Harijans, the Catholics, does not save them from these mundane sufferings which call for unity of all toilers."[19] Given that such economic interests are assumed to overshadow religion, the politicization of these interests is expected to occur in a sphere distinct from community and religious identity.

In certain instances, unions have acknowledged the existence of the distinct interests of minority communities. Some unions have recognized that "the workers coming from oppressed caste and minority communities have disabilities and grievances in addition to the grievances common to all workers. Sometimes these are of greater importance in their daily life than common trade union demands. They do not feel enthusiastic about them [unions] if the trade unions do not champion their special demands."[20] However, these grievances are still represented as needs that are "special" and therefore implicitly external and exceptional aspects of the working classes.

This notion of the working class must be understood in relation to national political discourses. The early development of the state was based on a form of secularism that attempted to set a boundary between the public, political realm of the state and the private sphere of religion. National identity was defined through the secular notion of citizenship. However, this concept has proved to be inadequate in the face of the increasing politicization of religious, regional, and linguistic identities. State secularism has been unable to address the politics of identity and to resolve the subsequent conflicts of community. The result has been twofold. First, the attempt of communities to gain political leverage and access to state power has resulted in a rising level of intercommunity conflict. Second, communities that have not progressed economically and socially or have not received state support have grown increasingly dissatisfied with state policies. The formal state secularist ideology has thus become increasingly marginal to growing community-based movements.

The absence of a conceptual bridge that can effectively integrate cultural differences and community grievances within the framework of the state has resulted in a realpolitik approach to such issues. The interests of caste communities, religious groups, and tribal movements have increasingly become objects to be won or traded by political parties. Such excessive reliance on the politics of vote banks has not provided the stable foundation necessary to link community groups with the Indian state. The politicization of community has instead been largely reserved to violent clashes and riots on the one hand and grassroots political movements that have become alienated and disillusioned with the Indian state on the other.

The rise of the Bharatiya Janata Party (BJP), in part, reflects the failure of the Congress Party's version of state secularism. The BJP appears to present an alternative to what it terms the "pseudo-secularism" of the Congress-led state. However, the BJP seeks to integrate community within the nation-state through an exclusivist approach, one which defines nationalist India in terms of a narrow Hindu orthodoxy. Rising support for this approach has exacerbated community-based conflict and further alienated minority communities.[21]

The BJP-affiliated union, the Bharatiya Mazdoor Sangh (BMS), has also departed from the secularist framework by attempting to develop an interpretation of workers' identity and interests through Hindu conceptions and imagery. This project emerges in the concrete policies of the BMS, such as the demand to change the National Labor Day in India to Vishwakarma Day and in the interpretation of labor and society through the laws of Dharma.[22] The position of the BMS appears to counter the conventional opposition between culture and ideology on the trade-union front. However, this appearance is somewhat misleading. The BJP-affiliated union in fact continues to rely on a vision of a unitary working class. The implicit assumption is simply that the Indian worker is synonymous with the "Hindu" worker. Furthermore, the BMS has often not followed an explicitly communal approach. It has also focused on the economic issues of wages, unemployment, and retrenchment in order to compete with the other trade unions.

The trade-union movement has been unable to transcend the parameters of the national debate on "secularism" and "communalism." On

May 11, 1986, the central trade unions held a forum called the Trade
Union Convention of National Integration Against Communal and Divisive Forces, in which they declared a united resolution against communalism.[23] The convention, however, was unable to create an alternative
to the view of the working class either as a victim of divisive elements
or as a predefined secular object to be used to fight communal conflict.
The secular unions have rejected the sphere of religion without attempting to grapple with a conception of religion that is not based on the
exclusionary approach of communal politics. In trade-union ideologies,
community bonds and religious identities are at best part of the worker's
private, nonpolitical world and at worst divisive and threatening residual
elements of a feudal past. In effect, such union approaches to the working classes have represented a type of "derivative discourse" (Chatterji,
1986) that has been rooted in the national conceptions of secularism
and communalism. The unions' inability to confront the implications of
workers' community identities has prevented them from adequately addressing the critical role such identities play in shaping workers' political consciousness and behavior. As research in comparative contexts
has demonstrated, conceptions of religious or other forms of community identity represent the cosmologies through which workers interpret
their everyday work and life experiences and often constitute languages
of working-class resistance (Joshi, 1985; Ong, 1988; Taussig, 1980).

In the Indian context, the potential slippage between such languages
of resistance and the violence of communal conflict (Chakrabarty, 1989;
Upadhyay, 1989)[24] has prompted the central trade unions to retain a traditional secularist separation between religion and politics and between
community and class interests. At the local level, however, identities of
religion, ethnicity, and caste play a central role in the everyday practices
and politics of workers. Such processes continually confront and inform
local union practices but are lost in the interstices of the national union
discourses, a paradox addressed in Chapters 3, 4, and 5.

If the issue of the community identity of industrial workers has raised
the specter of "communalism," the question of gender has been viewed
by unions as a marginal concern. Conventional wisdom assumes that
since economic problems such as mass labor retrenchment, lockouts,
and closures are so immense, the position of women workers can only
be of secondary significance. The industrial labor force thus has been
viewed as the domain of male workers. Although the government and
the unions have stated a formal commitment to the inclusion of women
in the industrial regime, this commitment has been limited to identifying certain "special considerations" for women and appending these
considerations to formal agendas. Gender has not been treated as an

issue integral and central to the organization of industrial relations (Banerjee, 1991).

The male-dominated nature of trade unions can be understood in terms of three characteristics of the union organizations: First, during the post-independence period, union membership has shown only marginal increases in the percentage of women members. Second, the leadership of the major union federations has been largely male-dominated. Finally, while some unions have added issues regarding women workers to their list of demands, their policies have not placed these issues at the forefront of their agendas. Women workers are consequently excluded at the levels of membership, leadership, and policy.

The exclusion of women must also be understood in relation to the gendered discourse that has shaped union activity and allowed women workers to signify a "special" or particular category externalized from the "general" interests of workers. Consider, for example, the nature of the exclusion of gender from the central tenets of trade unionism in the discourse of the Left Front government in West Bengal.[25] The orthodox class-based ideology of the ÇPI(M) has sustained the notion that women can be subsumed within "larger" democratic and class-based movements (Basu, 1992). Trade unions have been reluctant to acknowledge that gender signifies relationships of inequality within the working classes. There has been a defensive rejection of the existence of a conflict of interests between male and female workers.

An extreme but not unusual version of the reaction of the leftist trade unions to the issue of gender is represented in the argument put forth in the fifth conference of the CITU:

If women's problems and demands are not taken up by the trade union movement, the reactionary circles, the government, and the foreign agencies who are already at work will utilize the situation to pit the women against the men and disrupt the united movement of the trade unions. The Conference therefore calls upon the state committees and the CITU unions to form coordination committees of working women under their guidance, ensure promotion of women in trade union positions and bring them in the same stride of the working-class movement in the country.[26]

This view signifies a pervasive problematic in which the CPI(M) party and union have tended to view the development of independent women's mobilization as a "western" and "bourgeois" phenomenon that represents a threat to the trade-union movement (Jayawardena and Kelkar, 1989; Sen, 1989). In response, the CITU has created a sub-organization, the All-India Coordination Committee of Working Women (AICCWW), to address the problems faced by women workers.

As the preceding excerpt from the conference indicates, however, the purpose of this organization has been to consolidate the existing position of the CITU rather than to transform the dominant paradigm of the monolithic working class that has guided union organization.

Some members of the CITU have attempted to bring up the exclusionary nature of trade-union activity. As one prominent leader argued in a moment of self-criticism: "It is a matter of shame that when thousands of women are being retrenched and thrown out of jobs, there is hardly a ripple of protest or action from the CITU and other unions. The trade union movement is not the preserve of men. Yet all kinds of hypocritical excuses, born out of feudal outlook, are to be found to explain away the neglect of the problems of working women."[27] Nevertheless, such issues have remained marginal in union analyses of the problems faced by industrial workers. Another prominent union leader admitted: "In theory we say a lot of things. We talk about reservations for women of 25–30%. But practice is another matter. In practice we are all chauvinistic."[28]

Such admissions from activists within the union indicate that there have been subtle shifts in union discourses regarding women workers. The attempt of the CITU to even admit the "special" needs of women represents an advance over the notion that the interests of women workers are purely a threat to unified union activity. Such "women's issues" nonetheless remain distinct from the general interests of the working classes. As Nivedita Menon has argued, this distinction is effectively symbolized by the sharply contrasting representations of the CITU's two weekly journals, *Working Class* and the *Voice of the Working Women*.[29] As Menon points out:

CITU's journal on women workers, *Voice of the Working Women*, was started in 1980. In the issues spanning the last five years [there] has been recorded a tremendous volume of struggle all over the country—peasants fighting against harassment of landlords, factory workers demanding better working conditions, middle class professional working women striking for higher salaries and better conditions of living, air hostesses against discriminatory terms of employment. In the same period, CITU's official journal *Working Class* reflects none of this powerful political activity, so that in effect *Working Class* is the journal of CITU's main members and *Voice* of the female.

The representation of the working-class and "main" membership is transformed in this process into a gendered category.

Trade-union conceptions of gender have been based on assumptions similar to union approaches to questions of religion and community. This belief in a monolithic "working class" has been shared by unions of differing political affiliations. As with the case of minority communities, women have also been accorded formal "special" considerations. However, unions have rejected a recognition of gender both as a conceptual tool necessary for an understanding of workers' interests and as a form of structural inequality that must be confronted when organizing the laboring classes.

State discourse on labor as embodied in the protective legislation developed for women workers has mirrored this compartmentalization of the issue.[30] This series of acts has been divided into three categories. The first category consists of a policy to protect women from discrimination through the Equal Remuneration Act (1976) and through general guidelines indicating the need to protect women's rights. The second group is comprised of policies to assign specific additional benefits to women laborers, including maternity leave, maternity benefit payments, and the provision of separate washing facilities and crèches in factories. The third category purports to protect women from specific situations deemed dangerous for women workers by prohibiting them from working during night shifts (from 7 P.M. to 6 A.M.), carrying heavy loads, working inside mines, and cleaning or operating machinery that could result in injury.

An analysis of the effects of such legislation confirms the insights of recent feminist research pointing to the limits and contradictions of state legislation designed to "protect" women (Alexander, 1994; Baer, 1978; Brown, 1995). In theory, protective labor legislation for Indian women workers is a comprehensive set of laws aimed at improving the position of women workers. In practice, these laws are inadequate. The absence of implementation and the lack of effective machinery for enforcement of the acts have made the laws ineffective. Moreover, these acts and the assumptions that have guided their development have proved detrimental to the interests of women workers (Viswanathan, 1992). Employers, trade unions, and scholars have held that facets of the legislation have been leading causes in the reduction of employment opportunities for women in the organized sector. On one hand, employers, unwilling to incur the extra costs that the legislation entails, simply do not recruit women workers. The legislation has provided an economic rationale for the prevalent social and cultural notions that emphasize women's domesticity and assume that a man's need to work outweighs that of a woman. On the other hand, the legislation has not included any protection of employment opportunities or job security for women workers.

A critical problem in state policy rests on the conception of "protection" that guided the original formulation of the legislation. "Protection" has been predominantly oriented toward the "special," that is, the biological attributes of women, rather than against discrimination due to cultural, social, and economic factors. The guiding assumption that influenced the initial development of this approach is embodied in the view that "women workers in all countries require special treatment because they need more protection than men in their working environment in view of their tenderness, sensitiveness and their influence in the home, including reproduction function and in bringing up future generations of the country."[31] The biological determinism of the government's approach implicitly placed the burden of responsibility on the woman worker rather than on gender discrimination linked to an economic, social, and cultural context.

Government discourse on women workers has undergone some change since the 1980s. There has been an increasing attempt to reassess the nature of discrimination faced by women. The sixth Five-Year Plan (1980–1985) marked a transition from a welfare-oriented approach to a view of women as a distinct social group that had been adversely affected by processes of economic development. Furthermore, responses to this issue were based on questions of women's rights and development rather than on "protection." According to the plan: "The main drawbacks in women's development have thus been mainly preoccupation with repeated pregnancies without respite, in physical workload, lack of education—formal and informal—and a preponderance of social prejudices along with lack of independent economic generation activity or independent assets. The strategy thus has to be threefold—of education, employment, and health."[32] The three proposed strategies of economic advancement, educational advance, and access to health care and family planning thus marked a significant shift in the understanding of gender discrimination.[33]

Despite the shift in the government's approach to women, the traditional gender-biased assumptions have continued to shape the organization of industrial relations in India. As the Ministry of Social and Women's Welfare has acknowledged: "Various cultural and traditional factors have led to the clear demarcation of economic roles between men and women. The labor market is not neutral. Males are considered for certain jobs while females for others. . . . Women's work is evaluated according to traditional perception. Most employers see the contribution of women as being less in value than that of men."[34] There has been little improvement in the employment of women in the industrial sector, whether in terms of opportunities for employment, job status and security, or implementation of government legislation.

State and union discourses converge in their juxtaposition of the general interests of workers and the special needs of women workers. This invention of a monolithic working class has subsequently facilitated the reproduction of hierarchical relations within the working classes. The assumption that the interests of women workers are special and therefore secondary has facilitated the displacement of women workers from industries in the organized sector. Industries such as the pharmaceutical industry (Gothoskar, 1992), cotton textiles, jute textiles, and mining, which employed a significant proportion of women workers in the colonial period, now employ a marginal number of women workers at the industrywide level (Jhabvala, 1985; Banerjee, 1989). As Renana Jhabvala observes, women in the 1920s formed approximately 20 percent of the work force in cotton textiles and 38 percent in the collieries; by the 1970s they constituted only 2.5 percent in cotton textiles and 5 percent in the collieries (1985: 22). Meanwhile, in the jute mills, the percentage of women workers has dropped from approximately 20 percent of the work force to 2 percent of the work force. This pattern of displacement acquires particular significance given the fact that the manufacturing industries have historically provided the site for the development of the labor movement in India (Chakrabarty, 1989; Das Gupta, 1994; Simeon, 1995) and have been characterized by the presence of strong union activity. How, then, can we understand the role of unions in this process of retrenchment? More specifically, how have the unions' construction of hegemonic boundaries of the working class shaped union activity and contributed to the transformation of the industrial working class into a primarily male working class?

Producing the "Working Class": Class "Unity" and the Displacement of Women Workers in the Jute Mills

The jute workers provide a striking case of two simultaneous movements. Jute unions have demonstrated the ability to mobilize in the name of unified class interests even as the jute labor force has gradually transformed into a male working class through the systematic displacement of women workers from the mills. The class unity of the jute workers in effect signifies the exclusionary construction of a gendered work force. This paradoxical convergence of unity and exclusion becomes clear when we juxtapose two forms of working-class protest: a general strike held in 1992 during the period of my fieldwork and a series of autonomous protests by women workers in the 1950s in response to their displacement from the industry.

The jute workers are represented by eighteen trade-union federations.[35] The two leading jute unions are the Bengal Chatkal Mazdoor Union (BCMU), affiliated with the CITU, and the National Union of Jute Workers (NUJW), affiliated with the INTUC; the other unions tend to cluster around these two organizations when defining positions in industrywide strikes and negotiations. Trade-union leadership in the industry is divided into two levels.[36] The first, dominant level of leadership consists of the "office leaders" who are the industrywide representatives of the union. These union representatives are generally not factory workers, and they are based in city offices in Calcutta rather than in the industrial belts where the jute mills are located. The hierarchy between this union leadership and the membership base of workers is thus represented by a geographical division. The centralized sphere of decisionmaking is both structurally and spatially separated from the rank and file of the union. This division is bridged by a second level of union leadership, consisting of factory-level leaders who are generally members of the jute labor force. These local leaders run branch offices based in the working-class communities and are responsible for grassroots organizational work, including recruiting members, collecting membership dues, informing workers of decisions made by the office leaders, organizing union meetings, and other political activities. This organizational hierarchy coincides with an ethnic and class-based hierarchy. Office leaders are generally middle- or lower-middle-class Bengalis, and local leaders are usually working-class migrants from Bihar, Uttar Pradesh, or Orissa. The higher class position of the office leaders has to a certain extent served an important role in enhancing trade union strength. These leaders have been able to provide resources (such as funding, education, and time) to the trade unions which the migrant workers may have lacked. However, the class divisions in the union's organizational structure nevertheless represent an important constraint on worker participation in union decisionmaking and leadership.

At both the office and local levels, the leadership was composed primarily of male activists. In my many visits to the central city offices of the major unions I never encountered a woman working in any capacity in the office. This gendered nature of union organizational activity was reflected by the unspoken surprise most union activists displayed each time I entered the office. I should add, however, that in most cases my own gendered position did not obstruct my attempt to interview leadership representatives. The more important factor in gaining access to union leaders was the political position the union occupied in West Bengal. Consider, for example, the methods I had to use to gain access to the office leadership. In the case of the CITU leadership, I was able to gain an interview with the leader of the jute federation only when a prominent national CITU representative intervened on my behalf. The All-India representative in question had to set up the appointment and call the office at the designated time in order to ensure that the jute federation leader would indeed speak with me. In the case of the other major unions that were not affiliated to the CPI(M) (the leading party of the Left Front government)—and therefore those less politically powerful—the jute-federation leaders were readily accessible in their offices. The CITU in this context represents the central union, which has been incorporated in a hegemonic bloc with the CPI(M)-led government in West Bengal.

A second important characteristic of the jute unions is the nature of their membership base. The precise membership support enjoyed by each union is a subject of much debate. The BCMU claims a membership of 110,000 jute workers, and the NUJW claims a membership of 96,000 workers.[37] Membership returns are not necessarily an accurate measure of trade union strength or worker support, however, for claims are often exaggerated and membership returns may not represent active or existing members.[38] Furthermore, as one central trade union leader pointed out: "There are about one lakh, eighty thousand [180,000] workers in the industry. But if you add up all the claims you have about five lakhs [500,000]. Though there is a reason for this. The workers are also smart. They become members of many unions. So one worker can be a member of CITU, INTUC, UTUC, or any other union." Whereas each union has a core group of active cadres, general union membership of the jute workers has often been based on utilitarian needs rather than on political or ideological affiliations. The notion of "support" as represented by membership thus requires qualification.

The organizational activity of the jute unions presents an important case for analysis because historically it has been characterized by high levels of political activity. The West Bengal jute workers have a long history of organized strike activity. The jute labor movement can be traced back to early protests in the colonial period that culminated in the general strikes of 1929 and 1937 (Das Gupta, 1990; Goswami, 1987). Since independence, the jute unions have organized seven prolonged industrywide strikes.[39] In contrast to the political fragmentation of the national labor movement, the jute unions have demonstrated an increasing ability to cooperate and unite on a common platform and have gained substantial increases in wages through the corresponding settlements.

While the general strikes appear to signify a strong capacity for organized labor resistance, the effects of this activity in fact conform to the model of business unionism. Consider, for example, the case of a general strike that shut down the industry for fifty days in 1992. This strike was supported by the jute federations of all eighteen trade unions. Approximately one hundred and fifty thousand workers participated in the strike, and forty-seven factories were shut down.[40] The result was the complete closure of the private sector of the industry with no violent or conflictual incident for the duration of the strike.[41] This case demonstrates that the operation of Indian trade unions is shaped by two central characteristics. First, trade-union activity has largely focused on protecting the interests of particular sections of the work force: unions have been preoccupied with maintaining an existing base of support rather than with attempting to extend their organizations to include unorganized sections of the work force, where, as Mamkoottam (1984) has noted, the growth of registered unions has been greater than the growth of union membership. Second, the organizational activity of trade unions in India has increasingly diverged from a mass participatory movement.

On December 6, 1992, all the unions effectively sponsored a one-hour "ceasework" in each shift in the jute mills and presented mill managements with a common list of demands. This initial protest was designed to serve two purposes. The initial aim was to display unity and strength to mill owners and management. Local leaders organized joint rallies during the ceasework, and speeches were given by the main leaders in the various mills. In addition, the ceasework was intended to mobilize the support of workers for the potential, indefinite, strike. As one local leader argued: "The maliks are not giving us our due. We know how hard we work. And what do we get? The malik has gone from owning one mill to nine mills, because of our hard work. They have this wealth because of our toiling. It is a question of our honor. We must get our due. That is why we are putting our demands." In their speeches during the ceasework, local leaders simultaneously launched an attack on the industrialists and presented a justification for the need to strike.

This occasion of joint action by the jute federations offers a deceptive image of organized unity. Their common demands in fact mask sharp differences among the unions' views of the actions required to represent the interests of the jute workers. Less than three weeks after the unified ceasework action, the unity shattered over the timing of the proposed strike. The Left Front unions led by the CITU were intent on launching a strike in January.[42] The INTUC, however, was hesitant to embark on a strike without first anticipating the effects a general strike would have on the precarious economic position of the industry.[43] According to the general secretary of the INTUC jute federation, the INTUC was opposed to the strike

because we know the whole industry position. First of all, before January the market is good. After January the market is down, so we knew the strike would be prolonged. Secondly, in West Bengal jute mills, three types of wages are functioning: (1) mills paying correct wages, including all benefits, according to industrywide agreements, (2) mills not paying fringe benefits, PF, ESI, gratuity, and (3) mills paying less wages. We told CITU that in the first attempt it would be better to introduce wage parity. Otherwise, if we go on strike these mills paying correct wages will be more loaded, and in future these mills will get locked out.[44]

The CITU and its allies, meanwhile, argued that it was imperative for workers and unions to attempt to win some gains from the recent economic boom of the industry.[45] Furthermore, jute-mill employers had been engaging in other illegal practices, such as systematically defaulting on social security payments so that workers were unable to receive their medical or retirement benefits and breaking prior settlements by reducing wages and retrenching workers.[46] Moreover, the president of the CITU jute federation argued that a delay in the strike would undermine the workers' strength because it would begin during the slack season of the industry.[47] The discord between the two unions was underlined when the CITU-affiliated unions served notice, without any agreement with the INTUC, for an indefinite strike to begin on January 17. The divergence in political strategy was based on significant ideological differences over the relationship between the interests of workers and the economic interests of the industry.

Despite the ideological conflict between the INTUC and the CITU, the INTUC ultimately joined the strike call, and the jute unions were able to present a united front. However, their unity arose from pragmatic political considerations rather than from a desire to overcome party divisions and develop a unified movement. According to the general secretary of the INTUC jute federation, the INTUC joined the strike in order to avoid the adverse consequences of interunion clashes:

First, if we didn't strike it will be our obligation to run the mill. This is not possible in West Bengal because CITU has the support of government, police, and anti-socials. So there will be a clash. Some mills can be run. But CITU can control one department in the mill. They can go to workers' houses and threaten them there. There can be a clash at the gate. INTUC leaders will be injured without help. In that position there will be a lockout by management. The government and management will think that in West Bengal CITU is more powerful. CITU will finalize the agreement. With an understanding between CITU, government, and management, there will be an "X" amount increase in wages. Then CITU will organize a meeting and will say that, because of INTUC, "X" amount was not increased as much as it could be.[48]

The INTUC's change in position was largely based on the pressure generated by the nexus between the CITU and the CPI(M)-led government in West Bengal and on the fear of losing worker support to the CITU. The "unity" of the INTUC and CITU jute unions in the 1992 general strike was thus a product of the party-oriented union organization that characterizes the Indian industrial-relations regime. The case also reveals that, given a sympathetic state government, trade unions are able to launch a unified strike action despite the politically fragmented organization of labor in India. Nevertheless, the state continues to assume a critical role in shaping the direction and effectiveness of trade-union activity.

I have examined the "unity" that governed the jute general strike in terms of the positions articulated by the leadership of the central trade unions. However, the central trade union leaders represent the city-based "office leaders" of the workers, distinct from mill-level leaders who work and live in the factories. The charter of demands and strike notices are drawn up and served by these office leaders. The organizational link between the central jute federation leadership and the jute workers is sustained by the mill-level unions. The positions of the local union leaders reflect the decisions of their affiliated central trade union organizations. These plant-level leaders are responsible for the mobilization of worker support for union decisions regarding the general strike. The central methods used by the mill unions are demonstrations and gate meetings held outside the factory and meetings held in the labor lines where the jute workers reside.

The local leaders generally supported the 1992 strike decision of their central union officials. As one local CITU leader stated, "No malik has ever given one paisa easily. It does not happen without fighting, without struggle. So the strike has to happen." Even while leaders with different allegiances expressed a public statement of support for the strike, however, they privately acknowledged that they would prefer to avert the strike and avoid the economic hardship the workers would endure. In the case of one mill, union representatives and workers unsuccessfully attempted to gain exemption from the strike. According to one report, "The [union] representatives said that more than 5,000 workers were once again earning their livelihood since the re-opening of the mill—which was locked out earlier—in June 1991. An indefinite strike at this stage would ruin them and their families."[49] Seven out of ten unions at the mill, including the INTUC and the CPI union (AITUC), opposed the strike. The CITU federation, however, claimed that the majority of workers supported the strike.

The gate meetings held in the period immediately preceding the 1992 strike sought to mobilize worker support through a class-based conception of the conflict. As one local INTUC leader's speech declared:

Our money is being stolen. Big industries are being built through our labor. Crores of rupees are being earned. But we are getting nothing. We are the workers. We are the ones who toil in the factory. Our jobs will be there but we must get our fair wages. We have tried to talk to the maliks. We have had meetings with the maliks and the government. But the maliks do not agree to our demands. So we have to struggle. We don't want a strike. But unless they give us wages worth our toiling we will fight. We are the ones who work while the maliks make crores in profits.[50]

This speech contains two crucial points. First, it is significant that the class-oriented analysis of exploitation is being presented by an INTUC leader. I noted earlier that the INTUC's formal approach to unionism has been governed by a liberal reformism that rejects the Marxian notion of class conflict. The local leader's speech, however, departs from this orientation. Although factory-level and official leaders must uphold the same formal ideological position, factory leaders often recast these positions through their local political discourses. Local leaders follow the decisions of the central leaders, but their interpretation of such decisions is grounded in their experience as workers in the mill. Hence, the ideological orientation of union leadership is often contingent on the class position of the leaders. The second significant point lies in the leader's focus on the responsibility for the decision to strike. According to media reports, a significant portion of the workers was opposed to a strike.[51] As one worker argued,

We are even prepared to take less money but we don't want the mill to close. If the mill closes everyone will lose. The mill will lose, we will lose, the country will lose. It is bad for everyone. The leaders are doing this, not us. They want to win even if the whole public loses. Until they have money in their pockets they will not be satisfied. They won't listen to anybody. The unions want to strike. We don't want to strike.

The local leaders were faced with the task of convincing the workers that the unions were opposed to the strike but had no choice in light of the owners' actions. The critical foundation for mobilization within the mill rested on the justification of the unions' action to the workers.

The strike lasted for fifty days with no incident of violence in the various mills. Although barricades and tents were put up at the front gates, management and families living within the mill compounds had no trouble entering and leaving the factories. With large segments of the workers having returned to their villages outside West Bengal, the mills assumed a deserted appearance.

The political dynamics of the 1992 strike reveal that the role of workers is contained within a predefined pattern. Decisionmaking, the development of strike agendas, and negotiation are the prerogatives of union leadership. Local leaders are responsible for assessing the workers' attitudes and communicating their response to the central leaders. There is a network of information and communication among workers, local leaders, and office representatives. In this context, workers can and do put pressure on local leaders. Meanwhile, workers are informed about plans to strike two months in advance so that they can budget for the loss of wages. Formal decisionmaking power with regard to the strike, however, rests with the central industrywide union leaders rather than with workers or local factory-level union leaders. The agency of workers, then, is embodied in their ability to withstand the prolonged strike period without wages.[52] This form of agency is distinct from the participation of union representatives in the process of negotiation and settlement within the confines of the formal industrial relations regime, confirming the notion that "Indian trade unions may be more appropriately called 'leader unions' rather than 'worker unions'" (Mamkoottam, 1984: 37).

The gulf between trade union organizations and worker participation that comes to light through the events of the 1992 strike has a deeper foundation than the particular authority structures and decisionmaking processes of the jute unions. Throughout the mobilizing gate meetings, rallies, and union speeches, political discourses bore a striking resemblance to an ideal, typically Marxian language of class resistance. Both unions and workers called attention to the relationship of exploitation between the *maliks* (owners) and workers. As we have seen, this language of the unified interests of the jute workers also characterizes the larger national discourses of the central trade unions. I suggest that the significance of this conception of workers is deeper than the strategic necessity of displaying a form of worker unity during a general strike. The inability of the unions to adequately confront differences within the industrial working classes has in fact prevented unions from transforming their organizations into mass-based participatory movements. While unions have focused on increasing wages, such economic gains primarily benefit only selected groups of workers—for instance, permanent, male members of the work force.

The meaning of the "unity" expressed through the jute workers' strike changes when we examine its operation within a different field of power, one that has implicitly rested on the marginalized position of women workers. In this context, hegemonic discourses on the "working class" have been articulated through a gendered political process that has facilitated the displacement of women from the jute labor force.[53] In this process, the jute work force has increasingly been transformed into a largely male working class. The jute industry, once the largest industrial employer of women, is now comprised of a marginal percentage of women workers. During the colonial period the proportion of women workers was approximately 20 percent; it is now less than 2 percent of the total work force (see Table 1).

The retrenchment of women workers has been noted in studies and publications by government, unions, and academics. Various committees and reports have described, denounced, and attempted to examine the causes of this decline of women in the jute work force.[54] These retrenched women have been depicted as passive victims of larger eco-

TABLE 1. Percentage of Women Employed in Jute Mills in India.

Year	Percentage of women employed
1950	20.0
1956	7.7
1957	6.4
1958	5.1
1959	4.6
1960	4.4
1961	4.2
1962	3.0
1971	2.5
1976	2.5
1977	2.5
1978	2.5
1979	2.4
1980	2.4
1981	2.4
1985	2.2
1991	2.0

Sources: 1950 figure is from the IJMA; 1956 figure is from the West Bengal Labor Directorate (1961); figures for 1957–1981 are from the Ministry of Labor, Labor Bureau reports (1965; 1973; 1984); figure for 1985 is from the Government of India Statistical Profile on Women's Labor (1990); figure for 1991 is estimated from my fieldwork interviews.

nomic and technological changes in the factories.[55] Government officials, unions, and employers have argued that the displacement of women workers was primarily a result of the implementation of modernization programs in the jute mills.[56] During the 1950s the initial stages of the jute production process were modernized in order to sustain the declining competitiveness of jute products as paper and synthetic substitutes began to capture the global and domestic markets. With the introduction of new machinery, a number of manual tasks were made obsolete. Industry and union representatives argue that, since women were concentrated in these unskilled manual jobs, their jobs were made redundant by the technological changes. This argument, however, does not account for the continual decline of women's participation in other occupations in the mill. Furthermore, in individual mills, actual increases in employment followed the modernization phase of the 1950s. Yet women generally are not recruited or hired to work on newly installed machines, since unions and managers share the belief that the operation of machinery is "men's work." Furthermore, a focus on the

impact of technical change does not address the question of why women
workers have not been recruited in the years following the initial period
of modernization. Arjan de Haan has demonstrated that employment
levels have shrunk and increased in waves rather than in a steady trend
toward reduction. Thus he argues that production rose after the reduction of the work force in the 1950s:

During the first half of the 1960s, employment and production increased. The
number of workers declined in the second half of the decade, and there was a
trend from retrenchment to closure: workers were thrown out of employment
on a mass scale between 1967 and 1970. In the mid-1970s employment was again
at a relatively high level. In the second half of the 1970s it first decreased, then
increased again because of the temporary recovery of the industry, and declined
rapidly in the 1980s.[57]

Nevertheless, the employment of women workers in the mill has declined steadily, and for all practical purposes the recruitment of women
stopped with the first wave of retrenchment in the 1950s. The question of the displacement of women from the industry evidently cannot
be explained adequately either by processes of rationalization or by
recourse to the economic crisis that affected the industry in the post-
independence period.

A second scholarly explanation for the retrenchment of women jute
workers rests on the implications of the state protective legislation designed for women. The argument states that employers have been unwilling to assume the extra economic burden that such legislation entails. Employers do not want to bear the cost of maternity benefits and
paid maternity leave. The weight of this argument is confirmed by both
management and unions and represents insight into one dimension of
the employers' rationale. In interviews I conducted at various factories,
managers consistently argued that it was not economically rational for
them to take on the extra burden of providing maternity leave; they
also cited fears that should they hire more women they would begin to
organize and demand crèches. Furthermore, they argued that the protective legislation barring women workers from working the night shift
caused additional scheduling problems. Both managers and unions asserted that male workers resented working additional night shifts in
order to substitute for women workers.

In actual practice such laws are generally not observed—the jute factories do not provide crèches for example; moreover, according to a
labor officer in one mill, women are sometimes simply recorded as male
workers in order to avoid payment of additional benefits.[58] In addition,
women who have worked in the industry have rarely filed claims for ma-

ternity benefits. Thus, although the legislation appears to provide an economic rationale for the displacement of women workers from the jute mills, the actual extent of the burden of the "protective" laws is debatable. Nevertheless, the retrenchment of women has served the larger goals of rationalization in the industry; state legislation has provided a convenient explanation and justification for this process.[59] The effects of such legislation must be understood in terms of the gendered social and ideological responses it has engendered—responses that serve as a reminder of some of the stark limitations of what Wendy Brown has termed "the politics of protection and regulation" (1995: 169) permeating state-centered social policies. Union-management conflicts over labor cutbacks in an economically declining industry have occurred at the expense of women laborers. Consider the following case of night-shift employment in one jute mill:

The male warp winders of ——— Mill who were continuously employed on the night shift refused to report for duty on the 20th and 21st of September, demanding transfer to day shifts. As the warp winders employed in the day shifts are all women, the management could not accede to this demand. In this connection a tripartite conference was held at the office of the Inspector of Factories, Barrackpore, on the 22nd of September. After examining the details, the Inspector of Factories told the representatives of the ——— Mill Union, who took up the case of the winders, that the management had no other alternative but to employ the same set of warp winders regularly in the night shift. The Government official advised the union representatives to try and persuade the female winders to accept alternative employment so that the vacancies thus caused may be filled up by winders working in the night shift. The union representatives agreed to act according to the advice of the Government official. Normal work by the male warp winders on the night shift was resumed thereafter.[60]

The precise nature of this "persuasion" is lost in the gendered silences of documentation and history, but the case unveils an implicit alliance among the state, employers, and the "traditional" male working class.[61] This alliance closely parallels the case in the cotton textile industry, where the federation of textile labor unions (TLA) colluded with the employers' association, the Ahmedabad Millowners Association (AMA), in the retrenchment of women workers (Jhabvala, 1985). In 1935 the TLA and AMA signed an agreement stating that rationalization would occur only with safeguards in place to protect against ensuing unemployment. However, as Jhabvala notes, the agreement specified that the only forms of unemployment admissible in this process were for employees of less than a year and married women whose husbands would benefit from rationalization (1985: 30). The notion that an acceptable compromise could be created at the expense of married women was also reflected in official resolutions and positions taken by trade unions in the industry (Jhabvala, 1985: 30). The gendered resolution of the effects of rationalization thus has not been limited to the West Bengal jute mills.

In the case of the jute mills, the unions failed to organize any industry-wide actions to counter the retrenchment of female workers and also often participated in the displacement of women. In her study of the increased marginalization of women workers in the pharmaceutical industry, Sujata Gothoskar argues that "issues of recruitment and promotion are not defined clearly as bargaining areas today. . . . But also more disturbingly, the unions do share some of the prejudices managements have expressed against women and women workers."[62] Gothoskar argues that in the case of the pharmaceutical industry, when the state protective legislation began to have adverse effects on the employment of women, women workers developed specific proposals that would extend the legislation to cover both male and female workers (for instance, by providing paternity leave for workers). Unions, however, were not responsive to such suggestions. In general, unions have tended to ignore specific issues pertinent to women workers, such as equal pay or maternity benefits (Ranadive, 1976: 64). When such concerns are included in formal union agendas, they are treated as secondary issues and are excluded from the focus of union strike activity and tripartite bargaining. In the case of an industrywide jute strike held in 1992, for instance, every trade union had placed the issue of low recruitment of women workers on their list of demands prior to the strike. However, union leaders I interviewed readily admitted that the issue (which is generally placed near the end of a list of approximately twenty or thirty demands) would never be discussed during tripartite negotiations.

Another dimension of the gendering of union activity is seen in the unions' inability to effectively support or incorporate the independent militancy of women workers into existing union organizations. Historically, women workers in the jute industry have often engaged in militant forms of resistance. Tanika Sarkar explains that in the early decades of the twentieth century, women displayed a significant degree of militancy, particularly in the general strikes of 1928 and 1929.[63] Militancy among women workers has been further confirmed by union leaders. A central trade union leader narrates the following incident:

[In 1953] I used to go and sit in the union office every day. People used to walk by every day. The men used to walk by. The women used to walk by. I used to just sit there, waiting for someone to peep in. They used to say, "Who is that crazy *babu* who sits there?" Then one day there was a strike. There was picketing outside the gate. I was picketing alone, as a symbol. No one else was there. Then the police came in a big truck and picked me up. At this point, a big group of women were just walking by the mill. They saw me being taken in the truck. One of them said, "Look, that is the *babu*" and they all just jumped onto the truck and said, "Take us too." The police couldn't do anything, there were so many of the women who jumped on. In the middle of that I managed to slip away. These women had never come into the office. I had never talked to them. They just knew who I was, and that was enough for them to jump up and help me.[64]

Such instances of militancy have not been integrated into the formal organizational activities of labor unions, as Sarkar asserts: "There was no extension of such militancy in union building or strike organizing activities which remained in the preserve of men and middle class women from outside."[65]

Despite the exclusion of women's concerns from union agendas, attempts to retrench women workers were often met by strong autonomous resistance from the women themselves, as the following report illustrates: "Fifty-six surplus women workers of Anglo India Lower Mills who had been laid off in October 1954 pending the permission of the Tribunal to retrench them surrounded the Manager in the department and demanded that they should be provided with continuous employment or be paid immediately retirement benefits for thirty years' service."[66] The immediate significance of this act of protest is twofold. First, the case represents a form of resistance independent of existing union organizations. Second, the form of protest described, the *gherao*, represents one of the more militant types of organized action.

The report documents the attempt to resolve the conflict:

The Labor Advisor of ——— Group of Mills discussed the situation at his office with the Manager and the newly elected members of the Works Committee. The Association's [IJMA] labor officer also attended this discussion. The women workers continued to sit outside the Manager's office with the object of forcing the management to accept their demands. It was agreed between the representatives of the workers and the management that the laid-off workers would be offered temporary and *budli* [casual] employment as long as they were available or until the permission of the Tribunal was obtained to retrench them. The women workers dispersed quietly when the mill closed in the afternoon. On the following day the workers' representatives, however, refused to sign the agreement. A notice has been put up warning the women workers concerned that disciplinary action will be taken against them if they indulge in indiscipline.[67]

The negotiations did not include representatives from the women workers involved in the process. The "representatives of the workers" identified in the report are the elected worker representatives from the Works Committee, who are usually also representatives of the central trade unions. There is a clear separation between the agents responsible for the organization of the gherao and the agents "representing" the women workers. In effect, although the women workers were organizing an independent protest, this autonomous organization was not given legitimacy within the bargaining process.

The separation between organization and representation has allowed women's militancy to be effectively dissolved within the boundaries of the formal industrial relations regime. The central trade unions operating within the bounds of the formal regime have provided one means for a dissolution of women's resistance. In one such situation,

Double shift working at ———— Mill was extended in the Batching to Winding department of No. 1 mill. Simultaneously, a corresponding number of machines were closed in the affected departments of No. 2 mill. One hundred and thirty workers were rendered surplus while thirty-six others were absorbed in alternative vacancies. About twenty-five laid-off workers were given budli jobs and permanent jobs were found for twelve others. Some laid-off female workers continued to stay at their machines throughout the week and demanded that only those workers whose machines had been stopped should be laid off. It was suggested by the union that to solve the redundancy of women workers, those who had completed twenty-five years of service or had reached the age of superannuation should be retired. Negotiations between the management and union in connection with the proposal were still in progress during the week.[68]

Pressuring women workers to accept retirement has been a central method to displace women from the jute industrial work force. In the period following modernization, retrenchment has taken the form of a gradual but steady decline of women through such localized cases. Female workers' refusal to leave their machines represents a clear form of resistance to this process of retrenchment.

The independent organization of women workers has also been concerned with workplace issues. However, such instances have usually been met by condemnation from union representatives. In one situation, "The female handsewers of ———— Mills refused to work on B twill broaded bags on 20/8/63 unless *coolies* were provided by the management for the purpose of carrying the bundles from the branding machine to the press house. At a special meeting at the Works Committee on the same day, the action of the handsewers was deprecated and the worker-members of the Committee advised the handsewers to resume work immediately."[69] In the face of pressure from unions and managers, women workers were often unable to achieve their demands. Nevertheless, their actions often represented a rejection of both the authority of management and the leadership of unions. In such cases, the women workers conflicted directly with state power. In one instance, "some female workers of ———— Mills surrounded the labor office on the 2nd morning [in August] and kept the labor office staff confined till 12:30 P.M. The advice of the trade union leaders and the Works Committee members to the demonstrators to disperse was of no avail. Ultimately, the police had to intervene to clear the mill premises."[70]

On some occasions, local union leaders did take up the demands of women workers.[71] The lack of success in such cases was due in part to strong employer pressures and large-scale retrenchment that also affected male workers.[72] However, as an Indian government report clearly stated, "It is apparent that the rate of reduction of female workers is higher than that of the male workers." There is a critical point of intersection between the way in which the "special" concerns of women workers have been added to state labor legislation and the way in which women's interests have been appended onto union agendas and activity. The discourse of "protection" that has classified women workers as a special group and the politics of gender as extraneous to the working class has facilitated the transformation of the jute labor force into a primarily male working class.

The presumption of class unity, in effect, serves to produce a unitary working class, one that is marked by exclusion and hierarchy. The paradox of this discursive and ideological production is that in practice workers do not behave in such a singular or unified manner. The practice of labor politics in the jute mills, as we shall see, centers around negotiations of power over the boundaries between gender, community, and class.

Chapter 3
Shop-floor Politics and the Production of the Labor Market

A cursory view of the jute factory creates an impression of a masculine space. In the Calcutta mill where I conducted ethnographic research, groups of male workers often gathered in the factory compound during breaks or before their shifts, but women workers were rarely present. In the larger context of the retrenchment of women workers from the jute industry, we might expect the question of women workers and the politics of gender to be of marginal significance. Conditions in the factory, in terms of the state of technology and the harshness of working conditions, conformed to classic descriptions of nineteenth-century European industrial working classes. It would seem, then, that such work experience would underline the commonalities among jute workers on the shop floor and conform to visions of the unified interests and nature of the working class. In contrast to national discourses of the state and unions that have invented notions of a unitary "working class," shop-floor politics in the Calcutta jute mills in fact center on the politics of gender and community.

My purpose in this chapter is to deconstruct the assumption of a singular working class and demonstrate that, in contrast to national discourses, class is a product of dynamic and contested political processes at the local level of shop-floor politics. To this end, I present my analysis of gender and community within a single analytical space, deferring a more extensive analysis of the production of each of these categories and the distinctive ways in which they operate to Chapters 4, 5, and 6.

I focus first on shop-floor politics, the "traditional" realm of working-class politics, in order to demonstrate that the boundaries of class are constructed through the politics of gender and community; I then turn to other realms such as the family, ritual practice, and community organizations. Such processes of the construction of class on the shop floor involve both the "structural" and the "ideological-cultural" dimensions.

I move away from the longstanding assumption in research on labor that class structure retains a level of uniform, objective "purity" while other forms of social identity such as gender, religion, and ethnicity are symbolic or ideological forces that either divide or intersect with class identity (Edwards, 1979; Willis, 1977; Chakrabarty, 1989). My approach also requires a departure from a strict separation between the structural and ideological, or the "objective" and "subjective," dimensions of class, a demarcation that has been increasingly problematized (Hattam, 1993). In order to bridge this divide, I analyze shop-floor politics in the jute mill in terms of contests over space, time, and movement. The "structural" dimension of class can be thought of as the ways in which workers are positioned on the factory floor, through recruitment practices and a particular division of labor. This positioning of workers is contingent on the politics of gender and community, since such identities are instrumental in decisions regarding the positioning of workers; thus, gender and community are integral to the class "structure." Meanwhile, the gendering of space signifies particular kinds of class hierarchies between workers and managers and between male and female workers. Finally, I analyze the contested nature of class through the dialectics of authority and resistance among managers, unions, and workers in the factory.

The system of factory discipline presents a striking example of the Foucaultian paradigm of regimes of modern power: management attempts to produce subjected and docile bodies through a disciplinary model that "partitions as closely as possible time, space, and movement" (Foucault, 1979: 137). However, I rework Foucault's model to demonstrate that such strategies of power do not "avoid distributions in groups; break up collective dispositions" (1979: 143) in order to produce neutral, individual subjected bodies. Instead, the system of codification that controls time, disciplines movement, and partitions space codes workers' bodies through meanings of gender, caste, and ethnicity. If, as Foucault asserts, "discipline organizes an analytical space" (1979: 143), such techniques of power are in effect employed in the task of producing particular analytical and material borders between class, gender, and community.

The Setting: The Politics of Space in the Jute Mill

Driving up to the mill, one passes small tea shops where workers sit waiting for their shifts to begin. When the car turns to enter the gate, workers sitting and standing nearby stop their conversations and turn to watch. All attention is on the vehicle and its passengers. The car, whether taxi or private car, is a symbol of power. Only people affiliated with management, with the "big people," are driven into the factory. Workers

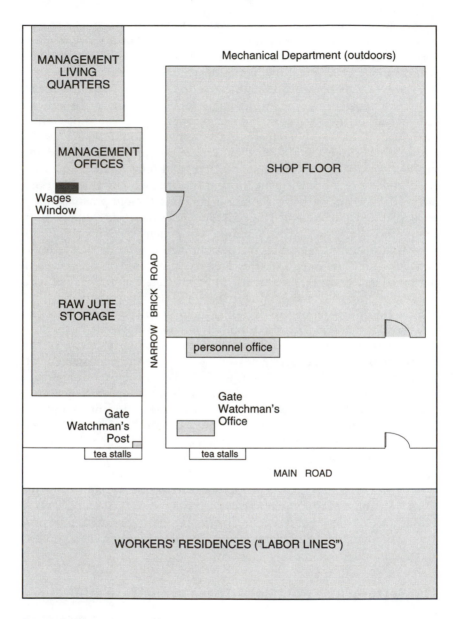

Figure 2. Shop Floor and Living Quarters in the Jute Mill

and lower-level supervisory staff walk in through the gate. To enter the factory is to enter a domain governed by a strongly codified system of power articulated through movement, space, and position. This representation of power "structures" politics and agency within the mill.[1]

The stage of jute-mill politics is spatially compressed within a clearly demarcated area (see Figure 2). On one side of the street lies the compound containing the factory as well as living quarters for management and supervisory staff; across the street are the worker residences or "labor lines" where about fourteen thousand permanent and temporary workers and their relatives live in seven hundred concrete quarters and makeshift shelters built out of metal, cloth, or other available materials. Workers and managers work and live side by side—the distances between the factory, the quarters of the general manager, and the workers' "bustees" are as short as a five-minute walk. Yet the wife or daughter of a manager living in the mill compound for twenty years is unlikely to have seen the inside of a worker's house.

Since the geographical proximity of the private worlds of management and workers does not permit class-based segregation of workplace and residence, gender codes become a central means to preserve class distinctions. This politics of space at the material level underlines the significance of the way categories of class and gender are carved out within a common theoretical space. For instance, the movements of women working in the factory are also restrained through the gendering of space. They are never seen in the tea shops or sitting in groups in the factory environs. This form of spatial representation in effect signifies the way the working class is produced as a masculine identity, one that marginalizes women workers and excludes them from access to employment as well as from a central role within the official public arena of factory politics. One of the ironies in my field research is that the only possible way for me to speak with women workers in private was to use the personnel manager's office during his four-hour lunch break. Even though I would lock the office from the inside during the interviews, a labor officer would often knock with the excuse of retrieving a file. This tactic generally resulted in minor theatrics: the women with whom I was speaking would quickly move from their chairs and stand or squat on the ground before the door opened. The officer would be reassured by the visual embodiment of hierarchy in our positions and by the mundane conversation we would have shifted to. After the officer departed we would return to our seats and resume our conversation. While the dynamic no doubt had an ironic overtone, the perception that a woman worker sitting on a chair was subversive provides a stark picture of the intensity of class hierarchy in the mill.

The congestion of the mill environment is reproduced in the spatial concentration of machines and workers on the shop floor. The mill produces jute (gunny) sacks for the domestic and international markets. The factory floor is characterized by high levels of noise and dust; in fact, the machines drown out all other sound, and managers and workers must shout in order to be heard. Workers and shop-floor supervisors tend to suffer from hearing loss. There is no ventilation or exhaust system, and jute specks and fiber dust often make visibility difficult and have led to a high number of respiratory problems among workers.

Production involves a serial process divided among nine discrete departments. The first three departments transform the raw jute into ribbons of thin fibers that will eventually be woven into cloth. First, raw jute is brought to the factory in trucks and classified into different grades of quality and placed into bales, *katcha* bales (weighing 148 kilograms) or *pucca* bales (weighing 180 kilograms). In the second department, the batching department, raw jute is softened in an emulsion. Workers feed the jute into a machine through which chemicals are applied, and then store it until it is ready for use. Jute that has not sufficiently softened is manually removed by jute cutters. In the third stage, the softened jute fiber must be transformed into "ribbons" through a "carding" process; here workers called "breaker feeders" feed the jute into the carding machine, which wraps the jute into a large, wheel-like roll. A worker takes this roll and feeds it into the finisher card, which straightens the jute by "combing" it with metal spikes until it becomes a narrow, ribbonlike strip. With continual management initiatives to raise production while reducing the work force, each worker in this department is responsible for four machines. Each machine feeds the jute strips into metal cans that must then be carried to the spinning department.

The spinning department is one of the most intensive sections of the production process in terms of the level of speed at which workers must move. Each spinning frame needs one hundred cans of jute and each worker is responsible for running four frames. In this phase, where the jute is spun into yarn and then wound around bobbins, the worker must ensure that threads do not break, and they must move quickly between the frames. The bobbins are then processed by the winding and beaming departments, which wind the bobbins onto spools that fit into the weaving shuttles. The weaving department is the largest department, and, in contrast to other sections, here each machine has a small chalkboard and a meter to measure worker productivity. After the cloth is woven in the weaving department, it enters the last phase of production, where it is ironed and cut in the finishing department and finally sewn into sacks in the sewing department. Finally, the finished sacks are bundled and sent to the buyers.

This production process does not in practice correspond to a sense of linear order in the factory. The shop floor tends to be crowded, for machines have been added at various stages in order to increase productivity, and there is very limited space between departments and between machines. As a result, the individualistic nature of work is markedly reduced and workers are often seen in small groups, particularly in the earlier stages of production and in the case of workers who must carry jute between machines. The spatial concentration of workers and machines allows workers to talk to each other on the shop floor and has led to numerous complaints by managers that workers tend to gossip and loiter. Such acts, reminiscent of the everyday acts of resistance that James Scott (1985) has analyzed, point to the contested nature of the production process and demonstrate that the control of time and movement through the production process represents a political and conflicted terrain (Stark, 1982).

Consider, for example, the chalkboards and meters installed in the weaving department. According to one senior manager, the chalkboards and meters had met with significant resistance from workers in the 1970s. Initially, according to the manager, all four hundred chalkboards would be broken every night. Management would reinstall a new set of boards, but the hidden resistance would recur, contesting management's attempt to intensify its appropriation of workers' time (Thompson, 1982). Eventually, management was able to quell the resistance by hiding a watchman in the factory who caught the worker in question; they then threatened to fire the worker unless the unions and workers guaranteed there would be no further damage to the chalkboards. Nevertheless, workers still attempt to resist the extraction of their labor by manually moving the numbers on the meter to increase the measured production. Management has retaliated by installing a second count that measures the cloth produced and by identifying "sabotage" if there is more than a 0.5 percent error between the two counts. Whereas such examples confirm the power of the hidden acts of resistance that Scott identifies, they also demonstrate that such acts do not escape the eye of management and are not necessarily more effective than organized union activity in circumventing repressive authority on the factory floor.

The regulation of time at the jute factory is not limited to the appropriation of worker's time on the factory floor but in fact encompasses the entirety of the worker's everyday life. Such regulation is most starkly manifested in the nature of the shift system that dominates all jute mills. The factory operates at full production twenty-four hours a day, six days a week, and operates for a half-day each Wednesday. Workers work for a total of eight hours a day and systematically rotate through different shift schedules six days a week, with one day off. The individual, family,

TABLE 2. Labor Force Estimates for the Jute Mill.

Regional Pattern of Labor Force (Percentage)	
Bihar	66
Uttar Pradesh	15
Orissa	7
Bengali	7
Andhra Pradesh	5
Religion (Percentage)	
Hindus	80
Muslims	20
Caste (Percentage)	
Goala	60
Dalit	25
Other (including upper castes: Brahmins and Rajputs)	15

Statistical data and records are not kept in a systematic fashion in the factory. These figures are based on estimates provided by management.

and community lives of workers are circumscribed by this schedule, punctuated by the piercing siren that regularly signals the shift change at the factory so that, as Foucault puts it, "time penetrates the body" (1979: 152). This regimentation of the worker's body occurs through a gendered process. Female workers switch between two shifts: the first runs from 6 A.M. to 11 A.M. and from 2 P.M. to 5 P.M., and the second extends from 11 A.M. to 2 P.M. and from 5 P.M. to 10 P.M. Male workers work a night shift from 10 P.M. to 6 A.M. in addition to the first two shifts. Although women workers are prohibited by state protective legislation from working at night, they must perform an additional shift of domestic labor following their work in the factory. Note that while management has adhered to the prohibition of women from the night shift, they have not provided crèches for women workers. In this selective enforcement of the protective legislation, management is in effect employing a specifically gendered mode of disciplinary power: it ensures that women workers will be positioned in the home at night so that they are able to perform their shift of reproductive labor. In response to my questions about childcare facilities, one manager argued that since the women currently employed were beyond childbearing age and new women were rarely hired, management did not need to provide crèches. Aside from the fact that several women whom I interviewed did have young children, the manager's response reveals a deeper point about the gendering of time—the manager actively projected the future of the jute working class in terms of an inevitably masculine terrain. The production of this masculinized space within the jute mill is perhaps most starkly evident in the fact that several of the mills I visited did not even provide toilets for women workers in the factory. These subtle yet significant distinctions between the experiences of male and female workers bring us to the question of delineating the relationship between gender, community, and class. Class politics, in terms of the movement, activity, and positioning of workers, do not occur through neutral processes but are constructed through and contingent on the politics of gender and community.

Gender, Community, and Class Structure: Constructing an Internal Labor "Market"

The class formation of the jute workers has been shaped by an internal labor market (Doeringer and Piore, 1971; Edwards, 1979; Gordon, Edwards and Reich, 1982) whose regulations and rules are constituted by distinctions of gender and community. Three primary characteristics define the internal labor market in the mill: job differentiation, recruitment, and the allocation of particular occupations to workers. The total daily work force of the mill (running at full capacity) is approximately four thousand and two hundred workers. The labor force is comprised of Hindu and Muslim rural migrants from Bihar, Uttar Pradesh, Orissa, and Andhra Pradesh, as well as a small proportion of Bengali workers.[2] Management is mainly Bengali, with the exception of several department managers and supervisors from the Marwari community. The caste composition is also diverse, with the main categories represented by the *goala* (buffalo herder) and *dalit* ("untouchable," literally, the oppressed) castes (see Table 2 above for estimates). A total of approximately one hundred and eighty women are employed in a work force of over four thousand workers.

One of the primary sources of differentiation that produces conflict and competition among workers in the factory lies in the determination of job status and security. Management has attempted to produce an ordered working class through what Foucault terms a form of "cellular power" (1979: 149) that places workers within an elaborate system of job classifications and ranks. Employment in the mill is thus divided into six categories in decreasing order of preference for employment: permanent status, "special *budli* (casual)," casual, temporary casual, seasonal, and extra temporary seasonal. Permanent workers are guaranteed full employment and all benefits as specified in the industrywide tripartite agreements. Special budli workers resemble permanent workers, for

TABLE 3. Employment Status of Workers Employed on a Daily Basis (Estimate).

Category of job status	Number of workers
Permanent workers	1904
Special budli	606
Casual (including seasonal, temporary casual, and extra temporary seasonal)	1607
Total daily workforce	4117

they are guaranteed employment for 220 days a year and also receive full benefits. The four categories of casual workers receive no guarantee of employment, although they may receive such benefits as the yearly bonus.[3] Casual workers must report daily at the factory gate in order to preserve their place on the casual work-force list. According to estimates of factory gatemen, an average of three thousand workers report to the mill on a daily basis. Although job status is not directly linked to seniority and there is no formal method for determining the employment status of workers, management is often able to link job security with worker production, efficiency, and discipline. It is perhaps not coincidental that a bulletin board in the general manager's office boasts a small poster proclaiming: "Fear of the Sack: Insecurity is the Key to Efficiency."

Employment and recruitment procedures in the factory are routinized through the mill's labor office. Run by the personnel manager, five labor officers, and clerical staff, the office is formally responsible for recruitment, disciplinary action, and the resolution of worker conflicts and grievances. In the determination of job status, there is wide leeway for decisions based on relationships of political patronage with both management and union leaders. It is not uncommon for some workers to gain permanent status if they have curried favor with a particular manager or if they have strong union ties, while others employed for thirty years remain casual workers.

The recruitment of workers occurs through several possible routes within the web of authority in the mill. Historians of working-class formation in the Bengal jute mills have demonstrated that the primary mode of the recruitment during the colonial period was represented by the *sirdari* system. Dipesh Chakrabarty has argued that in this system, the *sirdars* (worker-supervisors), who were given absolute authority over workers, recruited on the basis of community relationships.[4] As in the colonial period, the sirdars continue to act as agents of control over the labor force. In the contemporary period, sirdars are on occasion able to use their critical position as intermediaries between workers and managers to influence recruitment decisions. As one department manager explained: "The sirdars are chosen by the company's favor. The sirdar is part of the supervisory staff. It is important for him to have control over the workers. . . . The sirdars are not changed much. You have the same people over years. They are only changed after retirement." The permanence of the sirdar's status provides leeway for the consolidation of personal power. Sirdars may use their position to influence recruitment decisions and gain employment for their relatives or kin.

Although the sirdar is a symbol of authority in the mill and enjoys a clear position of power in relation to other workers, recent years have witnessed the decline of the sirdar's absolute authority. One union leader asserted: "They [sirdars] are basically *coolies*. They have to fix the machines and supervise about thirty workers. The supervisor just walks around. If a machine is broken they don't even stop to look at it. They don't bother. The sirdars have to see to the machines. They are like *mistris* [mechanics] now. The burden on them is big. They cannot manage. The machines are so old there is always something wrong." The leader's description of the sirdar as a coolie holds harsh derogatory connotations, as it casts the sirdar as a powerless, unskilled worker rather than a supervisor. This description is particularly significant since the sirdar's control over employment has generally been replaced by that of the trade union leader. Trade unions exert considerable control over recruitment procedures in the mill. According to one labor officer, the standard practice, when a large number of vacancies arise, is to divide the jobs equally between the trade unions. In the more typical situation of a single vacancy, a union leader will usually make a plea on behalf of a particular worker. In this situation, there are two ways in which a person can get a union leader to support his or her case. First, the applicant usually uses family or community ties, confirming the significance of kinship ties in the structuring of work forces that has been demonstrated in comparative contexts (Lamphere, 1987; Hall et al., 1987). A worker who is a member of a particular union may go to the leader and attempt to persuade him to employ a relative or a particular community member. Second, a person without union or community ties may make a payment to the leader and essentially purchase the job. Indeed, even workers who are union members or applicants with family or community ties may have to make a payment.

Supervisory and disciplinary staff are also able to use their own positions of authority to accumulate personal power and influence recruitment. In one case described by the personnel manager: "The *bara sahib* [general manager] had sanctioned the appointment of a worker's son. Even after that the worker still offered Rs. 100 to my colleague [labor officer]. They think that is the way here." Workers understand that the rules of employment and discipline are such that they must make a payment in order to gain an entry into the factory. Management retains formal authority over recruitment, but there is an informal understanding that it must consult with and satisfy the main trade union leaders.

The labor "market" poses a paradox for conventional economic theories,[5] since workers must first purchase the capacity to sell their labor. Employment is treated as a form of capital that is under the control of intermediaries such as the labor officer, the sirdar, or the union leader. This system of employment in turn consolidates the structure of authority within the factory. Workers often must take out loans at exorbitant interest rates, as high as 10 percent per month, in order to buy employment. In some cases, they agree to give a percentage of their salary to the "broker" in question. Hence, they never receive the full wages to which they are entitled, and in many cases they fall into a cycle of debt.

The result is a disjuncture between actual wages and the wages workers presumably receive based on tripartite agreements between unions and the employer association, the Indian Jute Mills Association. The official structure of wages in the industry was set up in 1963, based on the recommendations of the Central Wage Board for the Jute Industry, a tripartite committee of government, employer, and worker representatives appointed by the government of India. The board developed a wage system that has provided the basis for standardized wages across the industry as well as for a coherent internal structure of wages for different occupations within the jute mill. In the current structure, workers are placed in seven different wage grades that vary according to assessments of skill levels for various occupations and according to distinctions between time-rated and piece-rated workers.[6] Within each scale, the calculation of the wage is based on different components, including a basic rate that varies according to the occupation and the skill grade, a "marginal element" that exists for piece-rated workers (and represents the only link between wages and productivity in the factory), a "separate element" that is the same for all workers, and the dearness allowance, the portion of wages linked to inflation[7] that represents the most significant share of the wage packet.[8]

The link between this system of wages and particular occupations and "skill" is complicated, since wages vary within various departments as well as between departments. Within the batching department, for example, in the first phase of production in which raw jute is processed, the attendant for the tank containing oil is placed in a higher grade than the regular workers feeding the raw jute into the machine. In general, two categories of workers—weavers who operate looms and sirdars within each section—are placed in significantly higher grades. Women

TABLE 4. Sample Wage Calculation of Minimum Monthly Wages, 1991
(based on 1988 tripartite agreement).

Separate element	Rs. 105.00
Marginal element	Rs. 168.84
Basic component	Rs. 42.16
Dearness allowance	Rs. 1349.30
Total	Rs. 1665.30

workers do not usually work in these two categories, but otherwise there is no substantial discrepancy between the wages of male and female workers.

Aside from monetary wages, permanent workers in the mill also receive additional benefits, including a social security fund, called the Provident Fund, to which employers must contribute 8.33 percent of the worker's salary; health benefits under the Employers State Insurance Scheme; a House Rent Allowance of 5 percent of the worker's salary that is paid to the worker; and an annual bonus consisting of 8.33 percent of the worker's salary. In addition, workers receive fourteen days of paid leave if they work a minimum of 240 days during the year. The extensive additional benefits are the product of effective general strikes by the jute unions, and they are officially outlined in settlements with the Indian Jute Mills Association.

The official wage structure and additional benefits have contributed to a popular image of the jute working class as a relatively well-paid, secure work force. In practice, however, this level of economic security does not extend to all workers in the mill. For instance, substantial numbers of casual workers do not receive the additional benefits and do not receive the full amount of the monthly wage since they are not able to obtain full-time employment. Another significant departure from the official system of wages is a growing trend of employers not to adhere to the formal tripartite agreements. For instance, some mills systematically default on payments to the workers' Provident Fund, while other mills have used a strategy of factory lockouts to pressure workers to accept lower wages. This trend was confirmed by union leaders, managers, and representatives of the Indian Jute Mills Association (IJMA); according to the secretary general of the IJMA, such violations were placing other jute factories at a competitive disadvantage since the mills paying lower wages were able to cut their prices on jute goods.

Factory work appears to represent relative security and high wages when compared to jobs in the informal sector of the economy, but this notion is in fact misleading. Significant hierarchies exist within the

TABLE 5. Scale of Basic Wage Grades (Excluding Dearness Allowance), 1991.

Grade	Basic wage (in Rupees)	Annual increment	Final wage after 10 years of service (in Rupees)
I	211	4	251
II	216	5	266
III	220	6	280
IV	230	7	300
V	245	8	325
VI	265	9	355
VII	320	10	420

work force: some workers are relatively well off and can accumulate economic and political power in the factory; others are trapped in a form of bonded labor, never able to pay off their debts. These hierarchies are particularly significant, since moneylenders and job brokers are often rich workers employed in the factory. Notions of "free" wage labor, the "contract," and formal "rules" governing the labor market thus prove to be inadequate for our understanding of such forms of capitalism. The point is not that premodern or precapitalist forms of exploitation persist within the factory but that the system of capitalism is constituted by such forms of patronage and dependence.

There is a third dimension to the recruitment system in the mill. Given the declining economic position of the jute industry, the typical recruitment situation often involves hiring against "natural loss," that is, when a worker retires or dies, rather than large-scale hiring. The conventional procedure consists of what is called the *khandani* (heritage) system of recruitment, whereby the job is first offered to a relative of the deceased or retired worker. In exceptional cases the widow or daughter may be considered if she can strongly plead her case and demonstrate sufficient economic destitution; in general, however, the job is given to a male relative, preferably a son of the worker. Employment and the positioning of workers on the factory floor is contingent on male kin relationships. The idiom of family through the khandani (literally, family establishment/heritage) system is thus used to construct the working class. The labor market is therefore shaped by this patriarchal route to employment in which women are implicitly restricted from access to factory work. Recruitment through blood ties highlights the personalization of this process of the construction of the jute working class. The factory recreates the extensive ties of the joint family rather than the impersonal ties that are assumed to characterize industrial capitalism and wage labor. The result is a transgression of the line that presumably separates the "public" factory and the "private" family. The significance of this system of employment is that it is the primary, official means by which a person may obtain work in the factory. Workers (male and female), unions, and managers confirmed the centrality of this system, and the labor office also had specific written documentation that indicated that the khandani system would be used to allocate vacancies in the mill.

Meanwhile, the factory increasingly has been transformed into a male sphere through the dual processes of the displacement of women workers and the curtailment of any new recruitment of women, an industrywide trend. Management representatives justify their refusal to hire women in various ways, often basing their rationale on national discourses that cast women workers as a "special interest" group. The standard arguments are that women workers are more expensive since they are eligible for benefits, and that they cause scheduling problems because they are not allowed to work during the night shift. Thus hegemonic discourses are translated into everyday practices that then reproduce particular kinds of gendered hierarchies and exclusions. One high-level management representative elaborated on these factors at length and then finally asked me with a measure of annoyance, "If there is a large supply of male workers, why should we hire women?" Implicit in his response is the assumption that women form a reserve army of labor that can be relegated to the "private" sphere of the home and that women's employment needs are subsidiary to men's—an assumption that discounts both the subsistence needs of women in households headed by females and the importance of the economic contribution of working-class women to the survival of working-class families. Thus the "labor market" is constructed through a gendered ideology embedded within cultural and social codes of power and hierarchy.

Meanwhile, the positioning of workers in various production departments has resulted in a community-based and gendered classification of work on the shop floor. Certain tasks are thought to be performed better by workers of a particular community. For example, supervisors argue that work in the beaming department is best performed by workers from Orissa. Other categories of work are described as essentially male or female. Women, for instance, are said to be better at handsewing because they are more patient and have "nimble fingers."[9] The operation of cellular power in the factory, in terms of the distribution of workers to particular classifications of work, is consequently exercised through the construction of particular sets of relations among class, gender, and community.

This classification of work has to a certain extent been reproduced through the concrete practices of recruitment and training in the factory. As the general manager of the mill indicated:

We are supposed to recruit from the employment exchanges but in practice we just recruit from the unions and leaders. Jobs are sold and bought by the workmen themselves. Vested interests are created. But it is in the management's interest to let this be since then we don't have to worry about training. At the moment they [workers/leaders who recruit] help in training. If management stops this type of recruitment they will have to institute a training scheme. And money spent on training is viewed as a wastage. Management thinks, "let them be trained by a leader or a sirdar or by a father or brother or mother." With such training money always changes hands. Workers have to pay to get training.[10]

Job training also becomes a resource that must either be bought or acquired through family or community networks. In some instances, this process may result in the reproduction of caste occupations within the factory structure. Muslim workers from the weaving castes, for example, form a majority of the workers in the weaving department.[11]

Supervisors in the mill explain the classification of work in terms of the natural abilities of workers from different communities.[12] They argue that Oriya workers are employed in the beaming department simply because they are the most efficient in this work. As one supervisor argued, "In the weaving department, there are mainly Mohammedans. Mohammedans are more efficient. They know weaving better. It is according to history. They are generations of weavers."[13]

This process of naturalization is perhaps most evident in the gendering of work in the factory. Both supervisors and union leaders share a conception of certain departments as women's work. The winding, sack sewing, and finishing departments are considered appropriate departments for the employment of women. Furthermore, supervisors say that women are efficient as "feeders" of raw jute in the batching department. This classification contains an implicit logic that links gender, skill, and ability (Acker, 1988). The assumption that women are not capable of handling machinery has resulted in a concentration of women workers in unskilled, unmechanized work such as handsewing and finishing. The only machinery handled by women is in the winding section, where management and unions construe the task as the simplest and therefore most undervalued technical work. In the everyday language of mill work these departments are called *maghikal*, that is, low-level women's work. According to management, such work is looked down upon as the lowest form of labor on the shop floor and is devalued because it is considered "women's work." On the one hand, women are excluded from work that is classified as "heavy" or "hard" labor; on the other hand, it is assumed that work performed by women must be "easy" and therefore

TABLE 6. Estimates of Women Workers Employed by Department.

Department	Number of women employed
Batching	22
Winding	52
Weaving	4
Sack (hand) sewing and bundling	49
Finishing	10
Sweeper	5
Spinning	0
Beaming	0
Raw jute handlers	0
Total	142

of less value. The result is a gendered construction of "skill" and work where, as Joan Acker has argued, the "division of labor generates and reinforces the association of masculinity with mechanical and technical skills and femininity with patience and selfless dedication to repetitive tasks" (Acker, 1988: 482). This gendering of work is often couched in terms of the difficulty of the work and the physical strength needed to perform work in the mill, producing what Paul Willis has described as a "conflation of masculinity and manual work" (1977: 151). Certain occupations reveal the contradictions in such justifications, however. For example, handsewing is classified as women's work, but women are not recruited to operate sewing machines.

It is important to note that this categorization cannot be reduced to a rational attempt by management to divide workers. In my interviews, both local union leaders in the mill and industrywide representatives in the central union offices in Calcutta provided the same description and justification of this gender- and community-based typing of work. Ironically, union leaders subscribed to classifications embedded in modes of power that management manipulated to order and discipline the working class. Furthermore, though some leaders were willing to argue that workers could cross over the community-based categorization of work, they expressed significant resistance to the possibility of dissolving the separation between "men's work" and "women's work."

This gendered stereotyping of work, a type of "hegemony of commonsense" (Willis, 1977: 162), mirrors and feeds the national discourses that have carved out a restricted space for the representation of women workers in opposition to the "general" interests of the working class. In effect, as Aihwa Ong observes, "in modern industrial institutions circulating discourses/practices produce and reproduce, in daily conditions, cultural concepts of male domination and female subordination which are fused into and become the 'common sense' of power relations" (Ong, 1987:162). When unions and male workers engage in this reproduction of asymmetrical gender relations, they in fact produce a scattered array of local practices and discourses that maintain the national hegemonic construction of class. In this process, they do not merely use preexisting gendered ideologies but also actively manufacture gender through the creation of particular notions of masculinity and femininity (Ong 1987; Willis, 1977). Thus, the formation of class in terms of recruitment practices and the division of labor in the jute mill is fundamentally linked to the production of gender.

Lest one assume that such conceptions represent a unified form of consent to the division of labor in the factory, I should point out that there is significant resistance to the gendering of work. In my conversations with workers in the factory, several women emphasized that they could and wanted to work in any occupation in the factory. As one woman worker asserted: "If you allow a woman to work, if you give her a chance to be in any department, she can do it. She can operate any machinery." On occasion, women did express an unwillingness to work in mechanized departments, appearing to confirm the assumptions of management and union leaders. However, consider the following response of the only female sewing-machine operator in the mill when I asked her why other women did not run the machines: "The men will get angry, that's why. I got permission from the *bara sahib* [general manager], that's why I was trained. So no one could say anything. And my husband does not work. So the male workers don't mind. But otherwise there would be trouble. The men will say, 'We are not getting work and being trained to run machines, why are you giving it to them?'" Her response points to the underlying threat of coercion that accompanies the production of consent to the gendered division of labor in the mill. Likewise, another woman who was a handsewer explained: "They know my husband also works. So they would be very angry if I learned to run the machine. That's why women don't want to work the machines. They prefer to be helpers. You need permission from the *bara sahib* to be allowed to run the machine. There is no protection for us if we run the machines." These women express a form of ideological resistance that opposes the hegemonic conceptions of work and skill that shape workplace practices. Hence, the construction of class at the structural level, that is, through concrete procedures of recruitment, ensures that training and job allocation is a contested rather than a natural or neutral product of economic processes.

Contesting Authority: Tactics, Confrontation, and Organization

The dynamic, contested nature of class unfolds through a dialectics of authority and resistance, centered on political struggle over time, space, and movement in the mill. Surveillance and the control of time and movement form the basis for the preservation of authority and domination in the factory. The office is responsible for monitoring, classifying, and documenting workers. Identity cards with a photograph and signature or thumbprint are issued to all workers. The surveillance includes both workplace and home. Sirdars watch over workers in their departments, and supervisors and managers continually walk through the factory to ensure that workers do not leave their machines; the factory employs watchmen to oversee workers' residences in the labor lines (see Chapter 5). The most striking evidence of this process of monitoring workers' activities and movements is the Indian Jute Mills Association's documentation of every political meeting workers have held during the entire postcolonial period, from gate meetings at the factory to union meetings in the labor lines. This information is compiled in the form of private circulars and memos that are distributed only to jute mill owners who are members of the IJMA.

The modes of monitoring used in the jute mills do not include such technologies as video cameras and monitors, which are often present in factories in advanced industrialized countries. Nevertheless, I suggest that we can think of this process of surveillance as fundamentally linked to the regimes of modern power that Foucault discusses in his analysis of techniques of discipline in the prison (1979). For instance, surveillance in the jute mill is accompanied by routinized disciplinary procedures implemented through the welfare office. When a worker unsettles factory discipline—which according to one labor officer occurs through a range of actions from "wilful disobedience," theft, physical assaults, and wildcat strikes, to sleeping while on duty, absenteeism, and drunkenness—he or she will face a series of responses: an initial oral warning, two consecutive written warnings, suspension from work, and, finally, loss of employment. These elaborate disciplinary procedures provide a clear contrast to the colonial period before the legal recognition of trade unions, when, as both workers and managers I interviewed indicated, the primary means of disciplining workers was physical coercion. One supervisor who has worked in the mill for the past forty years admitted:

I don't like working in this industry. It is very tough. Standing in the factory for ten hours at my age. You know I am over sixty [years old]. I have two sons but I won't let them work in *chatkal kaam* [jute work]. Once we used to beat the workers, they would bleed in the mouth. We would kick them and still they would plead for work. I have seen this myself. Now we have to beg them to work and say nicely *kaam karo*. See how much things have changed? The workers have changed.

In the endeavor to transform the worker into "a productive and a subjective body" (Foucault, 1979: 26), there has been a clear shift from the manager's attempt to control workers through the "punishment" of brute physical force to the disciplinary power that observes, imposes on, and prescribes workers' movements.

To a certain extent the nature of surveillance inherent in this regime of power differs for male and female workers. For instance, women workers tend to engage in less visible movement on the factory floor largely, I suggest, because of the gendered conceptions of work and space in the mill. Furthermore, as I noted earlier, even in the process of documenting workers, management often classifies women workers as male workers (with false names) so that they cannot be held responsible for providing additional benefits to them. In some cases, male workers were officially employed by the mill, but their wives would often unofficially substitute for them on the shop floor. Factory surveillance and discipline seek to transform male workers into "docile bodies"; in the case of women workers, however, such techniques do not merely engage in the process of generating subjected workers, but in effect produce an erasure of women's bodies. The technologies of power are inextricably linked to particular gendered codes that distinguish between male and female bodies.

The success of attempts to produce obedient workers and to control the movement of workers on the shop floor is always partial and linked to various moments of worker resistance. For instance, management methods of surveillance are complemented by a form of counter-surveillance used by workers and union leaders to monitor the movement and activities of management. This subaltern surveillance is based on an extensive intelligence network in the mill. Information trickles down from management to clerks, labor officers, *durwans* (watchmen), union leaders, and workers in the factory. Workers and leaders also track the movements of management in the mill. If the general manager goes from the management building to the labor office, a durwan leaving the labor office will inform workers that the "burra sahib is in the labor office." The process is facilitated by the mill drivers, who are responsible for the transportation of all high-level management representatives. If management representatives hold a meeting at the owner's house, a driver immediately informs one of the durwans, who in turn spreads the news in the mill. As my position in the mill was routinized, I too was incorporated into this intelligence network. I was sometimes able to provide information regarding the whereabouts of a particular manager, and my research was facilitated by my ability to track down managers with the help of this network. I should also point out that my own movements were monitored both in the factory and in the "bustees," dispelling once again the omniscient aspirations of the field researcher.

This form of subaltern surveillance hints at the possibility of resistance to the power and authority that structures workers in the factory. Recent research questions the exclusive identification of politics with authority systems and social order and points to the significance of subaltern agency and resistance (Comaroff, 1985; Guha, 1984; Ong, 1988; Scott, 1985). This work reveals the limitations of defining politics through an exclusive emphasis on the state and formal political institutions and on mobilization through formal, large-scale organizations. Paradoxically, however, the upsurge of this literature has resulted in the attempt to widen the theoretical parameters of what counts as "resistance" and increasingly risks the possibility of transforming resistance into an all-encompassing concept that undermines its analytical rigor. Clearly, if the term "resistance" can be used to describe a union strike (Fantasia, 1988), a form of clothing (Hebdige, 1979), or a peasant's theft of grain (Scott, 1985), clarification is warranted in its usage. In my interpretation of resistance in the factory, I make three analytical distinctions—among tactics, confrontation, and organization.

The structuring of workers in the mill is continually subverted through everyday practices described by management as "loitering, gossiping, wasting time." Management notices continuously denounce "criminal activities" in which workers are allegedly "tampering with [weaving] loom pick meters, sitting and sleeping on the cloth, bags, rolls and bales in the finishing and sack-sewing department," and in which "leaving work on the pretext of attending nature's call/drinking water/to have tea . . . they spend 30–45 minutes in and around the canteen leaving their jobs." These acts represent the "tactics" (de Certeau, 1984) workers must use to negotiate within the fields of power that structure their workplace. I draw here on de Certeau's conceptualization of the tactic, which "must play on and with a terrain imposed on it. . . . It operates in isolated actions, blow by blow. It takes advantage of 'opportunities' and depends on them without any base where it could stockpile its winnings, build up its position, and plan raids. What it wins it cannot keep" (1984:37). Workers must seize opportunities to circumvent the eye of management or, as de Certeau has put it, they "must vigilantly make use of the cracks that particular conjunctions open in the surveillance of the propriety powers" (1984: 37) in order to combat high workload levels and circumvent the various rules that govern the factory. These acts never change the conditions that they resist, however, and in most situations they result in more stringent supervision and discipline. The temporary nature of the "winnings" of such tactics is evidenced in the management's response to the prolonged tea breaks taken by some workers:

It is notified that henceforth three tea vendors instead of the present two will serve inside the department in between 2:30–3:30 P.M. in the following places:
1. In between spinning and winding departments
2. In front of the quality control office
3. In [the] Sack Sewing Department
All workmen [sic] of the "A" shift are hereby directed to have their tea inside the department from the aforesaid places and such tea timings must not exceed 5–7 minutes for each worker.

The reassertion of management authority and discipline occurs simultaneously through the reinforcement of the measurement of time—as part of the struggle between the employer's extraction of time and the worker's claim for his or her "own time" (Thompson, 1982)—and through the spatial rearrangement of the tea break. There is an explicit attempt to dissolve the workers' collective social process during the tea break; the "off-time" must also be contained within the factory floor and divided according to departmental boundaries.

Worker resistance is not, however, limited to isolated, hidden tactics. One of the common forms of mobilization of workers in the mill occurs through spontaneous incidents distinct from both individual tactics and the planned organization of interests through trade unions. In such incidents, class conflict is often transformed into moments of open confrontation over the symbolic representation of authority. Consider, for instance, the following incident that occurred on the factory floor. A high-level management representative was conducting an inspection in the factory when a power failure occurred. During the blackout, three large bobbins used in the spinning department were thrown at the manager. The manager was able to grab a flashlight from an electrician and quickly make his way out of the factory. The force of the incident was embodied in the transformation of a part of the means of production, that is, the spinning bobbin, into an instrument of resistance. The attack momentarily displaced the manager from his position of power on the factory floor. After power was restored, the manager returned to the exact location of the incident, thus reclaiming the territory and reasserting his position of authority on the factory floor. He then summoned eight laborers who were working in the spinning department into his office, effectively dissolving the collectivity of workers in the department. Finally, he took them to his office, gave each of them a paperweight, and said, "Now hit me. Come on, hit me in the light. Why do you do your dark deeds in the dark?" The reassertion of management power thus takes the form of the symbolic appropriation of the act of resistance. Under the passive veneer, the manager in fact dictates when, where, and with what weapon the workers should resist.

Confrontations do not necessarily culminate in the victorious reassertion of management authority. In one instance, a worker was collecting his wages from one of the mill accountants. After receiving his wages, the worker went back to the clerk and claimed that he had been given Rs. 100 less than his allotted amount. The clerk denied the error, and a loud argument ensued. Within two minutes, approximately sixty workers had appeared on the scene, leaving their department to defend the worker. The swift transition from an individual argument to a collective conflict can be understood both in terms of the highly politicized nature of the work force and in terms of the spatial configuration of the factory. The wage window (which is part of the management building) is located at the entrance of the factory (see Figure 2), where there is a flow of worker traffic from the raw jute storage area to the factory floor as workers sort out the raw jute and move it to the first stage of production. Workers are able to assemble quickly outside the management building and transform this material space into a symbolic space of collective resistance. As Rick Fantasia suggests in his analysis of wildcat strikes in the American context, the spatial configuration of political conflicts, "manifested in the physical movement and positioning of the workers" (1988: 83), provides us with a sense of the ways in which such forms of resistance develop on the factory floor.

During the mounting tension of such incidents, the conflict rapidly shifts from the precipitating issue of money to the worker's honor. The language of resistance used in this incident emphasized the fact that the worker was a "poor man and an honest man." Meanwhile, a union leader appeared on the scene and quickly briefed a representative of higher management. The manager then went to the worker, gave him the Rs. 100, and told him to forget about the incident. The manager later admitted that the situation could have turned into a very serious conflict if it had not been diffused immediately.

The resolution of the incident was largely accomplished by the timely intervention of the trade-union leader. What, then, exactly is the relationship between trade-union organizations and the potential and practice of worker resistance? There were seven trade unions in the factory: the Center for Indian Trade Unions (CITU), the Indian National Trade Union Congress (INTUC), the All-India Trade Union Congress (AITUC), the Hind Mazdoor Sangha (HMS), the Forward Bloc, the Forward Bloc (Marxist) (regional leftist political party unions in West Bengal), and one independent union formed by an "outsider," that is, a non-worker. The CITU and INTUC were the most powerful unions in the mill, each claiming a membership of over three thousand workers.

Unions play a central role in the everyday processes of the resolution of conflict and the redress of workers' grievances. Daily union activities encompass a wide variety of concerns that range from raising workplace issues of leave requests and transfers between departments, to resisting management disciplinary actions, to facilitating requests for the repair of a worker's house. In addition, union leaders negotiate with management over long-term questions of workload and job status. Production levels and job status constitute critical issues of contention, since mill managers have been steadily increasing workload levels and reducing work forces in order to reduce production costs. In addition, mill management counters union resistance by linking increases in workloads to the job status of workers. For example, during the period of my fieldwork, the major trade unions were attempting to gain permanent status for five hundred casual workers. The management agreed to the demand, provided unions guaranteed their consent to the replacement of existing weaving machines by paired looms, a change that would double the workload of weavers. However, this agreement poses a paradoxical situation for unions and workers, since such increases in production eventually result in the retrenchment of workers.

The local offices of the unions are located in the labor lines so that workers have direct access to leaders and union offices. The factory-level leaders of the unions are, in general, workers employed in the mill, and in circumstances where a leader is not technically employed in the factory he (there were no women leaders) is usually a resident in the labor lines and a member of the workers' communities. Although local leaders are drawn from the communities of the jute workers, there are nevertheless clear distinctions of status between union leaders and regular mill workers. For instance, it is commonplace for leaders of the strongest unions to spend long periods of time each day negotiating conflicts in the management offices. During this time, leaders are able to leave their machines and take time away from production without fear of disciplinary action from management. One of the ironies of my fieldwork was that I was able to develop strong relations with particular union leaders simply by sitting in management offices and striking up conversations. Given the mediating role they often play between management and workers, the union representatives were able to understand my own attempts to find indirect ways to circumvent management controls in my research.

Although trade unions often engage in forms of militant protest (for instance, in their attempts to counter management offensives with regard to workloads and retrenchment and in the case of individual complaints of workers), the strength of particular leaders often implicitly rests on the authority of management. Management reinforces the leadership of trade unions, since managers generally do not listen to or act on grievances or issues brought directly by workers. This chain of authority functions even in the case of minor bureaucratic issues. In one situation, a worker brought a doctor's certificate to the labor office in order to account for his absence from work. The labor officer on duty refused to sign the document because it was the wrong form. At that point a union leader who happened to be sitting in the office nodded to the officer and asked him to sign it. The labor officer took the form and, turning to me, said, "See, because he is sitting here I will sign it." Workers must gain the help of a leader if their grievances are to be effectively addressed and if they are to survive the endless bureaucratic procedures that govern their work. One of the biggest worker complaints was that labor officers and management representatives were never available to take care of such bureaucratic tasks. My own observation confirmed the fact that workers were constantly being told to "come back later" when they tried to directly approach the managerial staff without the aid of a union representative.

In this process, management is in a position to indirectly "build up" particular leaders; if a particular leader is able to gain favors for his members, his support among workers is likely to be increased. As one union leader explained: "Several unions exist because of the *maliks* [owners/management]. They have no actual leadership, no organization, no rules, no existence. But management will say they exist. You can make a union even out of one person. But is that a union? If the maliks call a meeting, they will call all these people and so they become union leaders." The multiplicity of unions then plays an important role in undermining the bargaining strength of trade unions.[14] In recent years, unions in the mill have recognized this role and have demonstrated an increasing ability to cooperate or at least to restrict themselves to competing rather than engaging in outright violent clashes. Management is nevertheless often able to use a "divide and rule" strategy by playing on differences among unions and by favoring particular unions that do not significantly challenge the boundaries of their authority.

The dependence of unions on management is consolidated by the prevalence of bribery and patronage. It is common knowledge in the mill that union leaders, regardless of their party affiliation, use their authority to supplement their incomes and that they often preserve this source of income by accepting management norms and back-door deals. During my fieldwork, I personally witnessed the negotiation of one such transaction: the leader of the largest union in the mill received a "gift" of Rs. 20,000 for his daughter's marriage. Significantly, the language of gift giving is often used to formally characterize such transactions. Leaders often are not paid off simply to resolve a particular conflict or incident. The "gift" represents a form of insurance aimed at containing and directing the future actions of the leader in question. There is no guarantee that the leader will show restraint in every incident that arises in the factory.

Bourdieu's call for the introduction of temporality (1977: 5) in an analysis of gift giving offers useful insight into the politics of patronage and corruption. It is not sufficient to state that all union leaders are bought off and controlled by management, for this argument misses the timing and complexity of patronage and dependence in the factory. Since union leaders must retain workers' support, they must effectively defend the interests of workers. Management "control" of trade unions does not preclude protest or negate a leader's capacity to mobilize workers. However, the mobilization must occur within boundaries that are acceptable to management. Consider, for example, one manager's description of the union leader who had received the gift of Rs. 20,000: "We like him. He creates *tamasha* [drama] but then he makes it swing in our direction. We like that he creates this tamasha." This tamasha, then, is a form of worker mobilization and resistance. The game of politics involves an intricate balance of interests that must carefully define the timing of the mobilization of workers, the boundaries of these interests, and the nature of the resolution of conflicts between workers and maliks.

The dependence of unions and leaders on management produces an appearance of consent to management authority, but this consent is always complemented by coercion or the threat of coercion in cases where leaders do not obey the "rules" of patronage and acceptable labor-management conflict. More militant union leaders are classified by management as "riotous," and they are constantly under the threat of chargesheeting, suspension, and, eventually, unemployment. In these circumstances, the union leader has two options: he can undertake legal action, or he can attempt to mobilize workers and call a strike. In the first case, the courts generally take years to resolve a conflict and therefore they do not constitute an immediate practical strategy. The second option, though more viable, is also inadequate, since employers continue to use the factory lockout to deter strike activity. In the case of larger unions, a leader may use political pressure through political party affiliations to counter the threat of victimization.

The ideological contestations of a local leader of one of the smaller unions (with a membership of 350 workers) in the mill clarify the problematic nature of the consent of union leaders. The leader had been working in the mill for almost fifty years and had been a union activist for almost thirty years. When the leader was a young boy, a British manager had seen him playing football in a small field opposite the mill and asked him if he wanted a job. I was able to observe this leader engage in extended conversations in three contexts that were characterized by three different configurations of power.

Situation 1

In the first situation the union leader had come to the management building to speak to one of the company directors who was visiting the mill. The leader was asking the management representative for an increase in wages for a particular department in the factory because of recent increases in workload levels. The following dialogue ensued:

Leader: . . . We need money because we are working so much.
Director: You are not working, I am the only one who works here. *I* am working.
Leader: But you are the *malik*, it's not the same.
Director: No, the company is the *malik*. The company owns all mills. I am just working for the company. The head supervisor is not here. He is sick but he will come back next week. When he comes back, you go to him and talk to him.
Leader: But *sahib*, we want to talk straight with you, you can do this.
Director: I cannot remember all the figures, the complaints. You go to the supervisor, then he will tell me what you want, then I will look at the case and make a fair decision.
Leader: [silence]
Director: This is a question of love [*yeh pyar ka cheez hai*]. I give you this money with love. What you get is because of my caring. There has been so much *golmaal* [trouble] here but I have not closed this factory down. For the past seven years it has been running.
Leader: No, of course, because of you the factory is running. We are very grateful. We don't want to do *golmaal* here.

The leader in this situation had adopted an appearance of supplication, continually consenting to the authority of the management representative while attempting to insert his demand into the dialogue. However, what we see in this conversation is an ideological battle to define the nature of the power relationship between the manager and the worker-leader. The manager begins by denying the asymmetrical relationship of power by arguing that since he is "just working" for the company he is therefore just a worker and is in the same position as the leader. He reasserts the chain of authority in the factory by telling the leader to approach the supervisor, and he concludes by redefining the worker-malik relationship in terms of a patron-client relationship. The worker-leader must be *grateful* for the employment provided by the malik. The language of the director constructs the relationship as a form of paternalism rather than as a contractual relationship; workers are not given wages in return for the sale of their labor power—they receive employment out of the "love" of the owner.

The union leader is set up to lose the battle over the definition of the meaning of the worker-owner relationship. He must reproduce his position of subordination through the subtleties of tone, language, and body gestures. The manager sits behind the desk while the leader stands near the door and speaks. The leader bends and salaams[15] as he leaves, while the manager pointedly looks down at the paperwork on his desk. The appearance of servility is thus preserved, and the leader appears to consent to the authority of the director.

Situation 2

In the second situation the leader walked in while I was conducting an interview with the personnel manager in the labor office. He had come to lodge a complaint for a worker who had to share quarters in the labor lines with twenty-one other people. After five minutes of discussion the following conversation occurred:

Leader: Why are you sitting here listening to him [the personnel manager]? You want to know the main problem we face? It is the capitalists [*pujipati*]. The capitalists are the cause of all the troubles.

Manager: How can you say that it is because of the capitalists? In Russia they are pulling down Lenin's statues everywhere.

Leader: Communism is getting stronger. It is moving forward. I was just reading a newspaper from Russia, so I know.

Manager: What newspaper are you reading? Why don't you read our newspapers?

Leader: Communism is growing. You can pull down Lenin's statues but Lenin is alive. His words are alive. You cannot pull that down.

This debate continued for a while and began to take a humorous and dramatic turn. At the end, the leader left, saying that he would send the worker whose complaint he had lodged. Given these two situations, it would seem highly unlikely that they concerned the same worker-leader. The difference in positions can be explained by the fact that, in the second situation, the personnel manager occupies a lower position in the authority structure of the factory and is responsible for the resolution of daily conflicts and grievances of workers and leaders. There is therefore a wider political space for the expression of the leader's ideological resistance to the manager's authority. The incident reveals that the expression of class relations changes according to context. If each situation were viewed as typical of the leader's understanding, they would result in very different conclusions, for he displays a form of submission in the first example and expresses a revolutionary ideological belief in the second.

Situation 3

This situation involved my interview with the union leader. During our conversation his analysis of union organization and the potential for working-class resistance was far more skeptical than the previous situation would imply. He argued that union organization was becoming increasingly difficult because the owners could easily divide workers and unions, break legal agreements, and initiate changes in the workplace. When I asked him how the owners could do this, he responded: "Through greed. They give bribes. They give favors. If a leader talks properly and acts properly the maliks will give him favors, they will employ his people. If you don't talk properly, they won't give you work. If you are too strong and you don't behave the way they want they tell you to get out of the mill. They chargesheet you." He felt that it had become increasingly difficult to effect change through union activities.

At the end of the conversation he added: "I also had written some things before about such issues but it doesn't do anything. The maliks don't like to hear what is written. They won't change. It's no use." His response highlights the point that even a private conversation between the field researcher and subject is shaped by a particular configuration of power. This "private" conversation cannot be assumed to represent "real" or more authentic views of the leader that transcend the constraints of power. On the contrary, we could interpret the leader's reaction as a critique of my academic project.

The three situations represent three very different interpretations and engagements, ranging from supplication to "revolutionary consciousness" to pragmatic cynicism; the meaning of class becomes contingent on the context. Each of these situations taken in isolation would have led us to a very different conclusion regarding the nature of class relations in the mill. The situations taken together reveal the constant shifting between positions, discourses, and the understanding of class in the factory.[16]

If, as I have argued, union leaders must depend on and comply with management, what, then, is the nature of the legitimacy of trade unions and their leaders in the factory? Worker support for union leaders in the mill is consolidated by the strategic role of leaders in addressing daily grievances and conflicts in the mill. Unions remain a crucial resource for workers who must deal with the otherwise absolute nature of management authority. The organization of unions provides a basic level of protection for workers, and the approach of most workers to unions is utilitarian rather than grounded on formal ideologies. It is common for workers to become members of more than one union or to shift membership according to changes in the relative positions of power of the major leaders. This utilitarian approach is strengthened by the fact that union leaders often use their positions for personal gain, often charging workers for their services. If quarters in the workers' residences were to become vacant, for example, a worker would have to pay a leader to negotiate on his or her behalf. Such payments vary in amount, but they can be as high as one or two thousand rupees, the equivalent of a month's salary for a permanent worker.

As I noted earlier, workers must depend on the authority of union leaders since they are unable to approach management directly. This dependence is intensified by the system of discipline and regulation in the mill. One of the most basic manifestations of inequality in the factory is workers' literacy. Nonliterate workers are dependent on literate workers in the event of disciplinary procedures, for factory rules require that workers submit a response to a "chargesheet." If a written response is not submitted, the worker is threatened with suspension. A worker must pay a literate person, usually a union leader, to frame this response. The point is not that the worker is "ignorant" but that literacy is translated into a resource, a form of capital, that perpetuates a certain system of power and authority and that perpetuates the political vulnerability of a certain section of the work force. The position of union leaders as the legitimate representatives of workers is consolidated by this vulnerability.

Workers are in fact aware of the complex network of interests and patronage that links management and trade unions. This network permeates the work force and builds on and reproduces hierarchies between workers. I have already discussed the reproduction of ties of community and gender within the factory. These relationships form a crucial component of the material used to build networks of patronage between unions and sections of the work force. Trade unions, like most other formal organizations, do not exist at the abstract level of constitutions and ideologies distinct from cultural and social configurations of power and interests. In practice, unions build on relationships, identities, and hierarchies that exist within workers' communities. The positions of migrant jute workers within their villages are translated into the positions held by workers in the mill communities. Workers with land in the village form the majority of the permanent workers and the main base of union support. Sirdars and union leaders tend to occupy positions as community leaders and also occupy relatively privileged social positions in both their villages of origin and their urban communities. The social hierarchies that exist in working-class communities are then transformed into inequalities and forms of dependency within the capitalist system of power in the factory. The incorporation of gender inequalities by local unions provides a window onto the creation of networks of interests in the factory. Trade-union activity is marked by the relative absence of women's participation, particularly in organizational and leadership activities.[17] One woman worker in the mill described the nature of women's participation in union meetings in the following way: "We just listen. The women never talk. The men talk. But we go and sit. We don't do anything for the union. After the meeting we just go home."

   The gendered basis of the networks of interests between management, unions, and workers is not merely linked to the question of the "participation" of women workers. On the contrary, the existence of such networks rests on the exclusion of women workers and the re-creation of gender hierarchies in the workplace and in factory politics. For example, in one case management wanted to increase the productivity of sack bundlers working in the sack-sewing department. This section was comprised of one hundred and fifty women, each handling four hundred bags per day. Management wanted to increase the workload so that each woman worker would handle two thousand bags per day. Since sack production levels would be held at existing levels, the change would mean that only thirty women would be required in the bundling section of the department. One of the women began organizing her co-workers to resist these changes and took the case to the district commissioner. This organization was independent of the existing unions and was comprised solely of women working in the department, for the bundling section is classified as "women's work" and accordingly employs only women. The district commissioner then called a meeting that included the women workers, management representatives, and trade-union leaders. After negotiations reached an impasse, management indicated that they would close down the sack-sewing department for six months. The women signed an agreement to this effect in lieu of accepting the changes proposed by management.

   The result of this strategy was twofold. First, since the entire department was closed, workers in other sections, such as sewing-machine operators, were also affected by the decision. Management was able to do this legally since most of the workers employed in the department were casual workers who were not guaranteed work. Management therefore took enough orders to employ fifty permanent workers in the department. The manager who narrated this case admitted to the explicit use of a divide-and-rule strategy to quell the resistance. The result was that male laborers from other sections began to pressure the women workers to withdraw their resistance. Second, the union leaders withdrew their initial support of the women bundlers and began exerting more pressure on the women. While management was able to play on gender divisions within the work force, the unions consolidated this strategy by adhering to the interests of the male workers who formed the base of union support. In the resolution of the conflict, the women's resistance was dissolved, the higher production level was instituted, and the interests of management, unions, and male workers in the department were safeguarded.

The relationship between community and trade-union support is not manifested as directly as it is in the case of gender. Unions claim a range of support that cuts across identities of region, religion, or caste. However, community ties also provide material for the creation of relationships of patronage between unions and workers. For example, unions may compete for the support of particular powerful castes or communities by attempting to gain benefits for members of the group in question. Workers from Bihar belonging to the *goala* [buffalo herder] caste represent the dominant caste in the mill, and both the CITU and INTUC unions have been competing for their support. According to one mill manager, a small union consisting of workers from Andhra Pradesh and Orissa was formed to counter the underrepresentation of their interests. The manager indicated that "the union was formed on an ethnic basis because these are weaker groups and they were being browbeaten by the goala caste workers." In general, however, links between community and unions are represented through subtle investments in networks and interests rather than through a one-to-one correspondence of identity. Unions in the mill do not usually have an "essential" community basis, but interests represented by unions are defined according to the interests of dominant communities. The contradictions inherent in the nature of trade union organization once again problematize the meaning of resistance. Even as unions provide an important resource to workers, they have created their own bases of power contingent on social inequalities of gender and community.

In effect, the representation of "working-class" interests through trade unions is constituted by hierarchical social relations that exist among workers. An analysis of trade unions thus cannot be divorced from an understanding of the differentiation of interests within the working classes. In this process, the boundaries of class are both produced and contested by the politics of gender and community. The differences that persist within the working class are manifested not by a pluralistic set of class identities but by a political process in which class interests are articulated through conflict, hierarchy, and exclusion.

Chapter 4
Manufacturing Community:
Rituals of Hegemony and Resistance

The national discourses of unions have articulated a conception of worker politics that is distinct from the politics of religion. These discourses are reproduced by unions at the factory level. Local leaders in the jute mill assert, for example, that religious conflicts rarely arise among the jute workers, and that if such conflicts do arise, they are generally the product of management tactics to undermine worker unity. Paradoxically, however, trade unions and management regularly engage in ritual practices that produce and intertwine narratives of religious, class, and gender identity. The practices occur within the context of celebrations of religious festivals held in the jute factory and working-class residences. Trade-union leaders of a particular community organize the festival and subsequently invite management to attend the inauguration of the event. In this chapter, I analyze the dynamics of these practices to demonstrate that local unions continually attempt to reinscribe the political identity of workers through the temporal, spatial, and relational construction of such narratives (Somers and Gibson, 1994). An analysis of this process of construction allows us to problematize the notion that "community" represents a primordial or "natural" realm that implicitly opposes the "constructed" domain of class or gender identity. Instead, as we will see, community identity is created through a conflicted dynamic of hegemony and resistance, a process in which community simultaneously produces and is manufactured through narratives of class and gender within a contested symbolic terrain.

Consider the following instance of the Shivratri festival, held in a particular community of Hindu jute workers in honor of the deity Shiva. A senior management representative was asked by a trade union to serve as the guest of honor and inaugurate the religious ceremony. The manager arrived at the community in his car and was immediately surrounded by union and community leaders, and then taken to the house of the main leader of the trade union. According to customary practices during such events, the manager is first offered food and drink while workers wait for the ceremony to begin. However, the manager insisted that he was pressed for time and declined the offer of food. This refusal represented a minor social offense and the union leader responded sharply, "Of course, you own the factories. Whatever you say will be." This short exchange reflects the inextricable link between the social context of the ceremony and the class identity of the workers. The narrative operating in this incident is embodied in the social and cultural expectations of the relationship between host and guest. The leader, however, interpreted the manager's violation of his role as guest in terms of the manager's position within the factory, that is, in terms of a worker-owner relationship; the conception of the manager's cultural error was translated into the terms of a class relationship. The manager's refusal of food was interpreted as an assertion of his class position and a form of resistance to the leader's authority as both host and organizer of the event. In such situations, workers deliberately identify managers as "owners" of the factory and highlight the opposition between workers and owner-managers while underplaying divisions and distinctions between various levels of managerial authority or between managers and the factory owner.

After the leader and manager had conferred in private, the ceremony began. The manager was taken to a platform on which a representation of Shiva had been constructed; next to this construction a microphone had been set up and the union leader announced that workers should gather around the platform. After approximately seventy male workers had assembled, the manager was garlanded and asked to give a short speech to initiate the ceremony. Finally, religious rites were performed by a priest, and the inauguration culminated with a ritual procession around the representation of Shiva.[1]

The enactment of this ritual inauguration of the Shivratri festival contains entwined threads of power, authority, and resistance that are produced during ritual ceremonies held in the jute-worker communities. Consider for instance the complexity of the manager's position. On one level, the ritual re-creates the symbolic authority of the manager—he is the guest of honor, he inaugurates the ceremony, and he consequently bestows the ritual with status and legitimacy. On a second level, however, the ritual results in a subtle subversion of the authority of management. The union leaders are able to control and direct the movement and actions of the manager within the space of the religious ritual, in an ironic reversal of management's own direction and discipline of the workers on the shop floor. As the union leader directs the manager to stand, sit, walk, or speak during the ritual, a symbolic transformation of authority takes place through the control of time and space.

The significance of this subversion of authority is underlined by the fact that managers argue that they must attend such rituals in order to preserve peaceful relations with the various communities of workers. Management's depiction of the compulsory nature of their attendance at such ceremonies must, of course, be contextualized within contemporary national anxieties over the potential for intercommunity conflict in India. On the one hand, national political discourses have underscored the need to accommodate and negotiate between the interests of different communities. On the other hand, national discourses primarily articulated by the right-wing Bharatiya Janata Party have constructed Hindus as a marginalized community that has been sidelined by the supposed "special treatment" of minority (particularly Muslim) communities. The manager's presumption that he must attend the Shivratri festival held by a particular group of Hindu workers cannot be extricated from the influences of such discourses. Yet this situation cannot be reduced to national narratives of communalism. At the local level, for instance, the manager articulated his concerns not in relation to potential community conflict but in terms of specific workplace-based dynamics of class conflict. As the manager asserted, if he had failed to attend the Shivratri ceremony, the union's members would have retaliated indirectly by slowing down production or damaging materials on the shop floor. The potential for a form of oppositional class politics permeated the organization of the ceremony. That the threat of retaliation was sufficient to shape management behavior underscores the effectiveness of class opposition that takes the form of "everyday acts of resistance" (Scott, 1985), particularly since the union in question was a small organization without affiliation to any major political party and therefore without any significant formal political clout in the mill.

Meanwhile, the union leaders' ability to engage in a symbolic appropriation of management authority subsequently consolidates the power and legitimacy of the union. The male workers in the community play a relatively minor role in this theater of action, although they participate in the religious rites. Female workers and wives of male workers do not participate and remain within their homes during the inauguration. The subversion of authority that occurs in the ritual is instead aimed primarily at reinforcing the authority of the union leaders within this particular community of workers.

The synopsis of this ritual conveys, I hope, a sense of the concrete practices through which the politics and identities of class and religion are intertwined in the factory arena.[2] Because women workers and wives of workers do not participate in these public rituals, the narratives of class and religion are interwoven within a gendered political space. During this process, the traditional class-based union organizations produce a particular form of community that incorporates narratives of religious identity, gender, social celebration, and entertainment through a guest-host relationship between workers and management. Drawing on these multiple narratives, union leaders hosting the celebration are able to demonstrate their legitimacy in the eyes of both management and the male workers who represent the majority of their membership base. Management is able to participate in an event that presents a veneer of harmonious relations with workers, in contrast to the conflictual relationship between managers and workers on the shop floor. Such practices aid the production of a particular form of hegemony wherein workers recognize the authority and legitimacy of both union leaders and management. This hegemony is always partial, however, because the meanings of the rituals are continually contested as more militant union leaders attempt to reassert an oppositional relationship between workers and management.

Religious festivals play a significant role in the jute industrial arena. They are not minor or random occurrences but routinized annual events organized by union leaders and workers in celebration of major festivals in both Hindu and Muslim working-class communities. One of the prominent trade-union leaders in the mill stated that festivals have been held since 1969, the year of the first successful industrywide strike in the postcolonial period. Such practices represent the "invented traditions" that Hobsbawm has defined as "novel situations which take the form of reference to old situations" (Hobsbawm, 1983:2), rather than the lingering traces of a "precapitalist" rural migrant culture. The organization of the events often involves prolonged negotiations between unions and management, and between rival unions (in the event that several unions cooperate in the organization of a particular festival). The rituals have two dimensions: the inauguration, where a high-level management representative is invited to initiate the ceremony as the guest of honor, and the independent sphere of celebration, which involves only worker participation. I focus here on the first aspect of the ritual, for such inaugural events constitute important exercises in labor-management relations which reproduce the hegemony of managers and unions in the jute mill.

My analysis builds on the approaches to working-class politics that have shed light upon the "making" of class through ritual, religious traditions, and other forms of cultural expression (Sewell, 1980; Thompson, 1966). I specifically examine the ways unions themselves produce particular narratives of cultural expression. The invention of class in this context does not merely draw on predefined cultural resources but also constructs particular hegemonic forms of cultural identity. Recent developments in post-structuralist theory (Butler, 1990; Minh-ha, 1989; Nicholson, 1990; Scott, 1988; Stedman Jones, 1983) have effectively demonstrated that the consciousness, identity, and experience of groups such as classes can be understood as categories that are constructed rather than reflective of a predefined essence. In light of this approach, the case of religious rituals in the jute mills provides an understanding of the means through which trade unions produce particular representations of the "worker" by weaving together certain strands of class, gender, and community identity. This political identity is not purely a discursive form but is constructed by institutional practices as well as "signifying practices" (Comaroff, 1985: 6) that include but are not restricted to a discursive dimension. A focus on ritual practice as a site of identity formation underscores the fact that an analysis of the construction of identity cannot be limited to a purely discursive analysis; it must also address a range of social activities (Sewell, 1980), including forms of symbolic action, "spatial practices" (de Certeau, 1984: 96), institutional activities, and everyday acts of resistance. Meanings, expressions, and identities of class, community, and gender, while constructed and contested, are articulated through such practices and therefore can be conceived of as "social products" (Marx, 1978 [1932]: 158).

I link recent debates on the social production of identity with the insights of this research on the politics of ritual—a field of cultural "tradition" that at first appears to lie quite far from recent research on the fluid, constructed nature of identity. Indeed, a long tradition of research has drawn on conceptions of Durkheim and has depicted ritual as a means for the legitimation of social order and the exercise of authority (Geertz, 1973; Gluckman, 1965).[3] Clifford Geertz, for example, has argued that the enactment of religious ritual produces an integration between the "ethos" or underlying dispositions, moods, and motivations of the participants and the "worldview" or the conception of the "order of existence" (Geertz, 1973: 112). Recent research, however, has demonstrated that ritual may also serve as a form of resistance and as a means for the subversion of social order (Comaroff, 1985; Dirks, 1992; Ong, 1988; Sewell 1980; Taussig, 1980). This latter work has added a measure of political dynamism to anthropological studies by conceptualizing ritual as a site of contested meanings and practices. In my analysis, I draw on the insights of both streams of literature. I analyze the Durga Puja festival, one of the most important Hindu festivals held in the jute mills and in West Bengal in general, in order to demonstrate that the ritual celebration of this event serves both to legitimize and to subvert the authority of unions and managers. Unions attempt to reinforce their legitimacy through the organization of the festival in the jute mill, yet the hegemony of the unions and management is contested during the course of the ritual celebration.

By integrating this dynamic approach to the politics of ritual with recent insights on identity formation, I open up a theoretical space in which studies of the multiplicity of identity need not be exclusively limited to contexts or practices that we associate with conditions of "postmodernity." More significant, practices that often serve as a marker of (precapitalist) cultural or "postcolonial" difference can in fact provide us with general insights into the production of identity. I specifically use an analysis of the Vishwakarma festival—a festival observed by particular sections of Hindu working-class communities to celebrate their tools of labor—to demonstrate how unions produce class opposition through the religious boundaries of the festival. By constructing a conceptual space in which class and religion represent relational rather than necessarily antithetical identities, I read the Vishwakarma Puja as a ritual of resistance rather than as a remnant of a hierarchical "precapitalist" culture (Chakrabarty, 1989). I conclude the chapter by touching on the implications of local ritual practices for relations between Hindu and Muslim workers, particularly in the context of national discourses on "communalism" in India.[4]

Narratives of Community, Class, and Gender: Dialectics of Hegemony and Resistance

Local shop-floor unions in the jute mill adhere to the national discourses of trade unions, which articulate a clear separation between the politics of class and religion. The standard official position of local trade-union leaders upholds a strong belief in the separation between union activity and religion, a demarcation that constitutes the foundation of their conceptions of working-class unity. As one union leader explains: "The point is that if you see another worker, you must help him. When others are in trouble, if they need food, if they need help, you must give them this help. Workers must work together in their struggle in the mill, to fight the maliks. Everyone must follow their own religion. That is their right. Everyone must follow their own religion." This attitude, echoed by local union leaders across the ideological spectrum, maintains a notion of religion as a private sphere of activity, as opposed to the public class opposition between workers and maliks. In addition, leaders of various unions in the mill emphasized the fact that there were no conflicts between workers based on religious affiliation. This point of view was also strongly maintained by the industrywide jute union representatives based in the unions' city offices in Calcutta. These representatives asserted that West Bengal was free from the "communal" conflicts that have surfaced in other parts of the country. This interpretation is to a large extent corroborated by the relative success of the West Bengal government's official campaigns against communalism.[5] In addition, trade unions affiliated with the Bharatiya Janata Party have not enjoyed more than a marginal presence in the jute mills and in West Bengal in general. One local Congress union leader in a mill in rural West Bengal said that at times members of the Vishwa Hindu Parishad (an ally of the BJP) had attempted to recruit Hindu workers, but that on such occasions the Congress and Communist unions united to counter the threat.

In a few cases, leaders did acknowledge a potential for religion to act as a divisive force among workers. In such instances, however, union leaders argued, the divisions were often created or exacerbated by management strategies:

There are divisions between workers, mainly of religion. But in this the capitalists have a role. For example a supervisor will say to the sirdar, "This worker is Muslim, that worker is a Hindu." He will say, "What is happening in the mosque? What is happening in the temple?" Like that he will help the divisions. I'll give you an example in Bihar. This happened in Tatanagar in Jamshedpur, an industrial belt, in 1978 when there was a Janata government. For the birthday of Ram [the Hindu deity] there was a procession being organized. The police administration had told them which roads to go through. But one of these roads had Muslim communities staying there. There were fundamentalists in both communities, among both the Hindus and Muslims. The Muslims said, "They will not come by the mosque." The Hindus said, "Such a big procession has been organized, it must go through the road." So stones were being thrown by both sides. This affected the factories there. The Hindu worker would say, "There is a Muslim worker at that machine, I will not work there." The Muslim worker would say the same to the Hindu worker. The result was that the capitalists had the advantage. The workers' unity was broken. For seven years, maybe ten years, the workers' relations were broken because of this Hindu-Muslim quarrel.

The union leaders' discourses on the relationship between religion and the working class center on two narratives. First, the leaders echo a position that falls within the framework of conventional national conceptions of "secularism" in India. The official rhetoric of unions implies the privatization of religion and a clear separation between religion and politics. The second narrative invokes the Marxian notion that employers utilize religion as a tool to divide the workers.

In general, union leaders at both the local and industrywide levels do not stray from these official narratives regarding the relationship between religion and working-class politics. On many occasions during the course of my interviews, I found that union leaders were willing to speak about a wide range of issues but often resisted discussing the question of religion. Whereas leaders openly discussed questions regarding women workers and admitted failures of unions to adequately represent gender issues, such candid discussions were nonexistent with regard to the issue of religious differences.

In one interview I conducted with a local leader at the Calcutta jute mill, the leader indicated that religious divisions were not present among the jute workers. I then asked the leader to describe the workers' communities and places of residence. The leader responded: "See there are two sides when you go to the labor lines [worker residences]. When you walk there is a gate, then on the right side the quarters are clean and well kept. You go to the left side and it is dirty. There are many *jhupries* [squatter constructions]." When I indicated that I did not understand why there was such a difference between the two sides of the worker residences (particularly since I had not noticed the difference on my visits to the labor lines), the leader replied: "The right side, that is our Mohammedan quarters. On the left side, the Hindu quarters are there. The right side is very clean. We always throw water. The workers in our community join together to clean the quarters. That is why." The leader expressed the separation between the two communities through a spatial representation of community rather than through a direct answer to my earlier questions about the role of religion. The incident sheds light on the problem of basing an analysis of the relationship between religion and class on discursive responses to interview questions, for the issue of communalism is extremely volatile in contemporary Indian politics. The official story on religion and politics stands in ironic contrast to the interconnections between class and community that unfold with union participation in the sphere of ritual politics.

An analysis of ritual practices provides a more subtle and valuable understanding of the production and transgression of the boundaries between class and religion. However, it is critical to note at the outset that the meanings of such intersections cannot be reduced to a model of communal Hindu-Muslim conflict. Union leaders, for instance, did not view the organization of religious festivals as a contradiction of their ideology of secular worker organization. One leader admitted:

It is true that [inviting management to religious festivals] does not do anything. Before 1969 it never used to occur. But now this is the belief. We have our positions. You are a GM [general manager] and I am a worker. But the point is to leave aside your designation. You forget you are a GM and you come to the festival as a human being. In the name of humanity, we are the same. Otherwise, we do not believe in mixing religion and politics.

The leader's reference to origins was of particular significance, as 1969 was the year of the first general strike in the jute industry since independence. Meanwhile, according to the general manager of the mill, religious festivals have been organized since 1947—that is, since national independence was achieved in India. In this case, the "invention of tradition" was associated with the invention of the Indian nation-state. The significant point here is not the accuracy of either claim but the way in which the differing views of the origin of these festivals reflect a form of appropriation of such "traditions" within the two larger political movements of nationalism and organized labor. In both cases, the union leader and the manager attempted to contextualize the rituals within an acceptable arena of formal politics in order to underplay the "mixing" of religion and politics.

There is a persistent attempt to preserve a distinction between the public realm of politics and the private sphere of religion, even while this line is being crossed and dispelled. As we shall see, the construction of community identity through such rituals is usually interwoven with narratives of class relationships—in this leader's view, "to leave aside your designation" and momentarily negate stringent class hierarchies—rather than with the national discourses on relationships between Hindus and Muslims. Although such local practices cannot, of course, be decontextualized from the larger discourses, they are not mere reflections of national political processes. The meanings of social practices are shaped by the specificities of local contexts and the contingencies of everyday politics.

Rituals are dynamic processes that are "invented" and contested as they are performed. Such situations are fraught with ambiguity, particularly since they reproduce hierarchies and legitimize authority even as they provide arenas for contestation. As Nicholas Dirks observes, "It is precisely the political permeability of ritual that makes possible a succession of contested performances, readings and tellings" (Dirks, 1994: 492). The jute workers' participation in religious rituals in the factory cannot be explained through a unified, synchronic model of meaning. As an interpretation of the Durga Puja (the worship of the goddess Durga, which is held in the workers' residences) reveals, the making of ritual involves the creation of multiple layers of meaning.

The Durga Puja is one of the most important Hindu festivals in West Bengal. It lasts for four days and has been transformed into a public celebration that involves Hindu communities across class and caste. Public *pujas* (worship) are organized by clubs and community organizations in both working-class and middle-class neighborhoods. This public form of the puja is specifically associated with West Bengal, although the popularity of the festival has been spreading to other regions. Its popularity is also reproduced within the jute mill, where the Durga Puja is one of the most important religious and cultural events organized by management and Hindu workers (Bengali and non-Bengali). The event was organized by a formal "Puja Committee" comprised of union representatives as well as members of the clerical staff. Financial contributions to the committee were made by both managers and unions. In preparation for the puja, a large tent containing an image of the goddess Durga was constructed in the *maidan,* a small, barren stretch of land in front of the workers' residences, across the street from the factory.

On the evening of the first day of the celebration, I accompanied the general manager and personnel manager of the factory to the inauguration of the Durga Puja festival. We were driven from the mill to the maidan across the street; management must always arrive at such events in a car in order to preserve the appropriate distinctions of status and position, even though the distance between the mill and the maidan is less than a five-minute walk. As we exited the car, several union leaders who were responsible for the organization of the celebration immediately stepped forward to greet the managers.

The maidan had been decorated with fluorescent lights. Four or five long wooden tables with chairs had been set up in three rows; the managers and I were seated in the first row, the only one that had bright tablecloths covering the table. The prominent trade-union leaders of the mill were seated in the two rows behind us. Male workers are not provided with seats for these occasions, and they must stand around in a circle and observe the proceedings. The spatial arrangement of managers, union leaders, and workers encodes their relative positions of authority and subordination.[6] The position of women, meanwhile, is marked by their invisibility, for they are not present at the event.[7]

The ceremony began with worship of the image of the goddess Durga. After one of the puja organizers had announced the commencement of the event, the managers and union leaders stood up and walked to the tent that had been set up near the benches. Workers standing around and watching were hastily pushed aside by the union leaders so that management could avoid all bodily contact with the workers. Inside the tent was a wooden platform with a large statue of the goddess Durga seated on a lion. The goddess Durga is a warrior in Hindu religious legends who successfully defeated the demon Mahisha in a heroic battle. According to mythology, the demon had been invincible—all other gods, including Vishnu and Shiva, had been unable to destroy him. During this time, the gods had surrendered all weapons and powers to Durga. In the statue constructed by the workers, Durga is holding silver spears, which she is using to attack a demon. The representation signifies her victory over the invincible enemy of the gods. The ritual performed for the inauguration is very brief—each of the managers must climb onto the platform, place a garland at the goddess's feet, and briefly join his hands in prayer. As each representative performs the worship, his name is announced with a microphone for the benefit of the workers who are not allowed to enter the tent. The physical boundaries of the ritual space within the tent exclude the possibility of any form of worker participation. This worship of Durga's *shakti* or feminine power is particularly ironic given the fact that women workers are excluded from the public and political dimension of the ceremony.

This enactment embodies the crux of the politics of rituals performed in the factory and worker communities. The enactment of such religious rituals results in the reproduction of two forms of legitimacy: the first upholds the realm of management authority, and the second consolidates the leadership of the local union representatives. In this process, unions and management draw on common symbols and participate in a shared representation of power and legitimacy. Clifford Geertz describes this process of legitimation through ritual practice as one in which "the moods and motivations which sacred symbols induce in men and the general conceptions of the order of existence which they formulate for men meet and reinforce one another. In a ritual, the world as lived and the world as imagined, fused under the agency of a single set of symbolic forms, turn out to be the same world" (1973: 112). The question that then arises is whether this "fusion of the world as lived and the world as imagined" indeed represents an absolute and complete process; that is, can we assume that such religious rituals are successful in establishing the hegemonic authority of management and unions? To address this question, we must shift to the concern that lies at the heart of theories of legitimacy and hegemony—the issue of consent.[8]

The following incident occurred during the careful designation of seating positions in preparation for the inaugural ceremony. An old trade-union leader arrived at the gathering and began shouting at the managers: "So all the Brahmins are sitting here. This is set up for all the Brahmins. Where are we lower-caste people going to sit? This festival is only for Brahmins." The general manager immediately attempted to placate him by saying, "We are all equal. We are all Brahmins." The leader, grumbling to himself, ignored the manager and seated himself at the end of the first row designated for the primary rung of managerial authority. This twist in the proceedings of the puja sharply contradicted the myth of equality created through the joint participation of unions and managers in the festival; it also interrupted the naturalization of the symbolic, spatial representation of management and union authority. The leader's analysis of this process in terms of caste, wherein management becomes synonymous with the upper-caste Brahmin, is particularly significant since it resists the production of hierarchical unity through the religious ritual. My intention here is not simply to demonstrate the importance of "caste consciousness" or to argue that the incident reflects the interaction between caste and class.[9] Rather, the point is that the leader is able to use the category of caste in order to simultaneously dispel the image of an ordered, unified Hindu community that is being enacted through the religious ritual. The union leader's act of seating himself with the managers clearly defied this ritual creation of the hierarchical relationships among managers, union leaders, and workers. Furthermore, the leader constructed an oppositional relationship between workers and managers through this consciousness of caste.

Despite the attempt to consolidate the authority of management and unions within a distinct symbolic space, the ritual was only able to create a partial form of legitimacy. Consider the conflict over legitimacy that emerges through the speeches made by union leaders during the course of the inauguration. The union leader who had resisted the spatial representation of authority began his speech with an interpretation of the meaning of the religious ritual. He began by praising the goddess Durga, indicating that she, along with other deities of Hinduism, represented the "shakti of good over evil." He then transformed this interpretation of the religious significance of the festival into an interpretation of the role of the participants and the practices of the ritual. He began to interweave personal attacks on the mill owner and management with references to Durga's attack on evil: "The *bara sahibs* [big bosses] all sit in front. They are given drinks before the others. That's why we are brought here—to see this. Mr. ——— owns nine factories. Mr. ——— runs all these factories. But Durga is the killer of evil. Together Durga and Kali [goddess of destruction] killed the demons. There could be an attack on management." The leader was momentarily able to transform the ritual from an "officializing strategy" (Bourdieu, 1977: 40) that reproduced the authority of management into a confrontational tactic that focused on the oppositional relationship between managers and workers.

While the leader continued his speech in this vein, the managers and the other union leaders were becoming increasingly tense and angry. After two of the union leaders had conferred with management, one of the leaders finally interrupted the speech. The representative justified his interruption:

What I had to do to end [his] speech was not right, but what he was doing was also not right. The management came today at our invitation. We invited them to attend. They are our guests. To offend their honor is to offend our honor. It is a shame for the Puja Committee. That is why I am not sorry to have ended [his] speech. The puja today is for prayer and peace. We should be gathered here for prayer [*vandana*]. This is not for politics. We do not want to corrupt our celebration. We are here for a good reason. To offer prayer and worship. I ask you to be here in peace and prayer. That is the purpose of the puja.

This synopsis of the speeches elucidates the role of ritual in both the perpetuation of and opposition to particular forms of social hierarchy. The incident undercuts the assumption that the meaning of rituals can be cast in a single model. The clear disruption of the attempt by the unions and the management to reproduce a form of unified community associated with such "traditional" forms of activity confirms that such ritual practices represent "a social moment of liminality" (Dirks, 1994: 488) rather than an example of social stasis.

The making of the ritual involves conflict over the interpretation and purpose of the performance. The speeches of the two union leaders dispute the meaning of the religious ritual, that is, whether the ritual is one of "pure" worship and prayer or whether it represents the act of creating and breaking the codes of legitimate domination. This contest over the meaning of the religious worship of the goddess is interwoven with a dispute over the interpretation of the class relationship between management and workers. While the second leader's call for peaceful prayer and worship represents an implicit acceptance and reenactment of management authority, the first leader's emphasis on the destruction of evil creates a consciousness of an oppositional relationship between workers and management—a form of consciousness that recasts the ritual in terms of a labor-management conflict.

The dynamics of this inauguration demonstrate the way in which union leaders and managers attempt to use such ritual practices to assert their positions of authority relative to the jute workers. Meanwhile, the absence of any participation by women workers in this public ritual reinforces the underlying narrative of gendered politics that permeates the industrial arena. Ironically, the union leaders organizing the ritual responded positively to my own participation in the celebration, and such events played a large role in the legitimation of my own role and authority as ethnographer in the factory. In their speeches, union leaders often introduced me by name and indicated to the workers that my research was concerned with the conditions of workers in India. My participation therefore did not lead the unions to identify me with the management, but rather carved out a legitimate space for me in the political landscape of the factory. Union leaders interpreted my participation as a positive act in large part because I was breaking with gendered norms associated with my class position—clearly, middle- and upper-class women, including manager's wives and daughters and the female labor officer from the factory, did not interact socially with workers or visit the workers' residences. This participation, then, provided me with a means to transgress the socio-spatial distance between my location and that of the jute workers the management had been attempting to preserve. Yet it is also clear that my class position gave me the resources to override gender codes, an option working-class women did not possess. This underscored once again the need to confront the intersections between the categories of class and gender.

Sacred Spaces and Rituals of Resistance

The momentary transformation of the Durga Puja from a ritual of order to a ritual of subversion points to the need to examine alternative spheres of resistance. As James Scott points out, these spheres are often overlooked by traditional analyses of the formal realm of organizational activities (Scott, 1985). Although Scott's work effectively revises the conception of class precisely by expanding the understanding of what counts as class resistance by peasants, his vision of class is still presented in predominantly economic terms. As Nicholas Dirks observes, Scott's notion of "everyday acts of resistance" has tended to ignore the possibility of ritual as a source of resistance (Dirks, 1992). This oversight stems in part from Scott's conception of class identity. Scott acknowledges that class may be "reinforced or cross-cut by other ties" and notes that "class may compete with kinship, neighborhood, faction, and ritual links as foci of human identity and solidarity. Beyond the village level, it may also compete with ethnicity, language group, religion and region as a focus of loyalty" (1985: 43). However, such links with other forms of social identity are not incorporated within his theoretical conception of everyday class resistance. Thus, paradoxically, though Scott's project aimed at expanding the notion of class politics beyond the realm of formal politics, his implicit theoretical conception in fact retains the conventional juxtaposition between class and cultural identity that has shaped intellectual as well as practical (trade-union) visions of class behavior.

The process through which Scott's opposition between class and cultural identity obscures the sites of rituals of resistance can also be seen in Dipesh Chakrabarty's work on the industrial working class, specifically in his analysis of the Vishwakarma Puja celebrated by jute-mill workers. In Hindu mythology, Vishwakarma is the architect of the universe and the producer of weapons for the gods, and the puja is celebrated by workers who use metal tools. Chakrabarty's interpretation of the jute workers' celebration of this puja as historical evidence of the "peasant's conception of his tools, whereby the tools took on magical and godly qualities" (1989: 89) serves as a marker of the "pre-capitalist, inegalitarian" (1989: 69) culture of the jute workers. Chakrabarty does not, however, explore the possibility that such ritual practices may have served as a site of (class) resistance to the industrial discipline of the workplace or to the culture of capitalism being produced within the jute mill.

An analysis of the celebration of this festival in more recent times provides a contrasting interpretation that allows us to think beyond the opposition between class and religion or ritual and resistance. Since it involves the worship of tools, Vishwakarma Puja remains a significant festival for particular Hindu communities of the jute working class. The rituals of the festival are specifically oriented toward work and the meaning of labor.[10] The festival, which is held within the factory compound, consists of the worship of the god Vishwakarma with offerings of flowers and *prasad* (sweets) and celebrations with music. The politics of this ritual in the jute mill unfold on two planes of activity and meaning, or, as David Laitin has put it, "the two faces of culture" constituted by "the cultural ordering of political priorities and the use of cultural identity as a political resource" (1986: 11). On the one hand, the religious ritual delineates a sphere of politics distinct from the "formal" realm of industrial politics; on the other hand, the ritual is politicized by the action and interests of unions and managers in the factory.

In the first case, the politicization of the ritual occurs through the involvement of trade unions and management and their conflict over the organization of the terms of the activity on the shop floor. The performance of the ritual is centered on representations of the deity Vishwakarma that workers construct in the factory. The construction of these images of the god disrupts production, for workers' labor time is taken away for this process. For instance, when the festival was being planned during the course of my fieldwork, management indicated that their primary aim was to contain and centralize the process by authorizing the construction of one large shrine that would require only four or five workers to build the puja and organize the activities. Furthermore, management stipulated that the puja would be limited to the mechanical department of the factory.

The unions, however, insisted on the construction of several images of the god, since the leaders of each union wished to create their own sphere of power and ritual authority. Hence, there was a symbolic re-creation of the competition between unions through the construction of the shrines in the factory. Eventually, six separate shrines were constructed in the factory by separate groups of workers affiliated with each union. The representation of the deity was transformed into symbols of power of the mill trade unions. In this process, as the unions utilize the puja as a resource to represent and consolidate their influence among their constituents, religious worship becomes the signifier of the interests of particular groups of Hindu workers. With this politicization of the festival organization and the corresponding conflict between unions and management, unions in effect construct the workers' interests through religious identity. Unions contribute to an erasure of the boundary conventionally assumed to separate the class and religious identities of the worker.

The ritual practices that constitute the worship during the Vishwakarma Puja also represent a sphere of political activity distinct from the unions' politicization of the festival. I shift here from the way in which such religious activities become politicized by formal, secular organizations to the second plane of analysis, which involves the political nature of the religious ritual itself. On the day of the festival a large shrine was constructed next to the shop floor.[11] On either side of the construction, two amplifiers blared popular Hindi film songs, drowning out the regular sounds of the machines. Meanwhile, five smaller shrines were constructed in the mechanical department. In these sections, ritual practice prohibited workers from touching their tools and machines. Religion in effect altered the landscape of the mill both in terms of space and time. The discipline of time and space was also continually subverted by other sections of the work force. For example, workers from various departments were able to leave their machines at various points during the day in order to perform a brief worship of one of the deities in the mill. The puja thus represented an arena for a political battle over the control of labor through the structuring of time and space. One high-level manager indicated with a significant degree of annoyance, "I will stand in each department of the mill for half an hour tomorrow and make sure that they do not just leave their machines." This battle was not limited to the financial question of preserving production levels, but represented a conflict over the preservation of capitalist discipline in the mill.

Through this ritual, religious worship creates a space of autonomous worker activity on the factory floor that temporarily challenges the authority of management. Consider the following incident, which occurred when I accompanied a labor officer to the department where the shrines were constructed. One worker said to the officer, "This festival is for us to enjoy. Why are the sahibs coming to see it?" A management representative no longer retained the symbolic authority or right to enter the ritual space in the factory; our visit represented an intrusion into this arena. The ritual results in a transformation of the sphere of work into an inviolable, sacred space of the workers. I suggest that this delineation of a sacred space represents the creation of political boundaries— boundaries that produce a class opposition between workers and management through the religious ritual practices of the puja. In contrast, Dipesh Chakrabarty has interpreted historical instances of this ritual as evidence of the workers' "incomprehension of the running principles of the machinery" (1989: 89). He juxtaposes the "religious outlook" of the workers with the "science" of modern technology. Chakrabarty's point is that the "man-machine relationship inside a factory always involves culture and a techno-economic argument overlooks this" (1989: 89). However, Chakrabarty does not consider the possibility that this "religious outlook" in fact forms an intrinsic element of the creation of class consciousness and identity. In my alternative reading, the performance of the Vishwakarma Puja in the factory, through the workers' "worship of machinery," produces a reversal of the "alienation" of the workers from the means of production. The transformation of the mechanical department into a sacred space results in a temporary wresting of the control of the means of production from management. Such beliefs can be read as providing an alternative conception of social reality (Fields, 1985; Taussig, 1980) that contests the dominance of capitalist authority in the factory.

My analysis compels a reconsideration of historical understandings of the Vishwakarma Puja and, at the very least, a questioning of the assumption that the puja celebration represents a form of purely mystical worship "whereby the tools often took on magical and godly qualities" (Chakrabarty, 1989: 89). More important, however, my reinterpretation of the puja reveals that an assumption of strict divisions and oppositions between the categories and identities of class and religion can constrain our interpretation of the political nature and effects of cultural and social practices. In the contemporary context, the dynamics of the Vishwakarma Puja demonstrate how rituals weave together the worker's religious identity with an oppositional class consciousness. Whereas in the case of the Durga Puja we examined the way trade unions produced particular hegemonic narratives of community that legitimized hierarchical relations among managers, unions, and workers, in this situation we see that ritual practices in the factory provide the space for the production of a narrative of an oppositional class relationship between workers and employers.

Contextualizing Narratives of Class and Community

Questions of class and religion in the industrial arena cannot be removed from the context of wider national processes. No discussion of the politics of religion in contemporary India can avoid the implications of the recent rise of Hindu nationalism and religious conflict or, in the more conventional language of Indian politics, the rise of "communalism."[12] In practice, particular discourses on communalism and nationalism often impinge on the rituals I have been describing. Consider the following incident, which occurred during the course of the Durga Puja festival. The start of the ceremony was being held up for the arrival of the deputy commissioner of police, who had been invited to attend the inauguration. There was speculation that his absence could represent a new state government policy barring government representatives from attending religious festivals, since such an act could be viewed as favoritism toward a particular religion. Meanwhile, however, management representatives and union leaders were provided with round ribbons in the colors of the national flag. Such symbols and signs can be conceptualized as the means through which the nation is imagined (Anderson, 1983), particularly since most workers are nonliterate and are consequently relatively unaffected by "print capitalism." The imagination of the nation in this process is intricately woven with the practice of religion, while the rituals of class and religion are littered with signs of the representation of national identity.

The wider implications of these rituals are perhaps best revealed by the fact that one of the central platforms of the trade union wing of the Hindu nationalist party, the Bharatiya Janata Party (BJP), is the demand that Vishwakarma Day should replace May Day as the official national labor day in India. D. B. Thengadi, one of the prominent leaders and founders of the BJP trade union (the Bharatiya Mazdoor Sangh [BMS]) explains the rationale:

It was a matter of sad surprise that even after its existence for more than three decades the Indian Labor Movement had not found out or conceived of the National Labor Day. Even in the United States, which happens to be the birthplace of the International Labor Day, the workers celebrate their own National Labor Day on the first Monday of every September. In our country, Vishwakarma Day is being observed as a national labor day from time immemorial. (1992: 6)

This ideological position transforms the Vishwakarma ritual from a religious celebration of particular communities of Hindu workers into a national ritual of Indian workers; the "Hindu worker" then becomes synonymous with the "Indian worker." Furthermore, this process of nationalization divests the ritual of its potential as a form of resistance and autonomous worker activity and turns it into a symbol of unity and order. Thengadi defines the meaning of the Vishwakarma worship through a particular interpretation of the Hindu myth in which Vishwakarma was asked by the gods to create a thunderbolt to destroy his son: "It was a difficult choice, love for his offspring on the one hand and love for the nation on the other. But the gods had confidence that the patriotism of Vishwakarma would rise above everything. . . . This sacrifice of Vishwakarma is without parallel. In the circumstances of today it is an inspiring example for all Bharatiya [India] in general, and labor in particular" (1959: 48). Thengadi presents Vishwakarma as a symbol of patriotism in stark contrast to the ritualized class opposition created through religious identity. In the local context of the jute mill, the puja has not been absorbed into a narrative of communal politics, particularly since the celebration involves only Hindu workers from the mechanical department and does not produce an overarching Hindu-Muslim distinction among the workers. In the context of the BJP union's national discourse, however, the identity of the worker is cast as an essentialized "Indian-Hindu" identity. I present this transformation of the meaning of the Vishwakarma ritual within the context of national and communal politics in India in order to mark the limits of analyzing local "cultural constructions" or "cultural systems" as isolated, self-sufficient worlds dissociated from wider political processes.

Local practices of class and religion clearly exist in relation to specific asymmetrical relations of power that govern community relations in contemporary India. This point is perhaps most clearly evidenced through the case of the Id-ul-fitr festival, which is organized by Muslim union and community leaders in the worker residences and also attended by Hindu managers. At first glance, the participation of a Hindu manager in the Id celebration and prayers held in the workers' mosque contradicts the national narratives of Hindu-Muslim conflict. However, during the festival held in my fieldwork period, a rival Hindu festival was organized in a community that spatially bordered the Muslim community in the residences of the jute workers. The management representative who was attending the Id-ul-fitr festival first had to stop at this event. The manager indicated that if he had not stopped at this Hindu temple first, the workers would have said that he was "more of a Muslim." Although we cannot ascertain whether this in fact would have been a necessary consequence, the manager in question was drawing on specific national discourses that construct a threat of Hindu-Muslim competition and conflict. In this process, the manager was able to position himself above this situation as a neutral authority (much like that of the state) that must keep the peace between Hindu and Muslim workers. The meaning of the religious ritual was consequently recast by this national narrative on communal conflict.

Meanwhile, the competition of the Hindu festival was juxtaposed to a nationalist construction of Islam during the speeches made by Muslim leaders of the jute workers. One of the prominent leaders described Islam as a positive force of strength and unity in India that advocated the "unity between Muslims, Hindus, Christians, and Sikhs." The situation recreated the national categories of "secularism" and "communalism." In the midst of these symbolic contests, six policemen were present in the workers' residences in anticipation of any "incident" or conflict. Though undertones of conflict are often embedded in everyday situations, there is nonetheless an official denial of intercommunity tensions. Both management representatives and trade-union leaders argue that "communal" tensions do not exist. To a large extent, as I have noted earlier, the West Bengal government has been involved in a strong "anti-communal" campaign, and Calcutta has indeed witnessed relatively low levels of communal conflict in the contemporary period. Nevertheless, it is clear that such power-laden public narratives continually impinge on local practices and constructions of identity; the performance of the Vishwakarma puja in the mill as a ritual of resistance becomes unsettled by such larger political processes.

The enactment of religious rituals in the factory and communities of the jute workers has provided a concrete set of practices through which we can begin to address the political complexities of the points of convergence between the narratives of class and community. Such convergences do not simply rest on an interplay between autonomous strands of identity; rather, there is a process of mutual construction. Unions construct a particular form of community through their organization of and participation in religious ritual practices. This process involves the hegemonic construction of a notion of a unified community and simultaneous resistance to this unity. Within the space of such moments of resistance, community practices then produce forms of class conflict through the creation of an oppositional relationship between managers and workers.

However, an underlying subtext to this chapter is that the representations of both class and community converge in the reproduction of particular hierarchies of gender. Ritual practices employed by unions and community leaders create a gendered public space, one that rests on the exclusion of women workers. Both the construction of community and moments of class conflict are contingent on a gendered division between public and private forms of activity. What is the precise form of this relationship between the "public" and "private" in the jute industrial arena? How does this relationship signify the way in which boundaries between community, class, and gender are produced and contested in the factory and workers' residences? And finally, how does gender begin to operate in a distinctive fashion in relation to class and community? These are the questions I turn to in the next chapter.

Chapter 5
Gender, Community, and the Making of a Worker's Public Sphere

The construction of the workers' public sphere in the jute mills represents a culturally specific and gendered political space that exists alongside the "bourgeois public sphere" (Habermas, 1992) and constitutes an arena where "members of subordinated social groups invent and circulate counterdiscourses to formulate oppositional interpretations of their identities, interests, and needs" (Fraser, 1992). The jute workers' public activity is shaped by a particular socio-spatial continuum between workplace and residence in the jute factories characteristic of the absence of a geographical separation between work and home in the Indian industrial arena (Chandavarkar, 1994). The physical separation between the public world of work and the private world of home that is often presumed in the context of industrial capitalism (Katznelson, 1981) simply does not exist for the jute workers. This spatial continuum between workplace and home is also qualified by management attempts to incorporate the workers' residences within the purview of its regime of disciplinary power and surveillance. Workers must therefore engage in a continual battle to transform their communities into a "free space" (Evans and Boyte, 1986), one that can evade and oppose management authority and the social codes of the "bourgeois public sphere."

In this process, the jute workers' public sphere attempts to represent the general interests of the workers but in fact produces gender hierarchies that conflate the worker's identity with a particular construction of masculinity on the one hand and exclude the participation and interests of women workers on the other. In particular, this "subaltern counterpublic,"[1] to use Nancy Fraser's term, enforces particular models of the working-class family—for example, through the construction of single working-class women as disruptive of social order in the workers' community. The borders of this public sphere are the product of a gendered politics, one that is constructed through the public enforcement of the family as a social unit within the jute workers' communities.

Paradoxically, the subaltern counterpublic in effect converges with management discourses within the bourgeois public sphere which portray the jute workers' communities as sites of moral decay and social disorder. An analysis of such gendered processes not only documents the marginalization of women but allows a critical break from the assumption that the subaltern is an autonomous symbol that lies in a pure realm outside the hierarchies and modalities of power that shape authority relations and the world of elite classes.[2] This convergence between the gendered discourses of management and workers ultimately circumscribes the contestatory nature of the workers' counterpublic. Public activities represented through workers' community organizations, everyday practices, and social discourses in fact center on the reproduction of the "working-class family." Both unions and community organizations of the jute workers are complicit in producing a patriarchal form of the family that then recreates hierarchical relationships of gender. Workers, union leaders, and managers participate in and produce a gendered public sphere that rests on the political construction of the "working-class family" at the material, organizational, and ideological levels. The family is therefore the product of dynamic political processes rather than a preconstituted static category (Mohanty, 1991) that merely serves as a signifier of essentialized patriarchal cultural traditions that oppress Indian women.

I build here on feminist research that has demonstrated how discourses on the supposedly "private" realms of gender and the family have played a significant role in the making of nations, the creation of economies, and the reproduction of cultural traditions (Pateman, 1989; Parker et al., 1992; Sangari and Vaid, 1989). The family is no longer conceived as an isolated unit in the private sphere but as inextricably linked with political, economic, and cultural practices. Feminist studies have examined the relationship between domestic labor and wage labor and have shown a dialectical interaction between the reproduction of the family and the social structure. Research on the links among work, community, and family in comparative contexts compels us to reconsider the very boundaries of the "political" in the industrial arena and to transcend the distinction between the arenas of the "public" and the "private" (Barrett and Hamilton, 1986; Glenn, 1986; Hartmann, 1981; Lamphere, 1987; Tilly and Scott, 1978). Building on such work, I argue that the operation of gender hierarchies is central to the creation of the jute workers' public sphere and to the representation of their class and community interests.

My purpose here, however, is not only to analyze the purely discursive processes that produce the jute workers' public sphere but also to demonstrate the material and political consequences for specific groups of workers. The masculinization of space in the jute factory and labor lines results in the construction of single working-class women as a social and sexual threat to the community. I conclude this chapter with the life history of one woman worker in order to demonstrate the concrete material effects of this social construction. Through this history I show that a single woman who attempts to speak with a union leader about workplace grievances incites speculation, gossip, and rumors about her relations with the union leader in question. Even access to the political resources of trade unions is contingent on discourses of sexuality and the family. As this life history reveals, surveillance of the sexuality of working-class women and the construction of single women as a sexual and social threat to the jute workers' communities in fact reverberate with parallels to management's surveillance of workers in the residences and its attempt to produce order in the labor lines. The attempt to discipline women's bodies in the workers' public sphere echoes the logic of management's attempt to discipline workers' bodies in the factory and labor lines. The production of hierarchies of gender in this process forecloses the ability of the jute workers to create a "counter-public" that can successfully break from the bourgeois public sphere and the management authority that lies within this sphere.

The Jute Mill Labor Lines

The workers' residences are located across the street from the factory, and they represent a territorial extension of the mill: the residences and the land on which they are built are owned by the proprietor of the factory. In the nineteenth and early twentieth centuries, factories in India were faced with labor shortages, and they actively recruited rural migrant workers. Since employers needed to attract rural migrants, they generally provided housing for the workers. The result was the creation of an important relationship between housing and labor markets that has continued into the contemporary period. Meanwhile, one of the main characteristics of industrial cities in India has been an extreme shortage of space and the growth of vast "squatter settlements" that have not observed strict class boundaries between neighborhoods.[3] This scarcity of space has had important consequences for the development of working-class residences. In modern India, the shortage of space and the absence of an accessible, independent housing market has meant that industrial workers have built makeshift residences in areas immediately adjacent to the factories and places of work; the result is an absence of a clear spatial separation between work and urban residence.[4] This

situation has been compounded by the importance of the specific pattern of rural migration in industrial work forces. The work/home separation has often tended to correspond to the urban/rural divide, with
industrial migrant workers often preserving ties to their home villages.
Urban residences are therefore strongly tied to and crafted around the
workplace (Chandavarkar, 1994).

The jute workers' residences, rows of small houses constructed back
to back with no windows, were built by the British industrialists when
they first established the mill in the late nineteenth century. Since then
there have been no new construction or improvements of the quarters.[5]
Each house has a small veranda, a room that is four feet by six feet, and,
in a few cases, a small room for cooking. According to conservative estimates, approximately fourteen or fifteen thousand people are housed in
seven hundred quarters. The shortage of residence quarters has been a
significant issue of contention between trade unions and management.
As one union leader indicated:

They [management] say they don't need to build new quarters. They say there
are outsiders who use water, light. But the condition of the quarters is terrible,
they are very dirty. It is difficult to get electricity. In June, July, when most of
the workers leave, it is terribly hot. Management could not stay for one hour in
the heat. The quarters were built with no windows, there is no air—the English
didn't bother to put windows when they built them. It is very hot in the summer. The workers get all kinds of diseases like TB [tuberculosis]. Young people
of fifteen years become like old men. It is no condition for people who work
hard to live.

The politicization of the question of the residences of the jute workers
occupies a central place within the construction of the class consciousness of workers. Consider, for instance, one incident that occurred in
a mill I visited in a rural area in West Bengal. During my visit, the
leaders of one of the major unions indicated that they wanted to show
me the labor lines rather than sit and answer questions regarding the
factory. This suggestion was particularly significant because my visit occurred a few days before the 1992 general strike, and the leaders were
representatives of a union whose central organization in Calcutta had
been among the strongest advocates of a unified strike action. The local
leaders were not interested, however, in discussing the strike or such
workplace issues as wages. The general secretary of the union simply insisted, "You can understand the situation of the Indian working class if
you see the *katcha* [temporary] lines."

The incident exemplifies how the class consciousness of the leaders is
constructed through a consciousness of the politics of residence—what

Ira Katznelson has termed the "spatial imagination" (1992: 239) of the working classes. As one trade-union leader argued,

They [management] are making crores of rupees but they cannot do anything about the quarters. Their crores come from our blood and sweat, but this is what we live in. Look at the difference between the quarters on the other side of the river [management quarters] and these quarters. That difference will tell you everything. They live in big houses by the river and we have to live here. We have been asking them to do something for so long, but they refuse. They will not bother. And the mill is making such a big profit. . . . If there is anything called violation of humanity, this is such a violation of humanity.

In this vivid description of the spatial representation of the relationship between workers and managers, the language of class is articulated through the politics of residence. This consciousness of the conjuncture between workplace and home was most concisely captured by one of the leaders at the end of my visit to the labor lines when he said, "We have shown you the face of this mill." Despite workers' dissatisfaction with the shortage of space and poor living conditions, mill managers have not undertaken any improvements of the quarters, and the central union organizations have not focused on this issue in any of the general strikes they have organized.

In the absence of management action, workers and their families have attempted to negotiate this phenomenon of extreme overcrowding in a number of ways. Most of the existing houses have been divided into separate quarters, that is, each room, including the veranda area, is turned into a separate "house." In addition, the area includes a number of makeshift houses, called *katcha* housing, made out of mud, clay, sacks, or any other available materials. Finally, quarters may be shared by a large number of male workers who "sleep in shifts": the use of the room or house is rotated according to the worker's shift in the factory. Inadequate living conditions have often hindered women seeking to accompany their husbands or parents to the factory (women rarely migrate alone). The scarcity of space and the fact that a small room may be shared on average by eight people have deterred some male workers from bringing their families to the factory. Indeed, rural folklore has historically identified the Calcutta jute mills with the journey of single men from the village to the factory. As Nirmala Banerjee explains:

Songs of village women from Bihar describe the mills and Calcutta as the villains who separated them from their husbands and lovers. Going to Calcutta's jute mills was rather like going to the battlefields. If your man came back triumphant he would cover you with gold; but the Bengal soil may suck him in or he may be seduced by some woman there. So one waited and hoped but could never dream of following him there.[6]

Masculinization of the mill and the urban arena in Calcutta continues to characterize representations of the jute mills. Women do, however, reside in the labor lines. The factory employs approximately one hundred and eighty women out of a total work force of four thousand workers, and a portion of male workers have brought their wives and families from their villages. Patterns of migration have varied across ethnic groups, and the trend of single male migration does not hold for all groups of migrants. Male migrants from Bihar, for instance, in general did not migrate with their families, and women did not migrate alone, whereas in the case of workers from Andhra Pradesh and Orissa, entire families tended to migrate to Calcutta (de Haan, 1994: 181). In addition to rural migrants, some women residing in the labor lines were born to parents who worked in the mill. In one survey of the work force conducted at a public sector mill in 1979, it was estimated that 49.75 percent were residing with their entire family, 14.25 percent were residing with part of their family, and 36.01 percent had left their entire family in the village (Mitra, 1985). Based on records of the labor office in my own research site, three to four thousand people were designated as family members of workers residing in the labor lines.[7] It was impossible to gain access to precise statistics on gender composition or even exact numbers of residents, because reliable records are not kept by management. Any independent attempt on my part to conduct a formal survey (in contrast to the everyday conversations, in-depth interviews, and observations that I recorded) would have raised suspicion among workers, since such records could be used as part of management surveillance.

The workers' suspicion would have been particularly appropriate, since their residences in fact do fall under the purview of management surveillance and control. The modes of disciplinary power discussed in Chapter 3—the "partitioning" of space and the constant gaze of authority—have been extended to the workers' everyday individual and community lives in the labor lines. The residences are literally mapped by management, each row or "line" of quarters and each individual quarters are numbered, and records of quarters are kept by management. Surveillance is then conducted by the "line *durwans*," watchmen employed by the factory specifically to watch over the residences. The durwans must perform an intricate balancing act as they occupy an intermediary position between management and workers. On one hand, workers often view the durwans as management representatives; in some instances, workers do not speak as freely in their presence. On the other hand, however, since the durwans live with the workers in the labor lines, and share a class and community position with other workers, they also inform workers about management movements and actions.

In addition to these official representatives of surveillance, management relies on informal sources of information. As I have noted in Chapter 3, the industrywide cartel of jute industrialists, the Indian Jute Mills Association, has a record of every labor and union meeting and rally, including the names of the organizers and speakers, as well as summaries of the speeches, since the early decades of the century—a stark example of the exercise of modern power through the "political anatomy of detail" (Foucault, 1979: 139).

This exercise of managerial authority in the labor lines bears a striking resemblance to the evolution of disciplinary systems as analyzed by Michel Foucault. Consider his description of the control of a town besieged by the plague in seventeenth-century France:

This enclosed, segmented space, observed at every point, in which the individuals are inserted in a fixed place, in which the slightest movements are supervised, in which all events are recorded, in which an uninterrupted work of writing links the center and periphery, in which power is exercised without division according to a continuous hierarchical figure, in which each individual is constantly located, examined and distributed among the living beings, the sick and the dead—all this constitutes a compact model of the disciplinary mechanism. The plague is met by order. (1979: 197)

The spatial segmentation, supervision, and policing of the jute-mill labor lines reverberates with parallels to Foucault's model of disciplinary strategies. Such strategies converge with the modes of disciplinary power employed in the factory. The extensiveness of management's attempt to regulate the labor lines has perhaps contributed to a pattern of circular migration where even workers with marginal landholdings retain strong ties to their home villages and those who are landless attempt to acquire land in the village. Workers I interviewed referred to their village of origin as their home (*desh*, literally, "country"). The memory of home and the anticipation of return provided them with a means of coping with the harshness of the control and surveillance of their "private" everyday lives in the labor lines.

However, the control of the labor lines I reconstruct here does not correspond to Foucault's totalizing vision of the panoptical model of discipline. This control is continually encroached upon by the workers. As Michel de Certeau has argued, "Beneath what one might call the 'monotheistic' privilege that panoptic apparatuses have won for themselves, a 'polytheism' of scattered practices survives, dominated but not erased" (1984: 48). For example, workers continually construct "unauthorized" quarters, called *jhupries*, that defy the ordered mapping of the labor lines. Management periodically posts notices in the factory condemning the "illegality" of these constructions, but they cannot demolish these quarters without retaliation from the workers. One labor officer explained that in the beginning the company gave permission for the construction of such structures and of certain small-scale enterprises such as vegetable stands, small grocery shops, snack shops, small theaters, and alcohol shops. In recent years, however, the company has lost control over such processes. There are a growing number of non-workers (often relatives or kin of workers) residing in the labor lines who are classified by management as "outsiders" and "illegal" residents of the lines because they do not hold any direct relationship to the factory. In my interviews, managers emphasized that these "illegal" residents were a central cause of overcrowding and poor conditions in the labor lines. They argued that the outsiders were responsible for overconsumption of water and for problems with other infrastructural elements, such as toilets. In some cases, for example, workers had rented out space to non-workers as a means of supplementing their incomes.

Management's construction of the category of the outsider had significant underlying political implications, for union activists working in the labor lines would also fall within this definition. Such "outside" activists historically have played a critical role in labor politics, for they have had access to the resources (such as time, money, literacy) necessary to promote union work. Furthermore, the construction of this insider/outsider distinction reflects management's attempt to impose a symbolic conception of community in which membership is contingent on a link to employment in the mill. By this definition, only mill workers and their families would constitute "legal" residents and members of this working-class community, a circumscribed sphere that would remain comfortably within the purview of management authority. Indeed, the absence of official records and statistics regarding residents of the lines stems from the extent of this overcrowding and the workers' unwillingness to provide information regarding the exact numbers of family members and kin residing with them. This conflict over residency in the labor lines suggests that workers are engaged in a subtle form of resistance to management control over material space within the jute workers' communities.

The attempt of workers to create a "free space" (Evans and Boyte, 1986) for community life outside of the control of management is not limited to reclaiming material space in the labor lines. The "effective" practical control of the workers' residences falls under several layers of organization, including trade unions and various ethnic- and caste-based community organizations. Factory-level union offices are set up in the labor lines, and trade-union meetings and rallies are held in public spaces in the labor lines. Male workers are members of specific "community clubs" that organize a variety of social and leisure activities, including music programs and dramas. In addition, workers are able to watch a color television owned by a particular club and have access to public spaces in which to play cards and socialize.[8] According to workers, eight clubs were organized in the labor lines, including the Oriya club, Yadav club (for the goala caste workers from Bihar), Bengali club, Andhra club, Milan Sangh, Netaji Subhas Association, Mohammedan club, and Sri Hanuman Mandir club.

Although there are no "official" divisions in the labor lines, the residences and the public lives of workers are clearly differentiated according to community, both in terms of religious and regional identities. Religious divisions are reproduced through spatial distinctions between Hindu and Muslim communities. Such spatial representations of community are marked symbolically by the construction of temples in the Hindu communities and a mosque in the Muslim workers' community.

In recent years, given the increasing spatial pressures, workers in the mill have begun to secure spare land or housing without regard to community separations. As one worker suggested: "It started off that people lived in separate communities. But now it is difficult to get houses. People are glad to get a house anywhere. It doesn't matter who the neighbors are. There are no houses now so people don't mind not staying in their own communities. They will stay anywhere they get place." However, the social and cultural organization of workers in the residences is still shaped by the reproduction of community ties. The significance of community ties is due in part to the migratory nature of the work force. As I noted previously, a significant portion of workers are rural migrants who often own and farm land, and therefore retain strong ties with their village of origin. These workers regularly return to the village during the harvesting months, from May to August of each year. Meanwhile, even workers with marginal holdings return to their villages for weddings or to visit relatives. This pattern coincides with the economic cycle of the factory. The factory produces gunny sacks that are used for packaging such materials as food grains and fertilizer. The demand for the sacking products also drops during the months of May to August, since packaging materials are not needed during the harvesting months.[9] The entire industry operates according to a pattern of circular migration, which reinforces the workers' links with their village of origin. Workers then reconstruct their rural, community-based ties within the industrial arena. As one labor officer aptly argued, the reproduction of community is such that there seem to be "mini-Bihars or mini-Orissas" in the labor lines of the jute mills.[10]

The reproduction of such community and kin ties constitutes the social fabric that shapes workers' everyday lives. The implications of such ties, however, differ for male and female workers. Male workers, for instance, have access to public spaces for community life after their shift at the mill or on their days off, whereas women must begin their shift of domestic work at home. Everyday public life in the workers' communities is shaped by what Kathy Peiss terms the "sexual division of leisure" (1986: 5). Working-class women in the jute mills are not able to participate in the community clubs. They are also excluded from participation in the public life of the street, a central arena of working-class social activity (Chandavarkar, 1994; Peiss, 1986). Tea shops and liquor shops, including shops selling home-brewed alcohol in the labor lines, are inaccessible spaces for women. Working-class women, however, do have to cope with the consequences of such public activity. Alcoholism is widespread among male workers, and women workers often complain that their husbands spend their salaries on alcohol consumption rather than on necessities such as food and clothing. Thus, the daily lives of women workers are characterized by sharp distinctions from the lives of male workers.

Vast disparities also exist between more prosperous (permanent) workers and casual workers without stable employment. Richer workers display forms of consumption that mirror patterns of middle-class consumerism; for example, they purchase color televisions and radios and spend large amounts of money on weddings and on gifts and clothes during religious celebrations. Workers assert that weddings and dowries for female children make up two of their largest expenses, particularly during the month of May (the marriage season in the workers' communities). One woman worker pointed out that a dowry for a "poor man" without land in the village could run to Rs. 10–15,000, and could go as high as Rs. 50,000–60,000 for wealthier men (the minimum monthly salary is Rs. 1,600). Workers therefore often have to take out large loans and go into debt in order to finance their children's marriages.

Faced with such high expenses, workers in the mill often supplement their incomes through outside employment. Male and female casual workers seek work in the informal sector to compensate for long periods when they are unable to work in the mill. Although some children of wealthier workers attend school, it is more common for children to work in shops or even on occasion to replace a family member in the factory if the family member has other work. Meanwhile, more prosperous workers often operate small businesses to earn extra money, running small shops in the lines, selling buffalo milk, or even operating as moneylenders. Workers who operate such businesses are habitually absent from work in the factory. These workers are usually permanent workers (their consistent wages allow them to engage in small-scale entrepreneurship) and are therefore not under the threat of losing their jobs, since strong unionism makes it difficult for management to fire them. Chronic absenteeism perpetuates the factory's dependence on casual laborers and reproduces the hierarchies within the labor force.

The links between workplace and residence are manifested in a variety of ways. Workers continually move between employment in the informal sector in the labor lines and in neighboring areas. Moreover, management authority extends from the factory to the workers' residences through particular strategies of surveillance and control. The jute workers must continually negotiate the sociospatial conjuncture between workplace and residence that shapes their everyday public life. The workers' "public sphere" is therefore constituted by mechanisms and debates conducted in a political space that lies between the formal authority exercised in the factory and the "private" individual and community lives of workers. In this context, the construction of a subaltern counterpublic becomes contingent on the workers' attempts to create forms of public life that circumvent or contest the factory authority of management. The result is a significant paradox, for the contours of the worker's public sphere constitute an exclusionary terrain, contingent on the reproduction of gender hierarchies and the marginalization of working-class women. Although the distinctive subaltern nature of this space is contingent on an oppositional relationship to the sphere of management authority, workers in effect reproduce gendered discourses that coincide with management assumptions regarding women, the family, and sexuality. In short, the gendered nature of the workers' public sphere ultimately circumscribes its autonomy and its potential to effectively contest management's social codes and authority.

The Making of a Gendered Subaltern Public Sphere

The connection between workplace and residence in the Calcutta jute mills has fostered the continual transformation of community concerns and conflicts that occur within the labor lines into issues that are brought within the boundaries of the factory authority. The communities of the jute workers in the factory area are significantly shaped by the social relationships that exist within the village. Rural hierarchies and relations are reproduced within workers' communities. Conflicts that occur within a village of a particular group of workers may be translated into a conflict in the factory. For example, in one case a conflict over land ownership in a village in Bihar caused a series of clashes between groups of workers affiliated with the two parties involved. These conflicts often involve caste affiliations. One manager characterized the situation:

Then they bring their conflicts here. There will be some conflict about land in the village. That will come to the labor lines. The goala caste workers will go to their own community, their own organization. The Harijans will stick together. And they will fight each other. Then they will come to the labor office and tell us to make the decision. It comes down to community then, the unions fall away. We interfere because we have to. Their problems affect production. They will tell the supervisors, "Remove that man, we don't want him here." Like that the problems enter the mill. Their caste divisions cause many troubles for us.

Since management acts as the representative for the landlord (that is, the factory owner), community clashes, as well as everyday conflicts between workers in the labor lines, are brought to the labor office in the factory for resolution. This method of conflict resolution in turn reinforces management's ability to regulate the everyday actions and lives of workers.[11] The labor office becomes a form of community "court," and the personnel manager and his labor officers must arbitrate the conflicts, which range from personal disagreements between neighbors or between workers sharing quarters to disputes over the occupancy of a particular residential quarter. According to one labor officer, workers come to the factory with their grievances because they cannot go to the police and file complaints due to their fears of arbitrary intimidation. As a result, according to the personnel manager in the mill, the labor lines provide one of the biggest sources of workplace conflicts: "For example, yesterday a worker retired and his quarter became vacant. Now there will be a thousand applications. The unions will start making demands. Workers will pay the leaders to get it [the quarters] for them—maybe Rs. 500, maybe a few thousand rupees. The labor lines are our main source of problems." The allocation of residence is in fact one of the major issues in workplace conflicts, and it often involves direct negotiation between unions and management. The scarcity of housing provides a source of conflict among workers and once again serves to reinforce management's authority as arbiter and judge both in the factory and in the labor lines. This role is further consolidated by the fact that factory ownership of the labor lines defines management as landlords of the workers.

The transformation of the politics of residence into an industrial conflict also often engages the intervention of the state. Both unions and management have brought their concerns regarding the labor lines to tripartite negotiations. Issues concerning the residences are often discussed in formal negotiations among management, union, and government representatives. These negotiations have often resulted from management attempts to assert or consolidate their control within the labor lines. In one case, a proposal was jointly sponsored by management, corporations, and the police to remove three hundred buffalos from the worker communities, ostensibly to improve sanitation and the conditions of the labor lines. However, the buffalos owned by workers and "outsiders" represented a thriving business and a central component of the "bustee economy": Each liter of milk is sold for Rs. 7 per day; each buffalo produces 15 liters per day; thus the total income from 300 buffalos is almost Rs. 30,000 per day. There was therefore strong opposition to the proposed removal of the buffalos. The issue was one of several workplace-related issues being discussed in formal tripartite talks among trade unions, management, and the West Bengal government. Meanwhile, unions on occasion have attempted to press management to improve conditions in the lines. One union attempted to take the factory company to court in order to press management to repair and construct adequate quarters. Although the judgment in the case favored management, it is significant for our purposes that the case was legally classified as an industrial dispute[12]—that is, not a private issue between landlord and tenant but a union-management conflict.

The relationship between workplace and residence has hampered the workers' ability to create forms of public activity and community organizations that are relatively independent of management authority. For instance, management and trade unions developed a formal institutional mechanism to resolve the conflicts arising from the continuum between factory and residence. A formal organization called the Village Committee was established to arbitrate disagreements between workers in the labor lines and to handle specific grievances regarding the conditions of the quarters. The committee, comprised of four management representatives and two representatives from each of the trade unions active in the mill, met in the personnel office in the factory, and problems were to be discussed until an agreement had been reached. If no agreement could be reached, the fourteen members of the committee were to vote on the conflict. The committee basically functioned as a *panchayat,* a model of local political organization supported by government policies in rural areas in India.

One of the primary aims of the committee was to institutionalize a separation between community and residential conflicts from the workplace. Workers would bring their grievances within a restricted time and space rather than during the regular working hours of the personnel office. In one case, the committee attempted to negotiate with workers who owned buffalos in order to enlist their cooperation in preventing the buffalos from dirtying the labor lines. In another case, a woman brought a grievance against neighbors who were preventing her from occupying quarters in the labor lines. The woman's husband, a worker in the mill, had recently died, and she had obtained his job in the factory. Management specified that she and her children could continue to live in the veranda of her husband's quarter; however, other residents of the quarter were attempting to push her out. The woman in question was able to enlist the help of the Village Committee in retaining this space primarily because her husband had been an active member of one of the major unions in the mill. Her contact with her husband's leader provided her with access to protection through the Village Committee.

Although this case demonstrates that it was possible for women workers to bring grievances to the committee, the leadership of the committee did not consist of any women. Moreover, the case confirms the patriarchal pattern of women's access to support, where a woman worker is able to gain protection solely through her husband's position. The only other attempt of the committee to involve women workers in its activities came in the form of a proposal that the female labor officer in the factory organize a meeting for women workers in order to educate them and train them to clean up the labor lines. According to one memorandum, the committee decided that a separate meeting for women should be held so that women living in the residences could be told how "to help maintain cleanliness *in their way*." The decision assumed that cleaning the labor lines was a task that fell within the acceptable realm of women's activities. Women, in other words, would be helped to do a job for which they were naturally adept, "in their way." This comment is a particularly stark example of the gendering of this organization in terms of both the consolidation of male authority within the public arena and the corresponding attempt to reproduce social norms that define domestic labor as the natural duty of women. More important, this harnessing of women's bodies to extract their labor echoes the ways workers' bodies are harnessed within the factory.

The organization of this committee in effect reproduces hegemonic representations of both gender and community. On the one hand, women workers were effectively barred from any role in the committee; on the other hand, the organization reproduced the role of management authority in overseeing everyday neighborhood and community conflicts in the labor lines. The organization helped to extend management control over workers' community life despite the participation of union leaders.

During the course of my fieldwork, workers in the lines began to organize a significant challenge to the reach of management authority. Several male workers who had grown increasingly dissatisfied with the operation of the committee decided to form an alternative forum, an Action Committee that would replace the authority of both unions and managers. The composition of the organization was particularly striking, for it crossed caste, religious, and ethnic lines. Moreover, although the members were not union leaders, several of the participants were union members and the committee was not an anti-union organization.

The organization evolved from public dissatisfaction with specific problems in the workers' communities. One of the founders of the forum explained that several workers had become increasingly concerned about problems of alcoholism:

But the alcohol shopowners just met with the union leaders and gave them money. So the leaders took the money and kept quiet. Slowly the problem of alcohol has been getting worse. Before there were only a few places selling it. Lately it has been increasing. People who didn't drink before started drinking. Young boys also started drinking. This talk came up in our Andhra Pradesh Club. We felt we must stop this. We must stop alcoholism. We must stop all vices. So we set up a meeting and called members of all the clubs. In this way the committee was set up.

The organization grew out of a public debate held within the community clubs in the jute-mill residences. The intention of the forum was to carve out the sphere of the "social" as separate from the "political." As one worker described it, "This committee is completely separate. Management has nothing to do with it. The unions also don't have anything to do with it. We want it to be separate. We don't want any political parties to come into it. . . . Some of us are with political parties but we will not bring that into this work." These characteristics of the making of a *proletarian* public sphere provide an interesting parallel to Habermas's conception of the *bourgeois* public sphere:

With the rise of a sphere of the social, over whose regulation public opinion battled with public power, the theme of the modern (as opposed to the ancient) public sphere shifted from the properly political tasks of a citizenry acting in common (i.e., administration of law as regards internal affairs and military survival as regards external affairs) to the more properly civic tasks of a society engaged in critical public debate (i.e., the protection of a commercial economy). (1992: 52)

I would add that the construction of the workers' public sphere represents a battle both with the public power of unions and management and with the bourgeois public conception of critical discourse and social regulation, that is, with the bourgeois public sphere itself. In this process, workers try to construct an oppositional public sphere that would contest management's attempt to regulate social life within the labor lines both in terms of management's direct control and through joint management-union activity.[13] Consider, for example, the use of coercive tactics within this subaltern public sphere. As one of the committee members explained:

First we stopped the alcohol. We called a meeting with all the alcohol shop-owners and gave them a warning. We said we would beat up anyone who drinks. We have been doing that. If anyone is drunk we beat them up and tie them up. This way we got control of the alcohol. Then we did the same thing with gambling. First we gave a warning. Then we beat up anyone who was gambling. In this way we have stopped all the vices. Then we decided to clean up the lines. We called in all the shopkeepers and told them to put up garbage cans to throw waste in. So people won't throw garbage anywhere. The next thing we want to do is for the children in the labor lines. The children go and play in the railway colony. It is a shame for us that they have to go there and play. So we will talk with the Company [mill] about getting a playground for them.

Organizers of the forum were unambiguous about this use of coercion and independent policing of the labor lines. As another committee member emphasized: "We will beat up anyone who drinks. We have beaten up about seventy or eighty people. Even if it is a union leader or a president of a union it will be the same. Even if it is my brother or father. . . . This alcohol is not made in government [legal] shops. It is sold in houses." This reliance on force provides a striking contrast to social regulation associated with Habermas's notion of citizen participation and the rise of "civic" concerns.

But the significance of such methods of coercion cannot be understood merely in terms of a manifestation of violence and brute force. On the contrary, the success of such methods arose from the public, social humiliation of the targeted persons. Through the use of such tactics, the entire community knows or finds out that a particular person has been beaten for violating the social norms defined by the committee. The importance of the publicity of such methods is highlighted by other forms of social ostracism used by the committee. As one worker explained, "For one person we shaved his head and beard, put a garland of shoes around him, and paraded him through the whole colony." Such tactics are commonly used as methods of punishment in rural communities in India, and they reveal the culturally specific boundaries of the Habermasian conceptions of "publicity" and "public opinion" derived within the context of the European bourgeois public sphere.

The contours of the jute-mill workers' public sphere rest on the presumption of common interests of workers. As Craig Calhoun has argued, in the bourgeois public sphere "the very idea of the public was based on the notion of a general interest sufficiently basic that discourse about it need not be distorted by particular interests" (1992: 9). This discourse of shared interests has also characterized the construction of the proletarian public sphere. Consider, for instance, the vision put forward by one of the workers involved in the organization of the "action committee":

We have to do this for our children. We have to educate them, to try and raise them up slowly. Our people will throw away all of their money on liquor and gambling and will not even leave enough money for *dal* [lentils] and *roti* [bread] for their children. We have to stop this. If our children are not in school they run around and get spoiled. The young boys spend their time in video parlors watching bad films. They waste themselves.

This emphasis of the committee's agenda embodies the workers' attempt to invest in their future within the urban setting in Calcutta rather than to rely on their anticipated return to the village. The image of improving the lives of children in the labor lines was a vision of the reproduction of the urban community of the workers—and an attempt to imagine a community that could become independent of the politics and authority of union-management relations yet would not have to retreat to the memory of their villages of origin.

Notwithstanding this vision of a common purpose and future, the making of this public sphere relied on a gendered notion of the public, a conception that ultimately foreclosed the possibility of producing an "imagined community" (Anderson, 1983) that would contest the domain of management power. The public sphere constructed by the committee still rested on the exclusion of women's participation. For instance, like the management's Village Committee, the Action Committee had no women members, and the organizers of the forum indicated that they did not intend to deal with issues specific to women. The Action Committee did not contest prevailing notions restricting working-class women to specific domestic or socially acceptable spheres. Furthermore, the preoccupation of the committee with social order and the future of working-class children (specifically boys) rested on the significance of reproducing a particular model of the working-class family that would uphold existing codes of the appropriate behavior, activities, and spaces for working-class women.

Paradoxically, such conceptions of the workers' counterpublic sphere in fact converge with management discourses on the social disorder and disarray of the labor lines. Compare the following description of the labor lines by one mill manager: "The main problem is that we have only seven hundred quarters for about forty thousand workers. There are many *jhupries* [illegal constructions/squatter settlements]. There are about fifty illegal liquor shops. All kinds of vices, blue films are shown, prostitution. In the dock area there are many criminals." The manager's description casts the jute workers' communities in the stereotypical image of a dangerous, violent, and immoral space, one implicitly contrasted with the civilized morality of middle- and upper-class neighborhoods. In his conception, the problem is only one of numbers, and he uses a language implicitly linking social and economic disruption to overpopulation—a connection that perhaps strikes a familiar chord with national discourses that have linked family planning with economic development. References to prostitution and pornography stem from management discourses on the social and moral disorder that arises when male workers migrate to the city, leaving their families behind in their village. The problems and "vices" of the labor lines are linked to the disruption of the working-class family.

The focus on the breakdown of the jute mill working-class family has reinforced the construction of the urban arena as foreign, dangerous, and male. For example, one of management's stipulations when I started my research at the factory was that I not go to the labor lines and that I confine my movements to the factory compound because, they argued, the labor lines were unsafe. Although I was able to circumvent this regulation with time (and by taking advantage of the fact that managers could not afford to take time away from their factory surveillance in order to continually keep watch over me), this experience nevertheless reveals the masculinization of this space. This masculinization is further demonstrated by the fact that the only woman working as a welfare officer was told that she should not go to the labor lines, whereas male labor officers often went to the lines to attend cultural functions organized by workers.

Management's characterization of labor lines as violent and unsafe was interwoven with a gendered discourse of morality.[14] They pointed to alcoholism, prostitution, and crime as forms of a social disease that violated middle-class norms and their particular representation through Bengali *bhadralok* culture.[15] Such conceptions were also specifically linked to views on the family and appropriate roles for women. Daughters and wives of managers often referred to the supposed sexual promiscuity of women workers, insinuating that women in the labor lines whose husbands had deserted them were living with other men and violating acceptable social codes regarding marriage. These representations of workers' homes and communities as dangerous spaces rested on the juxtaposition between the "endangered lady" and the "dangerous woman" that Mary Ryan has discussed in the context of early-twentieth-century cities in the United States (1990: 73). Whereas management's discourses on working-class masculinity centered on the threat of violence and the protection of upper-class women, discourses on working-class women in the labor lines focused on the threat of unrestrained female sexuality.

The discursive construction of the labor lines in terms of moral disorder parallels the discourses and representations produced by the community activism of the workers' Action Committee. The irony of this convergence of gendered discourse is underlined by the fact that while management engages in a construction of the labor lines in terms of moral disorder, one of the cornerstones of social order in the working-class communities in fact lies in the reproduction of a patriarchal model of the working-class family. Dominant ideologies within the communities of workers do not permit single women to reside without the presence of family members, particularly male relatives, in the household. Working-class women likewise must adopt socially acceptable roles; they are responsible for performing domestic labor such as housework and childrearing, and they do not enter masculine spaces in the labor lines. Women are rarely seen in tea shops in the labor lines or near the factory, and they do not participate in public activities such as religious festivals. Furthermore, although trade unions play a central role in shaping the political and cultural spheres of workers, women workers also have been marginalized from this activity: they may attend union meetings, but they rarely speak. The point I am making here is not that women workers represent an essentially passive or subservient group, but that everyday social and institutional practices of workers produce exclusionary masculine spaces.

In this process, the bourgeois and workers' public spheres overlap, for they both produce gendered discourses of social and community order. In effect, the conception of the workers' counterpublic which the Action Committee produced was unable to break from the gendered politics that have shaped management discourses and union practices. This gendering of the workers' counterpublic was not limited to the exclusion of women's participation but also fundamentally centered on the production of a particular form of masculinity. As Kathy Peiss has noted in the context of working-class activity in the United States, the construction of workers' public culture is transformed into "a system of male privilege in which workers' self-determination, solidarity, and mutual assistance were understood as 'manliness'" (1986: 4). The use of coercive policing by male workers was a subtle reproduction of the notion that the future of their community rested on the adoption of aggressive strategies that could only be adopted by men. Just as management and union constructions of the mill as masculine, "heavy" work have led to an exclusionary representation of "the working class," so too the committee's focus on male strength and coercion has produced a gendered conception of the working-class community. The conflation of manual work and masculinity (Willis, 1977) converges with the conflation of community and masculinity in a new continuum between workplace and community that the committee had, ironically, been attempting to disrupt.

Management, union, and community discourses and practices participate in a shared understanding of the working class as a masculine construct. This shared production of hegemonic narratives of gender moves us away from romanticized notions of an autonomous "subaltern" sphere, whether in relation to union activity or community practices. It is precisely this gendered bordering of community that prevents the workers' counterpublic sphere from transcending the discursive boundaries of the management-union nexus and from effectively resisting the extension of factory authority over workers' community life; in this process, both class and community become exclusionary representations of the jute workers' identity and interests.

The Gendered Effects of the Subaltern Public Sphere

If, as I have argued, the workers' counterpublic represents a site of exclusion in relation to women workers, what then does "community" mean for women who continue to work in the mill and reside in the labor lines? Before turning to the general patterns of women's everyday lives in the jute mill in the following chapter, I present the life history of Rekha, a woman worker in the mill. Her history reveals how management, unions, and workers' community norms converge in the production of gender hierarchies and provides a unique view of the political and material effects on women workers. In particular, I examine how this creation of gender hierarchy centers on the enforcement of a patriarchal model of the working-class family—where the existence of a single woman represents a deviant figure and a threat to factory authority, trade unions, and community norms of social order. I maintain that the reproduction of particular patriarchal models of the family is not a natural process[16] but rather the product of enforced cultural and social norms within the public arena of working-class activity in the jute mills.[17] I do not intend to imply that the working-class family cannot represent a source of support for working-class women. The question that concerns me is how particular patriarchal models of the working-class family are reproduced and subsequently naturalized in working-class communities through a set of political processes.[18] Trade unions and community organizations participate in, produce, and enforce such models of the family through ideologies of domesticity, the invention of cultural traditions regarding the family within the public sphere of activity and discourse, and the reproduction of hierarchies that govern the lives of women workers in the jute mills.

Rekha's situation was unique in a number of ways and signifies a critical disruption of the hegemonic narratives of community and class. She was employed in the weaving section of the mill, a department that represents a highly skilled and traditionally male occupation. The context of my interview was also distinctive. In general, I sought interviews with women workers and arranged times when I could speak with them at length. In this case, however, Rekha sought me out and accompanied another woman with whom I had arranged to speak. As she later explained during the course of our conversation, she had paid someone ten rupees to take her place in the factory so that she could speak with me.

Rekha's father was a worker in the spinning department of the factory. Her parents had been landless laborers in Bihar, and they had migrated to Calcutta in search of employment. She was married to a man in Bihar at the age of twelve or thirteen (she was unsure of the exact age). Her parents then brought her and her husband to Calcutta. After two years, her husband deserted her for another woman, leaving her with two children (a boy and a girl) to support. It is at this point that she managed to obtain a job in the mill. As she recalled: "When my first husband left me I went to him [the general manager] for a job. I had covered my head with a sari but he saw the *sindoor* in my hair. He asked me, 'Are you married?' When I said yes he slapped his hand on his forehead and then laughed. Then he asked me 'Why don't you send your husband?' I told him my husband left me, and I touched his feet and I begged for a job." Management's reaction to her request is particularly telling since it highlights the pattern of patriarchal access to employment in the mill. His initial disbelief that a married woman would work stems from his subscription to the classic middle-class model of the family, according to which the husband must seek employment and the wife must confine herself to the domestic space within the household. Meanwhile, she must play on his paternalism and represent herself as destitute in order to gain employment—a common method used by widowed or deserted women. In this representation, the woman must present herself as a victim of circumstances beyond her control that prevent her from occupying a socially acceptable role within the family. A woman seeking employment must in effect demonstrate that she has tried to conform to this ideal middle-class model of family life when, in practice, working-class women and poor women in both rural and urban areas have always worked outside the household. From the very outset, Rekha was compelled to consent to a patriarchal and class-based model of the family.

Once she had managed to obtain work, Rekha's personal situation began to improve, for her employment provided her with some means of economic independence—or, as she put it to me with the benefit of hindsight, "at least I could put food in my mouth." Once she had begun to work in the mill, her family and community members began to pressure her to remarry, since it was unacceptable for her to live on her own. Cultural pressures on women to marry and stay within the household are often much sharper for Bihari women than for women from Andhra

Pradesh or other communities. Workers from Bihar generally prefer not to migrate with their wives, and a single woman working in the mill represented a significant deviation from social norms. Rekha began to face increasing pressure to marry again. Members of her community began to exert pressure on her parents, who were also workers in the mill. Rekha's single status became a source of dishonor for them. Methods of social ostracism and informal means of power, such as gossip and rumor, were also exercised in the labor lines. The intensity of this social compulsion was such that Rekha eventually agreed to marry an unemployed man residing in the community and subsequently undertook the economic burden of supporting him, his family, her two children from her first marriage, and two daughters and a son from her second marriage. As she described her situation,

After my husband left I didn't want to get married again. I just wanted to work. So I came to the mill and I begged for the job. I told my parents that I want to get a job, otherwise I will kill myself. So finally they said all right. But then later they made me get married. They said their honor depends on it. People were saying things. They were saying, "See this girl how she is—this is why her husband left her. . . ." So my parents forced me to marry. They said otherwise I will get no help from anyone. I will be left alone. So I got married. But I was better off not being married. At least I could work and put food in my mouth. My man is very poor. And I have to see to his sisters. I will have to get them married. I already paid 5,000 rupees for my man's brother's wedding. For the girls the dowry is very high. It will be ten thousand rupees or even fifteen thousand rupees even to marry a really poor man. I will have to see that all my brothers' sisters get married.

The social hegemony of the family was even able to outweigh her economic self-sufficiency. The economic burden of such social responsibilities reinforced her dependence on wage labor in the factory. However, this labor did not provide her with any means of economic independence because her social role was still defined by the structure of the family.

Rekha bore the economic burden of her husband's mother and sisters, but she did not receive any assistance from them, either financially or in terms of help with household work. For instance, whereas her mother would help her by taking care of her children, she felt that she could not rely on her in-laws for similar support. The patriarchal construction of the joint family structure in India is such that a woman must enter her husband's household; as a newcomer she is in a position of subordination and only begins to occupy a position of clear authority in relation to the daughter-in-law who eventually marries her son (if she bears one). Rekha was placed in a position of subordination in relation to her mother-in-law. As she put it, "My mother-in-law doesn't help. She only asks for money. She asks for money for dowry for her daughter, but where can I get the money from now? I tell her I don't have it, but she says I'm hiding it and not giving it to her." In middle-class households new brides are often pressured into additional amounts of dowry (either in terms of money or, increasingly, luxury items such as televisions or washing machines),[19] but Rekha was faced with a situation where her labor and earnings were being extracted within the household.

In the midst of this triple exploitation of wage work in the factory, domestic work in the household, and financial support of her in-laws, Rekha's relationship with her husband provided a measure of personal support:

When I come home from the mill I am so tired I just sit in a corner and start crying. Then he [her husband] tells me "Look, you are working hard in the mill. You lie down and I will cook the dinner." But usually I will cook the dinner and my husband will help me by taking care of the children. When I cry my husband will help me. Actually, I like my husband, but he is a poor man. He tries to make a little money by selling eggs—he is also a barber, so sometimes he makes ten rupees a day. But how much can you make with that kind of work?

Throughout our conversation, which lasted several hours, Rekha repeated that she liked her husband but that he was "a poor man." Given my discussion of the enforcement of patriarchal models of the family, it seems perhaps ironic that her husband was her only source of support within her immediate household. Rather than seek to erase such contradictions, I suggest that they can serve as a warning against false essentialisms, in this case in relation to the nature of Indian male workers. Rekha's husband's willingness to take on some responsibility for household work points to the possibility that individuals may disrupt hegemonic constructs through their everyday actions.

Rekha's history should reveal the manner in which the working-class community in question publicly enforced the family as a central organizing structure of the community. The social hegemony of the family can be understood as the product of dynamic processes constituted through everyday practices in worker communities. In other words, I am arguing against the temptation to identify the power of such conceptions of the family as lingering, static traces of traditionalism in Indian society. The persistent significance of this form of the family can be better understood as a product of gendered *political* processes rather than as a deviation from recent changes that are occurring in the family structure in the United States or in other Western societies.

These political processes are not limited to the sphere of community; they also include the practices and ideologies of trade unions, organizations that we classify as "modern," "formal" institutions. Shortly after

Rekha started work in the mill, she began experiencing harassment by two of the shop-floor supervisors; the supervisors threatened to fire her if she did not engage in sexual relations with them: "You know there are one or two sahibs who ask me to go places with them. They say, 'We'll go to this place and meet.' But I refused to go, so they stopped giving me work. For eight months I couldn't get work. If I would go to work they would say 'Why are you at this machine? Who told you to come to work?' I would just say, 'sahib, the machine was empty so I'm working here.' Then I would not be called to work." Her employment was contingent on sexual politics within the factory arena. Since she was a casual worker, the supervisors possessed the means to easily prevent her from obtaining work if she did not cooperate with them. As she described her experience:

I tried to tell Mr. ——— [a management representative]. I said "See, I am not getting work." He would always say, "Come back later." The labor officers would also say the same thing. . . . But I didn't tell them what the sahibs were asking me. I'm too ashamed to tell anyone. It will look bad on me. So I have not told anyone. They [the sahibs] would tell me to come to this room where the durwans stay in the mill. But I refused to go. They said if I went with them I would never have to worry about getting work. But even if I starve and I never have food in my stomach I will never go. A woman's *izzat* [honor] is in her hands. She can let it go, but once she does she can never get it back. Some women might do it. But out of ten women, two, three, or five, maybe more will not do it. But now I cannot get work properly. Right now I'm working because at this time there is need for me [it was the puja season when many workers were on leave and she is a skilled worker]. But soon again I will have to sit. Now they don't come near me. They don't say anything to me, they don't even look at me. No worker does this. The sirdars don't do this. Only those two sahibs.

She was unable to obtain any support from mill unions despite the fact that she was a member of one of the prominent unions in the factory. As indicated above, when she approached any of the leaders of this union they would abruptly dismiss her and tell her to "come back later." She then went to another of the union leaders with her grievance. After she had visited his office on a few occasions he told her to stop coming to see him. The leader indicated that people in the community were beginning to gossip and speculate on his relations with her.

The fact that a few visits of a woman worker to a union office should incite public attention and gossip indicates both the extent of the gendered boundaries of union activity in the mill and the gendered nature of public opinion. It further reveals the manner in which the "rational critical discourse" of the public arena centers on the politics of sexuality and the definition of criteria for the "appropriate" spaces for women. What we might conventionally classify as the "private" realm of the family is in fact sustained through public political processes that involve both the cultural hegemonic constructs of community and the institutional operation of trade unions; the construction of the family is reinscribed within and constitutive of the "public" realm. At a deeper level, the surveillance of Rekha's sexuality and the attempt to discipline her body through the enforcement of a patriarchal model of the working-class family converges with the regime of disciplinary power that management exercises in both the factory and labor lines. Just as managers attempt to turn workers into docile bodies through factory discipline, workers' unions and communities attempt to transform working-class women into subjected bodies through the regulation of their sexuality. The two processes are framed within a common analytics of power (Foucault, 1978).

Meanwhile, Rekha was able to keep her family at a subsistence level by performing domestic labor for some of the management representatives living in the factory compound. As she explained: "The other sahibs give me work in their houses. I clean their floors. I wash the dishes. I work in three or four houses. So when the mill is closed I can at least feed my children. They don't pay me money but they give me food, and if they have extra food they will send it to me." She was thus performing a double shift of unpaid domestic labor, in the management quarters and in her household.

To an extent, Rekha's persistence in supporting her household did increase her status among other workers. While her employment as a single woman had been frowned upon as socially deviant behavior, her role as the sole supporter of her husband's family brought her new support from other workers. As she indicated, "Sometimes the other workers, the men, will say, 'She is poor, she's just sitting there, why don't you give her some work?' They never trouble me. The men think I am good because I am taking care of my whole family. They think highly of me." Male workers were willing to identify with her as a "poor" person in need of employment; yet this shared class identity rested implicitly on her new position within a patriarchal family, where she was contributing to her husband's household. This collective class support was framed by gendered boundaries that might easily have been overlooked without placing the context of her work experience within her broader life experience in her community and family.

I have presented this life history to illustrate the burden upon women workers to negotiate a complex web of family structure, gendered practices in employment, and exclusionary practices of trade unions. Rekha's experience embodies the relationship between the system of authority in the factory and the institution of the family, the gendered ideologies of management policies regarding issues such as recruitment, and the exclusionary practices of trade unions.

Despite the power of this combination of institutional and ideological forces, however, Rekha was able to continue her work in the weaving department of the factory. The importance of this encroachment on the fields of power that have shaped the position of women jute workers is underlined by the fact that she was one of only four women working in this skilled occupation in the entire industry. During my visits to other factories, management and union leaders alike refused to believe that a woman was working in this occupation in the mill. They insisted that it was impossible: the weaving department was the toughest job (and most highly skilled) in the factory and therefore could only be performed by men. Given the fact that she was able to obtain and keep employment in this department without consenting to sexual exploitation by the management staff, I suggest that her actions must be understood not merely as survival but as resistance.

Although I am aware of the dangers of overstating the case for resistance, the significance of Rekha's ability to resist the managers' sexual harassment without the organizational resources of the unions or any support from her family or community should not be underestimated. Women's public silence on the experience of harassment could be interpreted as a form of consent to cultural (or perhaps political is the better term) codes that do not permit them to speak about the harassment even with friends or family members. This silence is particularly significant, since it allows sexual harassment and violence against women to continue; the implicit message is that a woman cannot speak about such experiences without bringing dishonor on herself as well as on her family and community. The continual creation of such silence forms the very texture of the "public" political realm. Rekha's decision to seek me out, however, represented an attempt to break the silence. During the course of our conversation she continually questioned me to make sure I was understanding everything she said. At moments when I would stop writing in order to listen to her, she would tell me to write down what she was saying, even as she made me promise that I would not disclose the information to anyone in the mill. Although I upheld my promise not to disclose her confidences in the mill, the uneasy (and insoluble) fact remains that my representation of her story in no way helps her situation.

In the context of these contradictions, I characterize Rekha's actions as having moved beyond survival. Despite the extreme structural constraints on her life, she displayed a strong consciousness of the extent of her accomplishment, as she indicates in the following interpretation of her labor:

The most important thing is to work. I want to work. I will do any kind of work. Anything I am asked to do, I will do. Any work. That is the only thing in life. If you work you can put food in your mouth. Marriage doesn't help. I became worse off after I got married. Before I was big and strong. Now I have become so thin since I got married. But I take care of my family. Even my mother-in-law. I take care of her. She is like my mother—I treat her like that. I will give food to everyone—my mother-in-law, her daughters, my husband—before putting food in my own mouth. See, for Durga Puja we had less money to buy new clothes. I bought clothes for everyone but myself. My husband told me not to buy him anything, to buy something for myself. But I didn't do that. I bought him new pants. Because I thought if he had a job he would have done that for me. He would have bought me a sari and not bought anything for himself.

This interpretation can be understood not as Rekha's misguided "consent" to the control of her labor but as her consciousness of the significance of her ability to economically support her family. Within a context of economic and social domination, she is able to transform her role into a source of empowerment and to survive the gendered ideologies that have classified factory work as "men's work" and transformed "the working class" into a male working class. This resistance must no doubt be qualified by the harshness of the circumstances she continues to face, and it perhaps also highlights the ironic reversal of the Foucaultian approach to resistance in Lila Abu-Lughod's reminder that "where there is resistance there is power" (1990: 42).

These fragments of Rekha's life signify the processes through which unions and community practices (re)produce consent to a patriarchal model of the working-class family. However, her ability to maintain her employment and interpret her survival as a sense of accomplishment provides a contradictory moment in the hegemonic gendered public sphere. This momentary point of contestation underlines the constructed and political nature of the boundaries that define the jute workers' counterpublic and prevents us from assigning women workers to a role of passive victims of oppression (Mohanty, 1991).

Let me return to the question with which I began this section—given the gendered representations of the workers' public sphere, what does "community" mean to women? If the Action Committee envisioned a future for the urban working-class communities in the jute mills which rested on the social order of the patriarchal family, what did the future signify to Rekha? In many ways her vision coincided with the one put forth by the leaders of the committee. She spoke at length about her children's future and about her desire to educate them. She spoke in particular about her daughters (without mentioning her son once during the conversation). This hope is mixed with her own memories of loss:

You know I studied till class eight. I passed all my exams. I still keep my certificates. I thought I could work with papers like this [she points to files on the desk]. I wanted to study more. But when I got married I had to stop. My [first] husband didn't want me to study. And then when he used to come to meet me at the school, people used to talk about me. They used to say things about me — they used to say I was going with this man. But then I showed them the sindoor in my hair and they realized I was married. But still they didn't like it. So I stopped going. I felt bad to go.

Moving from the past to the present, she asserted: "I want my girls to go to school. Then after that they can get married."

This decision to invest in her daughters contrasts clearly with the masculinized image of community organization. More significantly, whereas the male community leaders could envision the possibility of building a community within their residences, Rekha's hopes rested on the possibility of escaping this community as well as the mill. As she said: "I want to send my three-year-old to the hostel [i.e., put her in boarding]. So I can at least get her out of here. I will try and send her away." Her desire to send her daughter away is a severe comment on the meaning that "community" has for working-class women and their daughters. The notion of a unified "subaltern counterpublic sphere" within the jute working classes thus falters on the gendered terrain of community.

Rekha's life history both demonstrates the material effects of the workers' gendered public sphere and disrupts the production of the hegemonic narratives of gender, class, and community. As her history has shown us, the construction of the political boundaries that delineate these social categories does not only represent a discursive event, nor is it simply about the creation of different types of identity packages. On the contrary, such boundaries produce very real effects that structure the lives of workers in various ways and through conflicted processes — processes that constitute the "making" of labor politics in contemporary India.

Chapter 6
Stories of Survival: Location, Difference, and the Identities of Women Workers

Stories of women's experiences in the factory and at home reveal that the identities of women workers are produced through the unique structural location they occupy in relation to hegemonic representations of class, community, and gender as well as through the meanings they give to their particular location and experiences. My analysis throughout this book has rested on the assumption that identity and group formation are both conditioned through structural forces and produced through the discursive and symbolic meanings social actors use to interpret their lives. We are left, then, with a number of questions. Does the particular social location occupied by women workers enable them to contest the asymmetrical relationships of power embedded in hegemonic constructions of class, community, and gender? How does this structural location shape women's consciousness, the meanings they give to their positions at work and at home, and the possibilities for collective resistance? Finally, given my analysis of the political production of categories, how can we analyze "women workers" as a unitary group?

By analyzing the ways women workers negotiate and interpret their everyday lives, we can conceptualize links between the structural and discursive dimensions to identity formation. This chapter, then, concerns the life histories of women workers who continue to survive in the jute mills in Calcutta. I hope to demonstrate that structure does not represent a set of transcendental, objective determinants but is shaped by modes of representation and the meanings that social actors, in this case working-class women, give to their position and activities.

I point here to some of the general patterns shaping the "dailiness" (Apthekar, 1989) of women's experiences at work and at home—where women's lives center around the task of survival as they bear the burden of social reproduction in terms of everyday subsistence and in terms of the attempt to provide a future for their children. Women give meaning to their experiences at work and at home in varied ways; their identities are constructed through difference (Hall, 1990)—such as caste, or ethnicity—and their own often divergent interpretations of the politics of gender.

By taking seriously the significance of women's discursive constructions of their experience (Scott, 1992), we can avoid the assumption that women's daily experiences of patriarchy and capitalism automatically produce an overarching form of critical consciousness or collective resistance. Indeed, the subordinate location of women workers in the jute mills has substantially limited the potential for collective resistance by women workers. This does not, however, lead to a form of passive subordination, as women workers' interpretations of their everyday lives often provide them with the means to assess and interrupt the reproduction of hegemonic representations of class, community, and gender. In particular, women workers transform the meaning of their productive and reproductive labor into the means through which they attempt to imagine a future for their children which can transcend the structures of capitalism and patriarchy. An understanding of the politics of survival of women workers cannot be fully grasped either by recourse to the analytical category of resistance or by the assumption that structural constraints simply inhibit collective action and produce a form of individualistic survival. Instead, as their life histories reveal, women workers interpret their endurance through their everyday activities as attempts to disrupt the reproduction of larger structures of patriarchy and capitalism, even as their particular social location enables them to recognize the risks of overt protest.

The Politics of Everyday Life: Women, Work, and Family

I spoke with several women workers, in individual and group interviews as well as in informal, spontaneous interactions.[1] Initially these conversations most often took place in the factory at appointed times; later, some of the women I spoke with invited me to their homes. These interactions were usually splintered by the continual demands placed on them, for they could only spare limited periods of time between their shifts in the mill and their domestic responsibilities. Meanwhile, our conversations were also constrained by gendered spatial politics, marked by the relative absence of places where I could speak with women in private. I attempted to circumvent such spatial limitations either by conducting conversations with women workers at their houses when their husbands were working in the mill or by using the personnel manager's office (which I would usually lock during the interviews both as a physical and symbolic act of privacy). I attempted to engage with the women on a variety of topics, ranging from the ways they obtained a job in the mill, to their reasons for doing so, their family histories, their opinions about work in the factory, their participation in unions, particular problems they faced on a daily basis, and their sources of support. I have pieced together some of the fragments of the experiences women workers related through the course of these interactions. The meanings women workers gave to their daily lives and pieces of the life histories that they were willing to discuss form the narratives of a continual struggle for survival as they must negotiate the demands of work and family.

Consider first the story of Saraswati, a Hindu woman worker from Andhra Pradesh who has been employed in the winding department as a casual worker for the past fifteen years. Her parents had been railway workers in Andhra Pradesh, and she had migrated to Calcutta with her husband. She is an older woman, although she resisted disclosing her precise age (as did many women with whom I spoke). She has six children, two of whom have already married. Her husband has also worked in the mill for the past twenty-seven years. Saraswati first started working when her husband became too ill with tuberculosis to work. However, her husband is now a *mistri* (mechanic) in the factory with status as a permanent worker. Since both she and her husband are employed, they are relatively well off. Her relatively higher economic status is highlighted by the fact that she invited me to her home (her family occupied two rooms of a quarter) after we had spoken in the factory. In contrast, many other women workers with whom I spoke did not have adequate (*pucca*) living quarters and were only willing to speak with me in the mill.

Saraswati indicated that her relationship with her husband was relatively stable and that they both contributed their incomes to pay for everyday household expenses as well as to accumulate savings for their children's marriage and education expenses. They had been able to acquire such possessions as furniture, metal vessels, and *thalis* (metal plates), commodities workers often sell to take care of marriage expenses, pay off loans, or survive periods of unemployment. The nature of Saraswati's relationship with her husband came through in the dynamics of my interactions with her. I had spoken with her in the factory, but she wanted me to come to her house and meet her husband. When her husband joined the conversation, there was no shift in Saraswati's responses or participation in the conversation. She continued to assert herself, and they both presented shared interpretations of their experiences—in marked contrast to other situations where women did not want to be interviewed with their husbands. Such subtle dynamics are of particular significance given the political and spatial constraints on the everyday interactions of working-class women.

Both Saraswati and her husband indicated that they felt that daily life had become more difficult with time. They spoke in particular about inflation and the fact that prices for food and clothing had increased substantially. As Saraswati put it: "Before you got forty rupees for salary but you could buy everything for ten rupees. Now everything is expensive—you may get three hundred rupees but it is not enough. Before you could buy a nice sari like this very cheap. Now if I want to buy a nice sari like this it will cost two hundred rupees." Her response, which in effect presents a conception of "real wages" calculated in relation to inflation, is of particular significance given management (and public) discourses that attempt to construct industrial workers as a privileged labor aristocracy. She interpreted her activities of purchasing commodities for her subsistence in terms of wider economic problems rather than in terms of her own individual problems of saving money. Her construction of the meaning of her daily life did not cast her experience in individualistic terms but as part of wider, "macro" structures.

Saraswati and her husband also spoke at length about their children and indicated that their main concern was to send their children to school and to be able to pay for their marriages. They both asserted strongly that they did not want their children to work in the mill. They intended to send all of their children to school and indicated that one of their sons was studying until the ninth grade and the other was in the seventh grade. Saraswati, in particular, spoke about the costs of having a large family: "Now people have two children, then it is easier to manage. But before it was not like this. You had many children. So life is very difficult for us."

Saraswati's attempt to develop a joint family strategy with her husband in order to provide a future for her children highlights the significant role of the family in shaping the lives of women workers. Many women workers with whom I spoke explained, for example, that family members provided their sole source of support. In such cases, women indicated that their primary connection was with their husbands rather than with female friends or other relatives. As one woman told me: "He [my husband] is the person I go to, to ask what to do, to discuss things. In the house whatever he says will be. That's the way it is. He is my main support." Such responses corroborated the significance of family strategies (Lamphere, 1987) in shaping women's choices and the negotiation of their labor and everyday lives.

This appearance of "consent" to the family structure, however, must be contextualized within a conception of the family as a microcosm of patriarchal power relations.[2] Such relations of power are generally based on several layers of economic dependence and control that are produced within the family. For example, as in most cases of industrial labor, women perform domestic labor in addition to their wage labor (Barrett, 1988; Barrett and Hamilton, 1986; Hartmann, 1981; Mies, 1986; Sacks, 1984). Even in Saraswati's case, although her family life and relationship with her husband was more stable than those of many other women in the mill, she was still responsible for all of the household work. Like many of the women with whom I spoke, she felt that she had no help from anyone and had to manage both factory work and her domestic labor on her own. She complained at length about her physical exhaustion due to harsh working conditions in the factory and talked about her difficulties in managing her household labor. The combination of factory and family work left her little time for any leisure activities, underlining the everyday effects of the "sexual division of leisure" (Peiss, 1986). Even though Saraswati was able to negotiate a unified family strategy with her husband in order to provide for her children, her everyday life was nevertheless circumscribed by the gendered division of labor within the household.

Few of the women I interviewed portrayed a family life in which husband and wife cooperated and contributed jointly to household expenses or toward care for their children. Compare the situation of Salma, a Muslim worker from Bihar. She has been employed in the sack-sewing department as a casual worker for the past twenty years. Both her parents were also jute workers (her father is now deceased), and they arranged her marriage to another worker from the weaving department in the same mill. Her family did not realize that her husband already had a wife in Bihar. This is not an unusual situation; both Muslim and Hindu workers who leave their wives in their village of origin begin to live with or marry women in the labor lines. Salma explained that her husband sent all of his money to his first wife, and her own earnings go toward the maintenance of their household in Calcutta: "Sometimes he gives ten or twenty rupees. Otherwise I pay for everything." The financial burden she bears is particularly substantial since she has had three daughters and will have to pay for their dowries and marriages.

The circumstances of her marriage have also forced her to break off her ties with her village of origin, for her husband's first wife is from the same village and Salma has been socially ostracized because of her marriage. She expressed fear that if she went back, "they [the family of her husband's first wife] will beat me." In the past eight or nine years she has returned home for only one week, and she does not plan to repeat the visit. Her marriage has ruptured the rural ties most jute workers have retained as a form of economic or social support. Meanwhile, her husband obtained a factory job for her through his union leader and has now left her with the responsibility for the financial and personal burden of raising her children. Thus, contrary to the model of "housewifization" that is often assumed for working-class women (de Haan, 1994), Salma's marriage has compelled her to engage in wage work outside the house.

It is a common occurrence among the mill workers that women are sole providers for their family's subsistence, even when their husbands are employed. In such cases, the wages of women workers are used to take care of all household expenses, whereas the male worker uses his wage for personal consumption. As a result, industrial employment has not provided women workers with a form of economic independence. Instead, a form of economic extraction takes place based on gender relationships in the family. This parallels the class-based extraction that takes place within the factory (Deere, 1990; Folbre, 1994; Hartmann, 1981; Mies, 1986). Where surplus labor is extracted from workers within the factory, unpaid domestic labor and the wages of women workers are extracted by husbands within the household. We therefore cannot assume that the participation of women in industrial work has lessened the significance of the family in their lives or that women's wage-earning power has transformed the family into a more egalitarian structure (Zavella, 1987).

The prevailing relations of economic dependence call into question any assumption of a natural form of consent to the family. Women workers may indeed strategize and use the family in creative ways as a form of support whenever possible as they negotiate their everyday lives, but we can nevertheless discern and analyze the way in which the family also produces unequal relationships of power that further marginalize women workers. The particular circumstances of a woman's family life in the jute mills has important implications for her work experience, for her family situation often determines how her wages are spent and whether she can gain viable economic security.

Consider, for example, the circumstances of Uma, a casual worker who has been employed in the weaving department in the mill for twenty-four years. Her parents had been landless laborers in Andhra Pradesh, and they had migrated to Calcutta in search of work. She is married and has seven children—four boys and three girls. Her husband is a permanent worker in the mill, but he is an alcoholic; according to Uma he does not work regularly, and he spends his wages on alcohol. She has thus been left with the task of supporting their seven children, and all of her earnings go toward household expenses: "We had no money. Our children had no food. So I went to the manager and begged him. I fell at his feet and pleaded with him. I asked him how can I feed my seven children. Then he gave me this job." In addition to his alcoholism, her husband beat her when he was drunk. As she talked about her husband's alcoholism and abuse, she expressed a strong sense of betrayal, for her husband was not fulfilling his responsibilities toward her and her children. She contrasted her situation with an idealized vision of family life: "If my husband was OK—if he was earning money and taking care of me, I would not work. I work because of my *majboori*. It is not good for me to say this. Because after all this is still my house I am talking about. It is my honor. I should say that my husband is a good man. That he helps me and takes care of me."

During our conversation Uma continually emphasized the fact that she "should" say that her family life was good, underlining the personal risk of talking publicly about her experience of domestic violence (she had volunteered the information; I did not specifically ask questions about domestic violence). Yet at another level she was also providing an ironic commentary on social norms that urge women to uphold an idealized image of the family, everyday experiences notwithstanding, in order to preserve their honor. Uma's experience of violence at home and her struggles to make ends meet with sporadic work at the mill have left her with a critical view of such idealized models of family life. As she commented: "In life everything is tied to *paisa*—whether your mother loves you or your father loves you or your husband loves you—it all comes down to money. There is no such thing as love. There is no such thing as love [she repeated]. Everything depends on money. There is nothing else." Uma reiterated this view several times as she talked about being beaten by her husband. However, her view of family life contained subtle contradictions. As she talked about her life, she maintained that she continued to stay with her husband and pay for all of the household expenses because of her children. Although she discounted the importance of love and emotion in her family relationships, she gave meaning to her actions and her life on the basis of her identity as a mother. For instance, she insisted that regardless of her hardships at home and at the factory she would take care of her children. "I have to work for my children. What else can I do? I have to put food in their stomachs. I cannot leave them. My husband beats me. My life is terrible, but I have to care for my children."

Uma's acute sense of the responsibility of her role as caretaker and sole provider for her children was echoed in many of my conversations with women in the mill. In such cases, it was clear that the battle for survival did not represent an individualistic struggle but an effort to provide children with a future. The extent to which women engage in productive and reproductive labor in order to support and safeguard their children's future marks a clear contrast to the masculinized version of the reproduction of the future of the workers' communities that we saw in the previous chapter. Given the ways in which women have had to assume the burden of supporting their families when their husbands spend money on alcohol, it is particularly ironic that community leaders defined activities such as closing down alcohol shops and furthering the future of children through education as a male domain.

The three stories I have presented point to a number of general patterns that characterize the "dailiness" (Apthekar, 1989) of women's work and home lives. For instance, the primary reason women provided for their employment in the factory was economic need. As one woman worker bluntly stated: "I need to put food in my stomach, that's all. And I have children—six children." This type of response was reiterated, almost without exception, in all conversations and interviews I conducted with women in the mill.[3]

The ways in which women entered employment and their own views of their employment outside the home often differed starkly. Like Saraswati, some women had joined the work force in order to supplement the incomes of their parents or husbands. One woman described her initial entry into factory work: "One of the friends of my father said, 'Why are you keeping her here in the home? What good will it do you? At least send her out to earn some money.' So he arranged for me to come and work here at the mill." However, many other women workers (like Salma and Uma) were the economic heads of households and were taking care of all the household expenses. In some situations they were left with this responsibility when their husbands died or deserted them or when they were supporting an unemployed spouse. According to a survey conducted by Sisir Mitra at one public sector mill just outside of Calcutta, approximately 43 percent of women employed in the mill were supporting their families as heads of households (primary wage earners). Meanwhile, in families where women worked in the mill, 58 percent of their husbands were unemployed (Mitra, 1985: 155). In other cases, women assumed the financial burden simply because their husbands did not contribute to household expenses. As we have seen, even when a woman's husband was employed, his wages would go to personal consumption, whereas her earnings would go toward basic necessities such as food, clothing, and other household expenses. As one woman described the situation: "Sometimes a woman's husband leaves her, runs away, and she has to take care of herself and the children. Sometimes someone's husband dies. It is very difficult. We have to see to our own lives."

Consider the situation of Prithi, a casual worker from Andhra Pradesh employed in the weaving department of the factory for thirteen years. Both her parents had been jute workers in the mill, and she was born in and grew up in the labor lines. She used the khandani system to

obtain her mother's job after her mother died. Prithi has been working in the mill since she was sixteen. She is unmarried and lives with
her two brothers on the veranda of one of her neighbors (mill workers
from Bihar), which she has converted into separate quarters by building a wall. Her unmarried status is unusual, but she said that she is
unable to get married because she has to support her brothers. One of
her brothers is an alcoholic and does not work even though he is also
a casual worker in the mill. As she put it: "If three people work and
only one person's salary is used to buy food it is OK. If someone else
is working [she points to her brother who is passed out on the floor of
her quarters during the entire interview] it would be all right. But if
only one person is working, it is not enough money." Like most women
I interviewed, Prithi complained bitterly about the casual status of her
employment and her inability to gain regular work despite the fact that
she had worked in the mill for thirteen years.

In the case of married women, the trend toward employment in wage
work tends to correspond to their economic status relative to the wives
of poorer workers, who are more likely to work outside the house. The
wives of male workers employed in the mill often take on informal work
such as sewing in order to supplement their husbands' wages. Both male
and female workers often adhere to the middle-class model of family
life, according to which married women should not work outside the
house. They indicated that the status of the family and community was
lowered when women worked outside the house. Some women whom
I interviewed indicated that they would prefer not to work in the mill,
for they felt working outside the home was a source of dishonor. As
Salma indicated during our conversation: "I didn't want to work. But I
have no choice. I have three daughters. I have to get them married.
I have no son. What will I do? I have to pay for the marriages. . . .
I want them to get married. I don't want them to work. They want to
work. Women should stay in the home. For their honor [*izzat*]. They
should not work outside." To some extent, as Arjan de Haan has argued,
this pattern has varied historically according to community differences:
Hindu workers from Bihar and Uttar Pradesh and Muslim workers sub-
scribe to the notion that it is preferable for women not to work; workers
from Orissa and Andhra Pradesh tend to view women's work outside the
home as socially acceptable. However, these cultural patterns tend to
be contingent on the politics of class and gender, since poorer workers,
particularly women workers themselves, often argue against such stereotypical assumptions. Many women, regardless of community differences,
expressed pride in being able to support their families even as they
spoke about exploitative employment conditions. In such cases, women
workers argued against any potential difference between the social roles

of men and women. As one woman forcefully stated: "I have to eat. I have to keep my house also. Just like they [male workers] have to keep their house and eat. So why should they mind that I work? Why should there be any difference [between men and women workers]?" There was, in short, no discernible monolithic attitude to the question of women's work outside the household. Moreover, women often indicated that their objections to work in the mill had more to do with harsh working conditions than with the notion that women should be confined to activities within the household.

The paradoxical implications of factory work for women workers is vividly embodied in the response of Meera, a casual worker from Uttar Pradesh who has been employed in the finishing department of the mill for over twenty years. Consider her representation of her work experience:

Listen, it is like this. Suppose there is a bird flying in the air. It needs to be in the air. If you put it in a cage, no matter how much food you give it, it cannot survive. It will still die. The wings are made to be in the air. The legs cannot fit in the cage. That's how it is for us. We are people in distress [majboori]. We are in this world to work. We cannot live without work. We are poor people. We are nothing without work.

During the interview, we had been discussing the reasons that led women to seek employment in the mill, and Meera had been arguing that economic compulsion forced them to seek work outside the home. I had then asked her whether she would wish to quit working if her family's economic position were to improve substantially.

Her response to this question offers a microcosm of the complexities in the construction of gender and the consciousness and identity of women working in the mill. On one level, she was using the metaphor of the cage to represent the confines of the family structure. To retreat to a purely domestic role would present a severe restriction on her freedom. On a second level, however, her interpretation of this desire to work outside the home contested the notion that factory work provided women with a form of liberation. She pointed instead to the class implications of her labor, emphasizing the absence of choice for "poor people." This metaphorical analysis is a vivid embodiment of the complex interaction between the categories of class and gender; she recognizes simultaneously the constraints of ideologies of domesticity and the political implications of work in the mill. Her words are a striking example of the way the production of the experience and politics of class are themselves defined by gendered location in the household and in the mill.

The pressures of economic survival result in the articulation of the concerns of women workers through a form of class consciousness. Women conceptualize their employment in terms of the pressures of subsistence and their *majboori* (compulsions) as poor people. This understanding of their labor is, however, continually intertwined with their gendered position, particularly when they analyze their position within and in opposition to the family structure. Women did not articulate their economic marginalization only in terms of their class position but also through their particular experience within the family. The convergence between gender and class in the life and work histories of women workers who remain in the jute mills lies at this juncture between the experience of economic survival both in the home and in the workplace.

The enormity of this struggle for survival can perhaps only be grasped when viewed in relation to the fact that in some cases women I interviewed were not able even to ensure basic survival. In one situation, I had begun interviewing a woman from Bihar, employed as a casual worker in the sack-sewing department. Her husband had been a worker in the mill, but he had died, leaving her with three children to support. Her father, also a worker in the mill, managed to obtain her husband's job for her through the khandani system. She has no permanent house and presently lives in a *jhupry*, a makeshift dwelling. Her father does not support her financially, although he sometimes gives food to her children. As a casual worker in the sack-sewing department, she only got work for two weeks at a time and was otherwise living at a starvation level. As she said, "When I have no work I try to manage to feed my children something," but she would often go without food herself. I was not able to converse with her for long, for she was unable to continue to talk about her situation without completely breaking down. Her last spoken words were, "I don't know how I will survive." Perhaps it is this silence—of women who have not been able to survive—that must continually haunt the narratives of the lives of women workers, and which marks most forcefully the political boundaries of class, gender, and community produced in the Calcutta jute mills.

Identity, Difference, and Power

Given my continuing argument regarding the political construction of categories, to what extent do women workers represent a unitary group? Is this category marked by a politics of difference (or hierarchy) that permeates constructs such as "the working class" or the "subaltern counterpublic"? In order to address these questions, let me return momentarily to Meera's representation of her class and gender position. In her response, her emphasis that "We are in this world to work. . . . We are poor people" reflects an attempt to classify the oppositional and asymmetrical relationship between her position as a worker and my status as an upper-class woman and "interviewer." The irony of her emphasis on her construction of the "we" in an oppositional sense is lost in the written transcription of the words but was clear in the tone of her response. The gender consciousness of the woman worker in this context was constructed around a recognition of hierarchy and difference between our positions rather than any commonality that we might presumably have shared as "women."

Through her response, Meera was calling into question the notion that we can speak of women as a unitary, always already existing category with shared interests, an issue that has been raised in recent debates in feminist theory (Mohanty, 1991; Butler, 1990).[4] Clearly, her comment pointed to the class (and caste) hierarchy that characterized our relationship and the dynamic of class politics inherent in the interview process. Yet her response also raises questions regarding the category of women workers that I am using in this chapter. Do the particular structural locations of women workers and the recurring patterns that shape their everyday work and home lives imply a singularity of identity and experience?

In the following section I suggest that, although the lives of women workers are conditioned by their particular structural location within the factory and family, their position does not necessarily produce a shared, unified gender identity. On the contrary, as we have already seen, women with whom I spoke often interpreted their experiences in significantly different ways. In addition, relationships between working-class women usually tended to develop within the context of their religious, regional, and linguistic identities. Such distinctions mediate the ways in which women respond to and negotiate their particular experiences at work and at home. Since Prithi, for example, was a casual worker and had problems obtaining continuous employment, her neighbor (also a woman worker in the mill) often invited her to her house for dinner. In this way, her neighbor provided her an indirect form of economic support, allowing her to save on food expenses. However, Prithi indicated that her neighbor would not accept food that she cooked because the neighbor was of a higher caste than she was. Although this relationship represented a network of support that does exist between working-class women, it was nevertheless constructed around the boundaries of caste.

Meanwhile, women workers often reproduce the gender hierarchies that have circumscribed their own everyday lives. Consider, for instance, the case of one woman working in a mill I visited on the outskirts of Calcutta, in a rural area in West Bengal. Kamala is a permanent worker and has been working in the winding department for the past thirty years. Her parents had both been mill workers, and her mother had also worked in the winding department. Her husband was also a jute worker, but she is now a widow and supports her two sons and two daughters. One of her sons is married, but he and his wife continue to live with her. None of her children is employed, and she emphasized that she wanted her sons to obtain jobs in the mill. As there is no official training program in the mill, she was training her older son so that he could eventually get work.

She spoke strongly about the difficulty of finding jobs, particularly for women. After we had talked for a while, she wanted to show me the different departments in the mill. As we walked through the shop floor, she first took me to a section of the winding department that was closed (the machines were covered with dust since they were not being run), and, pointing to them, she said, "See—they are not running the machines. It is just lying there. We need jobs. We need work. They shouldn't shut down the machines." As we continued through the factory, she pointed to other departments in the mill where women were not given employment. Then she stopped in the bundling section and pointed to two male workers in this traditionally "feminized" occupation, and said, "They are even giving women's jobs to the men." Her commentary provides a striking reflection of both the constructed nature and the rigidity of the gendered boundaries of class. On the one hand, the political and constructed nature of the gendering of work is highlighted by the transformation of women's work into men's work in a situation where male workers needed employment (a process that has also been occurring in the other mills I visited). On the other hand, this shift is emblematic of the broader, unyielding, historical trend toward the masculinization of factory work in relatively high-wage, unionized manufacturing industries in India.

In the context of this trend, Kamala has effectively attained a sense of economic security for herself and her family, a position that has increasingly become the sole preserve of permanent male workers in the mill and that provides a striking contrast to the lives of most women who are employed as casual workers. As a permanent worker, Kamala has relative financial security and also has possession of two quarters—permanent pacca quarters and makeshift katcha quarters that she built herself. In addition to her employment in the mill, she runs a small-scale business by selling milk in the labor lines (an enterprise in which her sons help her). She owns four buffalos and earns about a thousand rupees every two weeks through the sale of milk (milk sells for eight rupees a liter).

Although she has been successful in achieving economic independence and security as head of her household, she continues to reproduce hierarchies within her family. For instance, when I visited her in her house in the labor lines, she continually supervised the household labor of her two daughters and her daughter-in-law as we spoke. Her elder daughter came out to meet me and began talking about her own wish to get a job; Kamala immediately told her to fold the clothes on her bed and later emphasized that she wanted to find work for her sons. Meanwhile, her daughter-in-law remained in the kitchen during the entire period of my visit; as Kamala herself indicated, her daughter-in-law was responsible for the housework, including all of the cooking and cleaning. Thus Kamala was able to achieve some success through her work and business, but she continued to reproduce gender hierarchies in her own family.

A recognition of such relationships of power between women is a central component in an adequate conceptualization of gender and in an analysis of "women's experiences." Just as an analysis of class cannot rest on an assumed identity of interests between "workers," an analysis of gender cannot focus on an unquestioned presumption of the "sameness" of women. An unquestioned assumption of "sameness" does not merely displace the possibility of differences between women, it obscures the asymmetrical relationships of power that exist between women and also operate within discourses of feminism. In this process, as Chandra Mohanty has argued, "the discursively consensual homogeneity of "women" as a group is mistaken for the historically specific material reality of groups of women" (1991: 56). Thus, while I have discussed the hierarchical representations of class and community in the mill, it should be clear that particular constructions of gender can also operate in a similar fashion.

Even at the methodological level, I was expected to adhere to social hierarchies and relationships of power. In the initial period of my fieldwork, if I was leaving an office and one or two workers were standing nearby, a member of the factory staff would physically push them away. Even while I was attempting to bridge the social space between my position and that of the workers (both male and female), management engaged in a continual battle to reverse this process, even if only by attempting to envelop me in an inviolable physical space. As one *durwan* [watchman] exclaimed when he witnessed a group of male workers taking me to the labor lines, "What is this madness?" Meanwhile, during my conversations and interviews with working-class women, they sometimes pointed out that I could ask them questions because of my privileged education, and they would sometimes resist responding to certain questions by indicating they did not understand. Even in situations where women were willing to talk and volunteered information about their lives, the dynamic of our interaction was always contingent on class and caste hierarchies. The hierarchies were often expressed in subtle ways—when I spoke with women in their houses, for example, they often ensured that they had brought a chair so that I did not sit on the floor. These incidents served as clear markers of the women's continual awareness of our asymmetrical social positions.

This articulation of difference among women is particularly critical since conceptions of gender serve as a means for the reproduction of relationships and distinctions based on social class in the factory arena. Social norms governing the behavior and movements of women of a higher class or status—female relatives of management or female members of the factory staff—served as important signifiers for their class and social status. Women of a higher status would be "protected" from contact with male workers and the male sphere of the factory. As Joan Scott has aptly argued, gender in this context can be understood as "a primary field within which or by means of which power is articulated" (1988: 45).

The case of Manju, a labor officer working in the personnel office and the only woman on the managerial staff, illustrates this process. Manju is the daughter of a woman working in the weaving department in the mill, yet she has managed to elevate her status by obtaining a managerial position as a labor officer, a significant accomplishment given the fact that it is highly unusual for a woman to be part of the managerial staff in this industry, even at the lowest rung of the managerial hierarchy. Her mother migrated from Bangladesh and has been working in the mill since 1955. Her father was once a shopkeeper, but he lost his shop (his goods were stolen by his assistants) and had deserted his family when she was still a child. Her mother was left with the responsibility of supporting the family through employment in the mill, and she was able to put Manju through school. Manju was able to pass the certification examinations necessary to qualify as a welfare officer and obtain her job in the personnel office.

One of the central methods Manju used to consolidate her upward mobility was her ability to adopt the social norms governing the "appropriate" behavior of a woman of higher status. She tried her best to avoid contact with workers; for example, she would not go to the labor lines and she would specifically avoid walking in the mill during the shift change in order to avoid coming into contact with a large group of workers walking to the shop floor. Her engagement with workers was limited to the time she was on duty in her office, a place where she was in a clearly demarcated space of authority. The gendered dimension of this behavior is underlined when it is viewed in light of the practices of the male labor officers (who were also members of upper-caste groups):

male officers had a significantly higher degree of contact with workers and, as noted earlier, often attended cultural activities organized by workers in the labor lines.

Manju had to uphold codes of behavior and attitudes that were socially appropriate for her new status as an upwardly mobile woman. She explained, "Certain sources tell me the workers are like this. They are illiterate. They will pass rude remarks. People say I should not go. They say after all I am a lady so why should I go. It is not right. I do not even go inside the factory [shop floor], as per instruction of management. Mr. ———— was told I do not have to go. I don't want to go. I am educated. If my job requires it and I am told to, then I will go." As a member of the managerial staff she had to act like a "lady" (*aurat*) in order to distinguish herself from the "females" (*janana*), as women workers were commonly called. This distinction was further pronounced by her upper-caste status; she was a member of the *kayasth* (warrior) caste—information she made a point of telling me.

Manju's strategies for coping with her newly acquired status as a "lady" within the mill reveals how the construction of gender and the identity of women often centers on the creation and reproduction of hierarchy.[5] Such situations suggest the limitations of conceptualizations of gender or feminism that do not account for questions of difference and asymmetrical relationships of power between women. In many ways Manju waged a successful struggle against patriarchal codes. Her consciousness of her own position as a woman working outside the home reflected a rejection of the notion that women should confine themselves to domesticity within the household. As she argued:

We are modern now. Why should women not work outside the house? Women have an aim and they should do it. I am doing it. At first I felt uneasy because there were all men only. I did not know whom to talk to. I thought, what will I do for eight hours everyday? But then I got into the habit. I got used to it. You get maternity benefits, maternity leave. So why should you not work? Anyway I finish work at 5 P.M. Then I go home and I do all kinds of work. I can do both.

Yet Manju's sense of accomplishment cannot be separated from the reproduction of a hierarchical relationship between her status as labor officer and the position of workers in the factory. Her situation is particularly ironic given the fact that her own mother is still a worker in the same factory. Yet her ability to transcend her working-class background was contingent on the adoption of gendered codes of behavior that distance her from both male and female workers. The social mobility that allowed Manju to transgress the boundaries of her working-class origins required a shift in the gendered codes that governed her behavior; the construction of her gender identity was inextricably linked to the preservation of a social distance from workers. This social distance also extended to her relationship with her mother, which became strained after Manju began work as a labor officer.

The construction of the identity of women workers, then, cannot be reduced to a shared experience of women's oppression. Rather, the stories of women's experiences suggest that the identity of women workers is conditioned by their particular social location—in the mill, at home, and in their community—but is always mediated through their own discursive construction of their particular experiences (Scott, 1992b). As Stuart Hall has argued, we must recognize that

events, relations, structures do have conditions of existence and real effects, outside the sphere of the discursive; but that only within the discursive, and subject to its specific conditions, limits and modalities, do they have or can they be constructed with meaning. Thus, while not wanting to expand the territorial claims of the discursive infinitely, how things are represented and the "machineries" and regimes of representation in a culture do play a *constitutive*, and not merely a reflexive, after-the-event role. This gives questions of culture and ideology, and the scenarios of representation—subjectivity, identity, politics—a formative, not merely an expressive place in the constitution of social and political life. (1992b: 253)

The production of the particular social location of women workers presents a striking example of this "constitutive" role of representation.

As we have seen, although women workers represent a distinct group in terms of their particular structural position, this phenomenon does not necessarily produce a unitary identity or shared form of consciousness or standpoint (Hartsock, 1984). I have pointed to relationships of power that exist among women and the role of gender as a signifier of class and caste hierarchies in order to argue against the assumption that the overdetermination of gender hierarchies means that gender is the most salient social identity for women workers in the mill. The structural position of women workers shapes but does not predetermine the meaning women workers give to their everyday lives. The positioning of women outside the hegemonic spheres of class and community politics does provide space for the development of a critical consciousness, and in some cases, an oppositional vision—one that is critical of both management practices as well as exclusionary union activities. However, the assumption that the social location of women workers naturally produces an expression of a critical or alternative vision of the social order undermines the intellectual labor that members of subaltern groups engage in when they interpret their experiences and construct meaning in their lives.

Critical Visions: Interrupting Hegemonic Narratives

The particular social location of working-class women provides the space for women workers to develop a distinctive critical conscious- ness through their interpretations of their everyday struggles. Women use their personal experiences and problems to assess management practices or workplace hierarchies. Consider the following discussion among two women laborers from the weaving and sewing departments in the mill:

Weaver:	After so long I cannot get a permanent job. Thirteen years I have been working here.
Handsewer:	We work for years but we still don't have permanent jobs.
Weaver:	Yes, she works for two or three weeks then for four weeks she has to sit at home. It is very difficult to manage. . . . [But] things are better now. Before, I could not even have rice and *dal*. Now at least I can have that. There was more sorrow [*dukh*] before.
Handsewer:	But we try to be happy. We try to forget our sorrow by being happy.
Weaver:	But it is important to remember our sorrow so we can see better what is happening today. We cannot see any happiness [*sukh*] if we don't remember the times of more sorrow.

This language of sukh and dukh was not limited to this conversation but was often the central means used by women workers to identify the meaning of their labor. Such "personalized" responses of women workers must be placed within the context of the relative absence of formal institutional channels of support as well as informal social net- works for women. Women workers in general argue that they do not have any sources of support. The response of one woman, "Who is there to help? I do everything alone" is echoed by many of the women I inter- viewed in the mill.

I suggest that this personalized interpretation of the experience of women workers does not imply that women are unable to analyze or understand the social or political implications of their position. On the contrary, their responses reveal a consciousness of the systematic ex- clusion of women from the public sphere of social and political power. Women workers in the mill display a critical consciousness of the cre- ation of a hegemonic bloc and the corresponding hegemonic discourse governing the production of a unified "working class." Their represen- tation of their personal experiences cannot be understood as a form of individualism but as a sharp critique of both union and management practices. One woman worker explained:

If you go to them [union leaders] they say come back later. Later. [The labor officers] also say the same thing. They say come back later. He [pointing to empty chair of the personnel manager][6] never has time. . . . We beg and plead about our problems but no one will listen. But if three or four of these big men go into the office and make loud noises they will immediately say come and sit down. And they will give them help.

This analysis presents a clear consciousness of the gendered nexus between management, unions, and a privileged (male) section of the work force. Another woman recounted an incident to demonstrate the absence of institutional support for women workers:

If someone is in trouble no one will help. I'll tell you one story about one woman I know. Last year one woman had an accident in the mill. She fell into a machine, her whole back was destroyed. She was in the hospital for three months. No one helped. The management did nothing, the unions did nothing. We went around and collected two rupees or three rupees from each person and helped her. No one else bothered. If there is something big that happens, the union will do something. If someone assaults me or beats me in the mill—if there is some incident with me, of course they will do something, if there is something big. Otherwise no one will help. If there is a problem or hardship we face, there is no one.

Women workers perceive the unions' definition of what qualifies as an "incident" as implicitly exclusive of the concerns and interests relevant to their lives and work. One woman expressed disbelief that anyone would be interested in interviewing her and discussing her views and concerns. As she said: "When ———— told me that someone was coming to talk to us on Thursday I thought she was joking. I didn't believe her. Then when she came to take two chairs—only then did I believe her." This comment embodies the extent to which women are marginalized from public discourse and representation in the industrial arena.

The consciousness of women workers of the exclusionary nexus between unions and management has reinforced the resistance of women to participation in trade unions. As one woman argued: "You have to give them money. . . . Whatever it may be you have to give them something. Even if it is ten rupees. I won't do that. I won't give money." Such responses shed light upon the question of women's participation in union activity. Low levels of participation and membership of women in unions in India and in comparative contexts (Cook, Lorwin, and Daniels, 1992) have often been interpreted as evidence of women's "apathy" and "passivity." I would argue that, on the contrary, women's rejection of union activity can be read as a form of consciousness of the exclusionary, gendered practices that have often characterized trade unions.

I have thus far been examining the manner in which women workers negotiate and interpret their experiences within the structural constraints of the workplace and home and in relation to the exclusionary boundaries of the hegemonic nexus between unions, management, and the state. Can we discern possible forms of autonomous resistance by women workers, or does the successful manifestation of this hegemonic bloc preclude resistance? I have argued that women workers are in fact conscious of the exclusionary gendered practices within the industrial arena and that they display a form of ideological resistance to this practice.[7] However, the question arises, is this ideological resistance transformed into a form of practical or collective action in the factory? That is, are there alternative forms of resistance that operate independently of trade unions or community organizations?

My study of women working in the mill reveals that the scope for independent collective action has been severely restricted. The combined forces of competition, dependence on employment, and the retrenchment of women from the work force limit the possibility for such action. This restriction is particularly evident in light of the fact that during the 1950s and 1960s women workers demonstrated militant opposition to their retrenchment from the mills. In the present context, the ability to gain employment is the most pressing issue for women workers. As one woman commented:

If three or four of us talk together and say we will go to the management and say something, the others will feel they will lose their jobs. So we don't do anything. We are afraid to say anything to management. . . . Each of us is so busy trying to see to ourselves. We have so many problems. We work for so many years but we are not permanent workers. I have to take care of my brothers. She has three children to take care of. . . . We cannot do anything to make things better. Anyway, we have no money to do anything.

The point is not that women workers are passive victims or that they are essentially incapable of engaging in collective action. However, structural constraints and an absence of resources severely limit the possibilities for organizational activity. As Bourdieu has suggested, the absence of resistance by members of a subordinated group often denotes the individuals' ability to recognize the immense structural constraints upon them and to gain a "practical mastery of the social structure as a whole" (Bourdieu, 1985: 728). This recognition of the immense odds they face compels women to adopt a pragmatic view of their everyday lives and reserves collective protest for the relatively privileged members of their community. In effect, women's lives in the jute mill are centered on the struggle to survive, a task that leaves little time or space for overt protest or organization.

Nevertheless, an exclusive focus on the structural constraints on collective action—without an analysis of the ways in which women workers interpret their own acts—does not fully capture the meaning of women's everyday struggles. Return for a moment to the life histories I presented earlier in this chapter. I have already pointed to the significance of motherhood for women like Uma, Hafijan, and Saraswati as they emphasize their concerns about their childrens' future and express hope that their labor will produce a better life for their children. In their perception of their productive and reproductive labor, these women understand their everyday activities as an attempt to interrupt the reproduction of structures of patriarchy and capitalism in the mill and in the labor lines. They emphasize their hopes that their children will become educated so that they will not have to work in the factory; they do not imagine a future in which their children will take over their jobs through the khandani system, which has inscribed patriarchal relations within the capitalist relations of production on the shop floor. In this discursive construction of their daily actions, the women I spoke with understood their practices as attempts to disrupt "macro" structures of power reproduced within the factory, community, and family.

The meanings women assign to their everyday lives provide us with the analytical space to move beyond a classification that constructs subaltern women either as clear resistors to or as passive victims of structural oppression. On the one hand, the struggle of women workers simply to survive cannot be adequately conceptualized in terms of the category of resistance. On the other hand, women workers interpret their labor as a means to provide a better future for their children, one that will move beyond the structures that have circumscribed their own lives. This imagined future and this investment in children prevent us from reducing women workers' practices to an individualistic form of survival. More significant, they do not perceive their labor as merely serving the needs of capitalism or patriarchy even while they are acutely aware of the implications and effects of such larger structures. In this context, we cannot then assume that women workers in the mill are simply victims or that women's reproductive labor can be reduced to the reproduction of these structures (Kuhn and Wolpe, 1978).

By taking seriously the ways in which women workers discursively construct their own social locations, practices, and experiences we can construct a third possibility, one that can inform recent research pointing both to the dangers of romanticizing resistance (Abu-Lughod, 1990) and the problems of presenting women as passive victims of structures of oppression (Mohanty, 1991). This alternative possibility allows us to analyze the very real material effects of hegemonic narratives of class, community, and gender without erasing the critical visions women workers produce. Such visions momentarily disrupt the regimes of power operating in the mill, community, and family, and remind us that the production of hegemony is always an incomplete, contested process.

In light of the complex hegemonic narratives of class, community, and gender that unfold in the factory and labor lines, it is an accomplishment for women workers simply to retain employment in the mill. This success is particularly significant given the fact that women's employment in the mill has followed the national pattern of traditional manufacturing industries and now constitutes only 2 percent of the work force. Nevertheless, these women persist in their struggle to obtain factory employment even though their largely casual status usually offers work only a few weeks at a time. Women's desire to work in the factory stems from bare economic survival rather than any sense that factory employment provides a form of economic independence (or any assumed liberation stemming from employment). The stories and fragments of women's lives and experiences form narratives of a continual daily struggle to survive in the face of harsh working conditions, job insecurity, responsibility for the maintenance of their household, and, in many cases, sole responsibility for providing for their children's future through investments in marriage or education. In this process, women workers must negotiate through the often unyielding hegemonic boundaries of community, gender, and class that unfold in the jute mill and workers' residences. Although their particular position does not produce a singular form of identity or consciousness, I have suggested that the social location of women workers provides space for a critical understanding of the implications of the political construction of the boundaries that circumscribe their work and lives.

The life histories of women workers point to the complex connections between the "micro" dynamics of the fluid, ever-shifting dailiness and discursive meanings through which they interpret their lives and the "macro" dynamics of the structures and hegemonic representations of class, gender, and community that constrain them. Thus, the boundaries that delineate the category "women workers" are produced through everyday social and political practices in the factory, family, and communities of workers. These boundaries are enforced by larger institutions and structures of power and are transformed into rigid borders constraining the lives of working-class women. Yet they always provide potential spaces for contestation, as women workers interrupt the reproduction of hegemonic narratives of class, community, and gender through their own visions of an alternative future.

Chapter 7
Conclusion: The Politics of Categories

My purpose in this book has been to argue that the representation of political identities and interests involves continual contests of power over the boundaries between categories. The study of politics, then, cannot limit itself to the question of which identity is mobilized or politicized within a particular historical context or about the way a particular category is discursively constructed over time; we must also interrogate the ways the boundaries of a particular category are produced in relation to other categories or identities. A more conventional approach to the study of political participation or collective action might investigate which identity or analytical category is particularly salient for explaining specific forms of political behavior and activity. My purpose has been to demonstrate that the attempt to reduce political activity or the representation of interests to a singular identity is in itself a political act, one that attempts to purify identities and categories that are always already marked by differences. The search for a pure category does not merely represent the need to preserve the analytical rigor of the theoretical models that we construct but constitutes the very substance of everyday politics; the search for purity in effect puts into play technologies of power that both designate and "police the boundaries" (Hall, 1992a: 30) of the category in question through hierarchical representations of other social identities.

I have used the case of the Calcutta jute-mill workers to analyze the ways the boundaries of categories can be understood as the product of political processes that unfold through institutional, discursive, and everyday social practices. Institutions such as the labor market, the family, and community organizations represent critical sites of political and social conflict. In this context, conflict does not merely arise out of predefined groups struggling over such scarce resources as employment or housing, but is centered on the construction of groups and their "interests," a process that involves the creation of particular meanings and relationships among gender, class, and community. This process has fundamentally turned around a dialectics of hegemony and resistance that highlights both the rigid and contested nature of such boundaries; social actors, such as unions, managers, and workers, have attempted to preserve particular hegemonic representations of class, community, and gender even as these representations are disrupted by moments of contestation.

Although trade unions manufacture a conception of a homogeneous working class, their articulation of class interests rests on hierarchical representations of gender and community identities. This process raises a critical paradox in the ways social, cultural, and political practices are classified. On the one hand, as we have seen in Chapter 2, unions are continually engaged in the production of class as a discrete identity that is subsequently antithetical to differences of gender, caste, ethnicity, or religion. On the other hand, the boundaries of class are created through particular meanings of gender and community, as we have seen manifested in the gendered division of labor or the intricate links between community and union organizations. Such dynamics produce a political paradox. Unions are engaged in a struggle to transform "class" into a homogeneous or "pure" category untarnished by differences or divisions of gender, caste, or religion. Yet in practice class has always already been marked by difference, as it is continually being manufactured through identities of gender and community, whether at the structural level on the shop floor, at the symbolic level as meanings of class are produced by religious ritual practices, or by a form of sexual politics that makes access to union resources contingent on the reproduction of a patriarchal model of the working-class family. The paradox lies in the fact that the boundaries used to construct distinct group identities (in this case, class) are founded on the existence of "other" identities (in this case, gender and community). The implication is that group identities are consequently never discrete or predetermined, and the attempt to produce a discrete, purified category in effect represents a strategy of power, one that is often involved in preserving a particular hegemonic representation of the category.

My point, however, has not been to juxtapose the contingencies of class with more "authentic" or "natural" identities of gender or community; the categories of gender and community are also created and contested. Thus, I argued that unions and managers employed religious rituals to construct hierarchical, gendered narratives of community. I further demonstrated that identities of gender were created through the reproduction of patriarchal models of the working-class family as well as through the potential challenge to those models posed by women workers.

Categories and identities are by no means easily mutable or arbitrary.

On the contrary, one of my central purposes has been to demonstrate that hegemonic representations of class interests or gender hierarchies are usually rigid and act as significant structural constraints. For instance, exclusionary constructions of the working class have effectively kept women workers from gaining access to permanent employment in the jute mills. However, this situation does not produce a form of natural consent. Women who continue to seek employment in the mill or who analyze the exclusionary nature of union activity are engaged in a process of identifying and contesting the boundaries drawn by managers, unions, and male workers. The constructed nature of such processes does not mean that the boundaries of categories are arbitrary or perpetually fluid. One of the tenets underlying my conception has been the notion that we must confront the structural conditions for group formation. In particular contexts, the relations between categories and the type of hegemonic representations produced are contingent on existing forms of economic, social, and cultural "capital" that are available to social actors (Bourdieu, 1985: 724). A recognition of such conditioning factors allows us to understand why particular types of representations become hegemonic. It also prevents us from transforming the concept of relationality into a laundry list of identities that randomly interact with each other. Thus, in the case of the Calcutta jute mills gender operates in a distinct fashion in relationship to class and community. Narratives of class and community rest on shared meanings of gender that place women workers in a particular location of marginality. In this context, however, gender does not transcend the politics of class and community, a fact perhaps most strikingly evident in the stories of survival of women workers.

Faced with this conclusion, we cannot simply acknowledge that social categories such as class, gender, and community occasionally "intersect" with each other. When we choose to analyze particular phenomena through the lens of one or the other category, we may ourselves inadvertently be producing political boundaries that simultaneously rest on and circumscribe the other categories. There is, then, a second dimension to the argument, one that considers what the implications of such political contests over the boundaries of categories in the jute mills are for the conceptualization of our own theoretical categories.

Time, Space, and Genealogies of Categories

I have implied throughout this book that a genealogical approach substantially enriches and recasts our understanding of particular forms of political activity. The genealogical approach I have adopted has rested on an understanding of the formation of social identities and categories through both temporal and spatial processes. Following Anthony Giddens's argument that time and space are "constitutive features of social systems" (1981: 30), I have attempted to analyze the ways in which categories are both dynamic, as their discursive meanings are produced through time, and material, as they are enforced in spatial terms. The question of temporality has operated in two forms in my discussion of the genealogies of class and gender. On the one hand, from the 1950s to 1990s, the steady displacement of women workers has transformed the jute mill working class into a primarily male working class. As I argued in Chapter 2, the state's and the unions' conception of a monolithic working class has in effect facilitated this displacement by refusing to confront differences and hierarchies among workers. From this perspective of the *longue durée*, it appears that the discursive construction of the purity of class interests has materialized; that is, if women have been displaced, gender may no longer be salient in marking the boundaries of class. By taking seriously the temporality of everyday experience and activity (Giddens, 1981: 19), however, I have shown that the production of boundaries between gender, class, and community continues to play a central role in the factory and in working-class communities.

By introducing this form of temporality into our conception of categories we can analyze the reproductive narratives that enforce particular representations of these categories while providing the conceptual space for an analysis of activities that may interrupt these reproductive practices. I have, for example, analyzed the ways in which managers, unions, and community organizations mark the borders of both class and community with hierarchies of gender. Yet in their struggles for daily survival, women workers may momentarily interrupt this reproduction of hegemonic boundaries by imagining a future for their children that does not rely on employment in the mill through the khandani system; in this process, they reject a future tied either to capitalist wage labor in the factory or to a form of security embodied in the patriarchal structure of khandani-based employment. By adopting a genealogical approach that reintroduces this form of temporality, we are able to recast the gendered history of the jute working class from a single event marked by victimized women retrenched from their jobs to a dynamic, contested process that both confronts the contingency of categories and links this contingency with systemic forms of power that structure the everyday lives of workers.

In order to adequately address this link between discursive contingencies and structural constraints, I have focused on the spatial representation of categories. On one level, the structural dimension of class formation is revealed in terms of the spatial positioning of workers on the factory floor. On a second level, this positioning of workers in material space is shaped by particular divisions of labor produced through discursive meanings of gender and community. This convergence between the symbolic and material spaces that mark class, gender, and community through the positioning of workers on the shop floor allows us to bridge the divide between structure and discourse without reverting to a reductive form of determinism in which the "economic" must inevitably outweigh the ideological or discursive. By thinking about space as a "practiced place" (de Certeau, 1988: 117), we can see how the spatial representation of categories is transformed from a static frame of analysis or technique of mapping to a dynamic process and a critical aspect of the genealogical approach to social categories.

Rethinking Categories, Recasting Explanations

A genealogical approach enables an important shift from an assumption that explanations can only be derived through specifications of particular causal mechanisms to a recognition that a closer examination of analytical categories that form the "context of discovery" (Harding, 1987; Somers, 1994) can significantly recast explanations of particular outcomes and specific forms of social and political behavior. Thus my analysis of the making of political boundaries in the jute mills has allowed a revision of conventional understandings of the displacement of women from the work force. I have argued for an explanation that does not rest on a single causal event, such as the onslaught of modernization or the economic crisis of the industry. Instead, I have suggested that the historical process of the retrenchment of women stems from daily negotiations of power over the boundaries between class and gender—negotiations that then become particularly acute and appear overdetermined in moments of crisis or disruption.

A central, underlying concern of this book is the framework of exceptionalism, wherein the inability of Indian workers to form a unified national labor movement or successful class-based national political party has served as a marker for the relative irrelevance of class politics in India.[1] By analyzing the production of the boundaries of class and examining their construction in relation to the politics of gender and community, I have interrogated the assumption that "the working class" can be reduced to a singular, monolithic entity with shared interests. Assumptions regarding the homogeneity and commonality of interests among workers have had a long history in both the Marxian and Weberian intellectual traditions. An unquestioned acceptance of such assumptions has frozen images of Indian labor politics within the framework of "exceptionalism" and subsequently allowed us to circumvent much of the empirical and theoretical richness of contemporary labor politics in India. On one level, a dichotomous framework that presents the politics of class in opposition to the politics of religion or ethnicity underestimates the significance of links among these categories. On another level, narrow definitions of class may lead us to underestimate the significance of class politics in various contexts. For instance, the assumption that languages of class are only articulated by trade unions or political parties has often led to this view in India. We begin to see that an analysis of the ways boundaries between categories are constructed can transform our understanding of particular political outcomes. In this endeavor, the issue becomes more than merely identifying a different pattern of class formation in India; put another way, my point is not that political culture in India or in Calcutta operates as an independent variable that makes workers act in a "different" or exceptional manner. Rather, by looking at the relationship between particular social identities, we begin to recognize that the languages of class may be expressed through a woman worker's resistance to sexual harassment by a manager, through an Action Committee attempting to create a workers' public sphere that circumvents management authority and surveillance, or through a religious ritual such as the Vishwakarma Puja that disrupts production and allows workers to break management control of time and space in the factory.

This recasting of the argument of exceptionalism is not limited to presenting alternative spheres for the analysis of class politics. Rather, I have suggested that an explanation of the relative weakness of working-class unions in India and their inability to serve as an effective independent force within the Indian political system does not stem solely from the institutional dependency of unions on the state and political parties (Chatterji, 1980; Rudolph and Rudolph, 1987) but from the unions' own inability to confront differences and hierarchies within the working classes as well. Consider, for example, the way in which discourses of "unity" operate within trade union activities. Unions often operate under defensive conditions in terms of their resources and political leverage; given this situation, unity among workers surely becomes one of the central means of maintaining collective action and bargaining power.

Despite this recognition of the "logic" of trade-union activity, I suggest that a focus on the issue of difference in the conceptualization of class politics is not merely a theoretical exercise. Trade unions (and state labor policies) that continue to assume narrow views of class end up simply acknowledging or attempting to add on "special" considerations for women workers, for example. The initial exclusionary structure or agenda of the union is left untouched. Hence, while Indian trade unions may have classified difference as division, the paradox lies in the fact that the unity of workers then rests on exclusion. It is at this point that unions begin to signify limited interest groups rather than a mass movement. The opposition in the discourses of trade unions between worker unity and the struggle for equality, on the one hand, and difference, on the other, permits a silent preservation of hierarchies within industrial work forces. As Joan Scott has argued: "Placing equality and difference in antithetical relationship has, then, a double effect. It denies the way in which difference has long figured in political notions of equality and it suggests that sameness is the only ground on which equality can be claimed" (Scott, 1988: 174). Meanwhile, this refusal to confront difference can foreclose possibilities for an emancipatory politics even at the local level in the jute mills.

The unwillingness of unions and workers' community organizations to confront gender hierarchies has hindered the ability of workers to develop an autonomous subaltern public sphere. When unions and workers uphold particular gendered codes of behavior, discipline women's sexuality, and engage in the surveillance of women's bodies, their practices inadvertently converge with management constructions of social and sexual disorder in working-class communities and with the particular modes of disciplinary power managers exercise in the factory and labor lines. Even at the local level, hierarchical forms of difference have been central to the making of the jute mill working class, even as unions have continued to insist that their political struggles must be achieved on the basis of sameness and unity. A central implication of this book is that if we begin to view the distinctions between class, gender, and community interests in terms of the production of political boundaries, we can no longer adopt such a limited framework for political activity.

My research suggests that this type of approach will enrich our understanding of the politics of labor in India as the economy undergoes particular structural transitions. One of the most significant issues in the economic restructuring of Indian industry in the 1990s is the "exit policy," the means by which workers are retrenched on a mass scale in order to enable restructuring. Given my argument regarding hegemonic forms of the "working class," I would expect this retrenchment to unfold through political processes in which the weak sections of the work force will be the first to lose their employment. As unions attempt to consolidate their membership bases during periods of restructuring, it is likely that a conception of the homogeneity or unity of workers will mask the hierarchies that will form the basis of this consolidation. In my interviews, leaders of the central trade unions across the ideological spectrum consistently argued that "women's issues" could only be of secondary importance given the extreme "macro" pressures of labor retrenchment and economic restructuring. I have suggested here, however, that such "macro" changes in fact center around the politics of difference and the ways in which the relationships among class, gender, and community are articulated.[2]

In the past, issues such as the retrenchment of women workers have often been explained in terms of the theory of the "reserve army" of labor. This approach holds that particular groups of workers, such as women, constitute a "reserve army" that is employed in times of labor shortages and displaced in periods of economic crisis. The economic functionalism that lies at the basis of this argument neglects the political dynamics that produce such shifts in the industrial work force. By conceptualizing categories in temporal, spatial, and relational terms, we can understand these shifts as ongoing political processes that are contingent on particular historical and cultural contexts, even as they are shaped by structural constraints.

I have pointed to the ways in which my interrogation of the "symbolic boundaries" (Hall, 1992a) between categories can enrich our understanding and begin to recast explanations of particular outcomes. This approach also allows us to engage with political outcomes and think through phenomena in comparative contexts—for example, the varying patterns of political participation in other social and political movements, such as that of women workers in unions and labor movements or of women of color in the U.S. women's movement. My purpose has not been to argue that Calcutta jute workers, Indian unions, or political activity in a postcolonial context is simply different from the theoretical visions of (European) social theory. The measure of postcoloniality, marked by the historical, cultural, and economic specificities of India or of jute mills in Calcutta allows us to rethink theoretical assumptions and deepen our understanding of categories, identities, and behavior in a larger comparative context. The "difference" of postcoloniality that marks my representation of the contemporary history of the Calcutta jute mill workers can provide the impetus for a revision of modernist assumptions that take for granted the technologies of power that produce categories of analysis and forms of knowledge (Foucault, 1980).

My argument that the boundaries of categories are manufactured through political processes (and the corresponding critique of a conception of a unified working class) signifies a deeper epistemological move that has questioned a series of juxtapositions: "class/culture," "modern/traditional," "capitalist/precapitalist," and "unity/difference." In this endeavor, I have drawn on recent innovations in social theory that use colonial and postcolonial histories to challenge these "paired oppositions" that have so often characterized social theory and that accord with the intellectual tradition of the Enlightenment. An interrogation of these binaries enriches our approach to the study of politics by moving us away from easy oppositions of "East" and "West" even as it challenges the boundaries between European social theory and the "Third World" case study.

The representation of social categories and the relationships among these categories have very real political and material effects. The "purity" of a category in this context is not a benign ideal type created to preserve the analytical rigor of our research, but it is in fact an effect of power—that is, a hegemonic representation whose boundaries are defined through other social hierarchies. The study of politics cannot simply require us to employ analytical categories to grasp social realities but must compel us to recognize that politics is about the production of distinctions and relationships among social categories. Contesting the boundaries of categories provides us with the theoretical force with which we can begin to confront the politics of identity without externalizing or exoticizing the politics of difference.

Notes

Chapter 1

1. The incident was narrated by labor officers in the mill. Note also that such cases have been historically documented by Dipesh Chakrabarty, *Rethinking Working Class History* (New Delhi: Oxford University Press, 1989).

2. See Radha Kumar, *The History of Doing: An Illustrated Account of Movements for Women's Rights and Feminism in India, 1800–1990* (New York: Verso Press, 1993), for a further discussion of the ways in which the notion of honor is used by communities and political parties in cases of rape and sexual assault of women in India.

3. On this point, see also Anne McClintock, *Imperial Leather: Race, Gender and Sexuality in the Colonial Contest* (New York: Routledge, 1995), p. 5.

4. Consider the way in which particular narratives of race and gender shaped public reactions to the Clarence Thomas and Anita Hill hearings. See essays in Toni Morrison, ed., *Race-ing Justice, En-gendering Power: Essays on Anita Hill, Clarence Thomas, and the Construction of Social Reality* (New York: Pantheon Books, 1992).

5. Candace West and Sarah Fenstermaker, "Doing Difference," *Gender and Society* 9, 1 (February 1995): 8–37. For critical responses see Collins et al., "Symposium on West and Fenstermaker's 'Doing Difference,'" *Gender and Society* 9, 4 (August 1995): 491–513. This exchange serves as one example of a growing intellectual discussion of the question as to how we can adequately address the relationship among different social categories and identities.

6. I use the term "resources" in my analysis in order to avoid theoretical confusion with Marx's use of the term "capital."

7. For an interesting critique of the distinction between structure and representation, see Timothy Mitchell, *Colonizing Egypt* (Berkeley: University of California Press, 1988).

8. See, for example, Chandra Mohanty, "Feminist Encounters: Locating the Politics of Experience," in Michele Barrett and Anne Phillips, eds., *Destabilizing Theory: Contemporary Feminist Debates* (Stanford, CA: Stanford University Press, 1992).

9. Karl Marx, "The Eighteenth Brumaire," in David McLellan, ed., *Karl Marx: Selected Writings* (Oxford: Oxford University Press, 1987), p. 317.

10. Karl Marx, "The Communist Manifesto," in Robert Tucker, ed., *The Marx-Engels Reader*, 2d ed. (New York: Norton, 1978), p. 480.

11. Ibid.

12. Marx, "The German Ideology," in Robert Tucker, ed., *The Marx-Engels Reader*, 2d ed. (New York: Norton, 1978), p. 179.

13. Marx acknowledged tension among members of the working class, but he characterized this difference purely in terms of divisive competition between individual workers.

14. Max Weber, "Class, Status, Party," in H. H. Gerth and C. Wright Mills, eds., *From Max Weber: Essays in Sociology* (New York: Galaxy, 1958), p. 183.

15. Max Weber, "The Distribution of Power Within the Political Community: Class, Status, Party," in Guenther Roth and Claus Wittich, eds., *Economy and Society*, vol. 2 (Berkeley: University of California Press, 1978), p. 927.

16. Ibid., p. 932.

17. Note that Weber did discuss the relationship between the economic and sociocultural realms. For example, in "The Sociology of Religion" he elaborates on such issues in his discussion of "The Religion of Non-Privileged Status" (in Max Weber, *Economy and Society*, p. 481). However, my concern in this discussion is specifically with Weber's formulation of the category of class.

18. For a more extensive discussion of the way in which this separation resurfaces in more recent labor history see Leela Fernandes, "Contesting Class: Gender, Community, and the Politics of Labor in a Calcutta Jute Mill," *Bulletin of Concerned Asian Scholars* 26, 4 (October–December 1994): 29–43. For a study that questions this assumption of unified interests in the United States, see David Roediger, *The Wages of Whiteness: Race and the Making of the American Working Class* (New York: Verso, 1991).

19. This layered approach is influenced by Katznelson's conceptualization in "Working Class Formation: Constructing Cases and Comparisons," in Ira Katznelson and Aristide Zolberg, eds., *Working-Class Formation: Nineteenth-Century Patterns in Western Europe and the United States* (Princeton, NJ: Princeton University Press, 1986).

20. This is most clearly reflected in the modernization literature of the 1950s and 1960s. See for example, Gabriel Almond and Sydney Verba, *The Civic Culture: Political Attitudes and Democracy in Five Nations* (Princeton, NJ: Princeton University Press, 1963); Lucien Pye and Sydney Verba, eds., *Political Culture and Political Development* (Princeton, NJ: Princeton University Press, 1965).

21. For an early critical reconsideration of this teleology see Lloyd Rudolph and Susanne Rudolph, *The Modernity of Tradition* (Chicago: University of Chicago Press, 1967). Recent literature has developed a critique of "modernity" and the "Western" assumptions that are transposed through the presumed universality of the category of "modernity." See, for example, Partha Chatterji, *Nationalist Thought and the Colonial World: A Derivative Discourse* (London: Zed Books, 1986).

22. Dipesh Chakrabarty, "Of Communal Workers and Secular Historians," *Seminar* (October 1990): 1–4.

23. Pierre Bourdieu, *Outline of a Theory of Practice* (Cambridge: Cambridge University Press, 1977).

24. Chandra Mohanty, "Feminist Encounters: Locating the Politics of Experience," in Michele Barrett and Anne Phillips, eds., *Destabilizing Theory: Contemporary Feminist Debates* (Stanford, CA: Stanford University Press, 1992); Joan Scott, "Experience," in Judith Butler and Joan Scott, eds., *Feminists Theorize the Political* (New York: Routledge, 1992); Stuart Hall, "What Is This 'Black' in Black Popular Culture?" in Gina Dent, ed., *Black Popular Culture* (Seattle: Bay Press, 1992).

25. The Communist and Left parties have never formed coalition govern-

ments in more than three states—West Bengal, Tripura, and Kerala—at any time in the postcolonial period.

26. The contours of the debate over exceptionalism and universalism have originated in the context of studies of labor politics in the United States and Britain, with the case of English working-class formation serving as the ideal type for the behavior of the "working class" and the United States serving as a marker of exceptionalism. See Edward P. Thompson, *The Making of the Working Class* (New York: Vintage Books, 1966); Gareth Stedman Jones, *Languages of Class: Studies in English Working Class History, 1832–1982* (New York: Cambridge University Press, 1983). Werner Sombart, *Why Is There No Socialism in the United States?*, trans. Patricia M. Hocking and C. T. Husbands (White Plains, New York: M. E. Sharpe, 1976). For a critical review of conventional explanations of "American exceptionalism," see Ira Katznelson, *City Trenches: Urban Politics and the Patterning of Class in the United States* (New York: Pantheon Books, 1981).

27. Such studies of these two variants rest on images of the "traditionalism" of the Indian worker. On one hand, the Indian worker is depicted as rural and illiterate and therefore different from the modern (Western) industrial worker. See, for example, Raman Rao, *Essays on Indian Labor* (Bombay: Popular Prakashan, 1965). On the other hand, such studies focus on the way in which precapitalist ties obstruct the class consciousness of the Indian worker. See, for example, Kuriakose Mamkoottam, *Trade Unionism Myth and Reality: Unionism in the Tata Iron and Steel Company* (New Delhi: Oxford University Press, 1982), p. 124.

28. This point has also recently been made by Rajnarayan Chandavarkar, *The Origins of Industrial Capitalism in India* (London: Cambridge University Press, 1994).

29. For discussions of the relationship between caste and class, see Francine Frankel and M. S. A. Rao, eds., *Dominance and State Power in Modern India: Decline of a Social Order* (New Delhi: Oxford University Press, 1990).

30. Katznelson, *City Trenches*, p. 16, and Katznelson, *Marxism and the City*; Ira Katznelson and Aristide Zolberg, eds., *Working-Class Formation*; Victoria Hattam, *Labor Visions and State Power: The Origins of Business Unionism in the United States* (Princeton, NJ: Princeton University Press, 1993).

31. See Patricia Hill Collins, *Black Feminist Thought: Knowledge, Consciousness, and the Politics of Empowerment*, (Boston: Unwyn Hyman, 1990), for a discussion of this stereotype.

32. Indrajit Gupta, *Capital and Labour in the Jute Industry* (Bombay: Trade Union Publication Series, All-India Trade Union Congress, July 1953), p. 2.

33. I am omitting the precise nature of the contact in order to preserve the confidentiality of the research.

34. See Rick Fantasia, *Cultures of Solidarity*, for a discussion of the limitations in using survey techniques in the study of class consciousness.

35. For a good critical overview of feminist literature, see Diane Wolf, "Situating Feminist Dilemmas in Fieldwork," in Wolf, ed., *Feminist Dilemmas in Fieldwork* (Boulder, CO: Westview, 1994).

36. For a critical discussion of the "self/other" binary, see Lila Abu-Lughod, "Writing Against Culture," in Richard Fox, ed., *Recapturing Anthropology* (Santa Fe, NM: School of American Research Press, 1991).

Chapter 2

1. My focus is on the central national trade unions. Smaller, independent unions offer alternative models for worker organization; for example, the Self-Employed Women's Association (SEWA) organizes informal-sector women workers. See Kalima Rose, *Where Women Are Leaders: The SEWA Movement in India* (Atlantic Highlands, NJ: Zed Books, 1992).

2. Indian Trade Union Congress, *Constitution*, 1957, p. 1.

3. Interview with INTUC leader, Calcutta, May 1992. "Tri-color" refers to the colors of the Congress Party as well as the Indian flag.

4. Ibid.

5. In the BJP's conception of Hinduism all religions "originating" within the territorial borders of India (including Sikhism, Jainism, and Buddhism) are embraced as Hindu and Indian religions. Islam and Christianity are excluded from "Indian religions" by this definition.

6. D. B. Thengadi, *Why Bharatiya Mazdoor Sangha?* (New Delhi: Bharatiya Mazdoor Sangh Publications, 1959) p. 10.

7. Ibid., p. 59.

8. CITU, *Constitution*, p. 1. The CPI(M) leadership represented the majority in the unified Communist trade union, and since the split both the CPI(M) and the CITU have taken the lead within the leftist/Communist spectrum of Indian politics. For a comprehensive political history of Communist Party politics, see Ross Mallick, *Indian Communism: Opposition, Collaboration and Institutionalization* (New Delhi: Oxford University Press, 1994).

9. Biren Roy, "CITU—A Critical Review," *Marxist Review* (1985): 209. Figures are in lakhs: 1 lakh = 1,00,000 = 100,000.

10. For a critique of the Left Front government's rural development policies, see Ross Mallick, *Development Policy of a Communist Government: West Bengal Since 1977* (New Delhi: Cambridge University Press, 1993). For an alternative view, see Atul Kohli, *The State and Poverty in India: The Politics of Reform* (Cambridge: Cambridge University Press, 1987).

11. West Bengal Department of Labour, *Labour in West Bengal 1977* (Calcutta: Government of West Bengal, 1978), p. 2.

12. Aditi Roy Ghatak, in *The Statesman*, Calcutta, May 1, 1991.

13. West Bengal Department of Labour, *Labour in West Bengal 1985* (Calcutta: Government of West Bengal, 1986), p. 178.

14. See his analysis of the case of the Calcutta Chemical Company, "Left Front Lukewarm to Workers' Cooperatives," *Economic and Political Weekly* (June 27, 1992): 1303–1304. Roy estimates that in 1991, 10 percent of industrial disputes were due to strikes, whereas 90 percent of disputes were due to lockouts.

15. West Bengal Department of Labour, *Labour in West Bengal 1979* (Calcutta: Government of West Bengal, 1980), p. v.

16. See Ajit Roy, "West Bengal: CPI(M)–CPI Relations, the Basic Issues," *Economic and Political Weekly* (May 20, 1989): 1081.

17. Note that this has not been the case for other trade unions in West Bengal.

18. Lloyd Rudolph and Susanne Rudolph, *In Pursuit of Lakshmi* (Chicago: University of Chicago Press, 1987).

19. B. T. Ranadive, *Working Class* (CITU newspaper) 18, 7 (March 1989).

20. B. T. Ranadive, *Working Class* 13, 12 (August 1984).

21. The growing strength of the BJP is reflected by the rise in its electoral sup-

port in the 1991 parliamentary elections. During the 1990s, the period of my research, the BJP is the single largest opposition party in Parliament.

22. Thengadi, *Why Bharatiya Mazdoor Sangha?*

23. The convention included the participation of the BMS.

24. Shashi Bhushan Upadhyay, "Communalism and Working Class Riot of 1893 in Bombay City," *Economic and Political Weekly* (July 29, 1989): PE69–PE75.

25. The All-India Democratic Women's Association (AIDWA), the women's wing of the CPI(M), has focused on some social problems, including dowry and bride burning. However, the AIDWA has not enjoyed a significant position of power within the political hierarchy of the CPI(M).

26. CITU Fifth Conference, Kanpur, April 13–17, 1983, quoted in *Working Class* 12, 8 (April 1983).

27. B. T. Ranadive, *Working Class* 12: 8 (April 1983).

28. All-India Trade Union Congress, interview by author, Calcutta, December 2, 1991.

29. Nivedita Menon, "Women in Trade Unions: A Study of AITUC, INTUC and CITU," in Sujata Gothoskar, ed., *Struggles of Women at Work* (New Delhi: Vikas Publishing House, 1992).

30. For a discussion of other forms of state legislation directed at women, see Flavia Agnes, "Protecting Women Against Violence? Review of a Decade of Legislation, 1980–1989," *Economic and Political Weekly* (April 25, 1992): 19–33.

31. Government of India, Labour Bureau, *Women in Industry* (1975).

32. In K. I. Thomas, *Labour in Indian Planning* (New Delhi: National Labour Institute, 1988), p. 424.

33. See Government of India, Ministry of Social and Women's Welfare, *Women in India* (April 1985).

34. Ibid., p. 31.

35. The precise number of unions may vary due to factional divisions within the major recognized trade unions in West Bengal.

36. This type of structure is characteristic of unions across the ideological spectrum. See Mamkoottam, *Trade Unionism,* for a similar study of trade-union structure in the Tata and Iron Steel Company in Jamshedpur, Bihar.

37. According to interviews with the organizing secretary, BCMU, and the general secretary, NUJW, Calcutta 1992. The AITUC jute federation claims 60,000 members, and the BJP federation claims 46,000.

38. For a report on the problems of trade union verification in India, see "Trade Unions' Verification a Farce?" in *Financial Express,* July 13, 1991. Note this point regarding the exaggeration of union membership claims has also been made by Kuriakose Mamkoottam, "Trade Unions: The Sociological Dilemma," *Social Action* 34 (January–March 1984): 39.

39. This includes general strikes held in 1969, December 1970, January–February 1974 (a thirty-three-day strike), January–February 1979 (a fifty-day strike), January–April 1984 (an eighty-six-day strike), January–March 1992 (a fifty-day strike), and January 1995 (a four-day strike).

40. *Economic Times,* January 29, 1992.

41. The four NJMC (public sector) mills and one mill run by a workers' cooperative, the New Central Jute Mill, were exempted from the strike.

42. There was some disagreement between CITU state leadership and the BCMU, the jute federation. See Nirmalya Mukherjee, "CITU Leaders Differ over Strike," *Financial Express,* January 4, 1992.

43. *Economic Times,* December 27, 1992.

44. General Secretary, National Union of Jute Workers, INTUC, interview by author, Calcutta, May 9, 1992.

45. The industry was going through a boom period. The rupee devaluation (in the context of structural adjustment policies) resulted in a rise in jute export earnings and a rise in profits for the mill owners.

46. Biren Roy, "Jute Mill Owners' Offensive Against Workers," *Economic and Political Weekly* (September 5, 1992): 1893–1894. Such practices were confirmed by my interviews with both union leaders and managers.

47. The strike had to start in January, when the market for jute goods was strong. Niren Ghosh, president, Bengal Chatkal Mazdoor Union, CITU, quoted in the *Economic Times* December 31, 1991.

48. General Secretary, NUJW, interview by author, Calcutta, May 9, 1992. This view was corroborated by the IJMA.

49. Ambar Singh Roy, "Majority of Angus Workers Opposed to Indefinite Strike," *Economic Times*, January 21, 1992.

50. INTUC leader, speech at gate meeting, Mill B, Naihati, West Bengal, January 22, 1992.

51. This was stated in reports in the *Statesman,* December 12, 1991, and the *Economic Times,* December 29, 1991, January 21, 1992.

52. The other partner in the waiting game—the owners—must withstand the period without production. But there are allegations of stockpiling of finished jute goods by mill owners so that orders are not affected during the period of the strike. Note also that mill owners are able to keep orders pending so they do not necessarily lose business during the strike.

53. Women have been increasingly pushed into the lower-paying and insecure jobs in the "unorganized" sector of the economy. See Nirmala Banerjee, *Women in the Unorganized Sector* (New Delhi: Sangam Books, 1985).

54. Government of India, Tripartite Committee, *Industrial Committee on Jute: Report on Women Workers,* IJMA circular, October 6, 1959; Padmini Sengupta, *Women Workers of India* (Bombay: Asia Publishing House, 1960). References and condemnations of this displacement of women workers are also often found in trade union newspapers.

55. For an analysis of the effects of modernization on women workers, see Mukhul Mukherjee, "Impact of Modernization on Women's Occupations," in J. Krishnamurty, ed., *Women in Colonial India* (New Delhi: Oxford University Press, 1989).

56. See Government of India, Labour Bureau, Ministry of Labour and Rehabilitation, Department of Labour, *Socioeconomic Conditions of Women Workers in Textiles, Khandsari and Sugar Products Industries,* Shimla, 1984.

57. Arjan de Haan, "Towards a Single Male Earner: The Decline of Child and Female Employment in an Indian Industry," *Economic and Social History in the Netherlands* 6 (1994): 145–167.

58. According to the Government of India, *Indian Labor Yearbook,* annual maternity benefits claims for the whole state of West Bengal were less than 2 percent during 1967–1980.

59. As de Haan has pointed out, while the Maternity Benefits Act was established in 1939, it was not until the 1950s that employers started to argue that legislation had made female employment too expensive. De Haan, "Towards a Single Male Earner," p. 157.

60. IJMA Weekly Report, Circular No. 62 L/D, October 1, 1960.

61. Note that the employers' interest in the displacement of women tends to be concealed mainly because the documentation of the case is produced by the IJMA.

62. Gothoskar, "Struggles of Women Workers in the Pharmaceutical Industry," in S. Gothoskar, ed., *Struggles of Women at Work*, p. 1339.

63. Tanika Sarkar, "Politics and Women in Bengal," in J. Krishnamurty, ed., *Women in Colonial India*, p. 232.

64. Secretary, AITUC, interview by author, Calcutta, November 20, 1991.

65. Sarkar, "Politics and Women," p. 234.

66. These reports are "internal," confidential reports circulated among mill owners and are not intended for public use or public relations purposes. All names of mills and trade unions have been omitted to preserve confidentiality.

67. Indian Jute Mills Association, Weekly Labour Report, Circular No. 13 L/D, February 9, 1955, p. 2.

68. IJMA Weekly Labour Report, No. 18 L/D, February 25, 1955.

69. IJMA Weekly Report, Circular No. 50 L/D, August 29, 1963.

70. IJMA Weekly Report, Circular No. 62 L/D, August 9, 1962.

71. In one case, for example, a central trade union leader led a procession of two hundred women workers demanding the reinstatement of displaced women workers. IJMA Weekly Report, Circular No. 40 L/D, July 9, 1958.

72. *Industrial Committee on Jute*, quoted in IJMA Memorandum, October 6, 1959.

Chapter 3

1. By speaking of structure as the codification of power through movement, space, and position, I mean to transcend the dichotomy of structure and agency. For theoretical discussions of the "structure-agency" problematic, see Pierre Bourdieu, *Outline of a Theory of Practice*; Anthony Giddens, *A Contemporary Critique of Historical Materialism*, Vol. 1, *Power, Property, and the State* (London: Macmillan, 1981); and William Sewell, "A Theory of Structure: Duality, Agency, and Transformation," *American Journal of Sociology* 98, 1 (July 1992): 1–29.

2. For an analysis of the historical origins and patterning of this migration, see Ranajit Das Gupta, *Labour and Working Class in Eastern India: Studies in Colonial History* (Calcutta: K. P. Bagchi, 1994).

3. Casual workers are not legally entitled to social security and other welfare benefits.

4. Dipesh Chakrabarty, "Communal Riots and Labor: Bengal's Jute Mill-Hands in the 1890s," *Past and Present* 91 (May 1981): 151. For a different view of the role of sirdars, see de Haan, *Unsettled Settlers* (Hilversum: Verloren Publishers, 1994).

5. One of the foundational assumptions of economic theory, whether originating from Adam Smith, *The Wealth of Nations* (New York: Modern Library, 1937 [1776]), or Karl Marx, *Capital* (New York: Vintage Books, 1963 [1850]), is that the worker sells his or her labor in exchange for a wage.

6. The original scheme based on Wage Board recommendations had eight grades.

7. This is based on the Consumer Price Index.

8. Note that the wage structure I describe is for shop-floor workers. Mechanics, drivers, and clerical workers are paid based on a different system of grades, characterized by higher wage levels.

9. Such stereotyping of women's natural ability in terms of patience and dexterity has been noted in other cases. See, for example, Maria Patricia Fernandez-Kelly, *For We Are Sold I and My People: Women and Industry in Mexico's Frontier* (Albany: State University of New York Press, 1983), and Aihwa Ong, *Spirits of Resistance and Capitalist Discipline: Factory Women in Malaysia* (Albany: State University of New York Press, 1988).

10. The manager was speaking in reference to all mills in the industry.

11. This does not imply that "caste is class" in India. On this point, see Partha Chatterjee, "Caste and Subaltern Consciousness," in Ranajit Guha, ed., *Subaltern Studies*, vol. 6 (New Delhi: Oxford University Press, 1989); and Francine Frankel and M. S. A. Rao, eds., *Dominance and State Power in Modern India: Decline of a Social Order*, vol. 2 (New Delhi: Oxford University Press, 1990).

12. This process has also been documented by Dilip Simeon, *The Politics of Labour under Late Colonialism: Workers, Unions, and the State in Chota Nagpur, 1928–1939* (New Delhi: Manohar Press, 1995).

13. For a discussion of the ways in which communities are transformed into classes, see Karen Sacks, "Towards a Unified Theory of Race, Class and Gender," *American Ethnologist* 17 (1990): 534–550.

14. The multiplicity of unions has been a defining characteristic of trade-union politics in India. For a lengthy discussion of this phenomenon, see Rakahari Chatterji, *Unions, Politics, and the State: A Study of Labor Politics* (New Delhi: South Asian Publishers, 1980).

15. The gesture of salaam, in which the leader touches his hand to his forehead, represents a sign of recognition of a figure of higher power and authority.

16. James Scott has effectively argued against theories of false consciousness in *Domination and the Arts of Resistance: Hidden Transcripts* (New Haven, CT: Yale University Press, 1991).

17. This marginalization of women in trade unions is also true of the wider national arena in India. See Vimal Ranadive, *Women Workers of India* (Calcutta: National Book Agency, 1976).

Chapter 4

1. Management leaves at this point, but the festival continues all day and night and involves celebrations that include the playing of popular Hindi film songs and alcohol consumption.

2. See Peter van der Veer, *Religious Nationalism: Hindus and Muslims in India* (Berkeley: University of California Press, 1994), for an analysis of how ritual practices produce religious identity in India.

3. For an extensive critique of the Geertzian conception of ritual, see Catherine Bell, *Ritual Theory, Ritual Practice* (New York: Oxford University Press, 1992).

4. The term "communalism" represents the conventional language used in India to describe exclusionary political activity based on religious affiliations, specifically with regard to the phenomena of Hindu-Muslim conflicts.

5. While the West Bengal government has been effective in preserving communal harmony, Calcutta was affected by the 1990 riots.

6. The significance of such symbolic representations of authority through the

spatial positioning of participants is reminiscent of rituals of colonial authority. See Bernard Cohn, "Representing Authority in Victorian India," in Eric Hobsbawm and Terence Ranger, eds., *The Invention of Tradition* (Cambridge: Cambridge University Press, 1983).

7. Note that even children are present at the event.

8. For a critique of the concept of consent, see James Scott, *Domination and the Arts of Resistance: Hidden Transcripts* (New Haven, CT: Yale University Press, 1990).

9. For discussions of the interplay between caste and class identities see Stefan Molund, *First We Are People: the Koris of Kanpur between Caste and Class*, (Stockholm: Stockholm Studies in Social Anthropology, 1988), and Frankel and Rao, *Dominance and State Power*. Dipesh Chakrabarty has pointed out the need to move beyond the notion of the "mix" of caste, community, and class in "Of 'Communal' Workers and 'Secular' Historians" *Seminar* (October 1990): 1–4.

10. For an analysis of the importance of this puja in contemporary popular culture, see Nita Kumar, *The Artisans of Banaras: Popular Culture and Identity, 1880–1986* (Princeton, NJ: Princeton University Press, 1988).

11. The Vishwakarma celebration does not represent an official state holiday. In West Bengal, May 1 is the official state holiday for labor day.

12. Bipan Chandra, *Communalism in Modern India* (New Delhi: Vikas, 1984). For an analysis of the historical construction of communalism, see Gyanendra Pandey, *The Construction of Communalism in Colonial North India* (New Delhi: Oxford University Press, 1990), and Romila Thapar, "Imagined Religious Communities?" *Modern Asian Studies* 23, 2 (May 1989). For an examination of the historical construction of communalism among the jute workers see Dipesh Chakrabarty, "Communal Riots and Labour: Bengal's Jute Mill-Hands in the 1890s," *Past and Present* 91 (1981): 140–169. For an analysis of the gendered implications of communalism, see Tanika Sarkar and Urvashi Butalia, eds., *Women and the Hindu Right* (New Delhi: Kali for Women, 1995).

Chapter 5

1. Fraser, "Rethinking the Public Sphere," in Craig Calhoun, ed., *Habermas and the Public Sphere* (Cambridge: MIT Press, 1992).

2. For critical discussions of the category "subaltern," see Rosalind O'Hanlon, "Recovering the Subject: Subaltern Studies and Histories of Resistance in Colonial South Asia," *Modern Asian Studies* 22, 1 (1988): 189–224; Gayatri Spivak, "Can the Subaltern Speak?" in Cary Nelson and Lawrence Grossberg, eds., *Marxism and the Interpretation of Culture* (Urbana, IL: University of Illinois Press, 1988), and Spivak, "Subaltern Studies: Deconstructing Historiography," in Spivak, ed., *In Other Worlds: Essays in Cultural Politics* (New York: Routledge, 1988).

3. There is often a struggle to preserve these divisions; consider, for example, Bombay, where the government has attempted to implement policies such as the bulldozing of squatter settlements in order to produce a form of "order" in the urban planning of the city.

4. This growth of urban squatter settlements is not unique to India; it is characteristic of many cities in "Third World" countries. See for example, Kemal Karpat's study of Turkey and *The Gecekondu: Rural Migration and Urbanization* (Cambridge: Cambridge University Press, 1976), as well as David Collier, *Squatters and Oligarchs: Authoritarian Rule and Policy Change in Peru* (Baltimore, MD: Johns Hopkins University Press, 1976). For research on "company towns" in the

United States, see Jacquelyn Hall et al., *Like a Family: The Making of a Southern Cotton Mill World* (Chapel Hill: University of North Carolina Press, 1987), and John Gaventa, *Power and Powerlessness: Quiescence and Rebellion in an Appalachian Valley* (Urbana: University of Illinois Press, 1980).

5. Management pays a "House Rent Allowance" that is part of the workers' salary and that is intended to serve as a subsidy for the workers' housing costs.

6. Nirmala Banerjee, "Modernisation and Marginalisation," *Social Scientist* 13, 10–11 (October–November 1985): 48–71. Banerjee draws on songs of Bihari women in the jute mills and coal mines quoted by D. P. Saxena, *Rururban Migration in India* (Bombay: Popular Prakashan, 1977).

7. The estimate is based on handwritten lists of workers and the number of family members residing in each quarter. However, even the labor office does not have an exact record, as quarters have been subdivided and temporary makeshift residences have been constructed in the lines.

8. More prosperous workers own their own televisions, a reflection of a growing trend of working-class aspirations to middle-class consumerism, particularly in the context of the economic liberalization program underway in the 1990s.

9. In the case of pending orders, the factory draws on the large casual work force that remains in the mill area.

10. This pattern is more pronounced in mills in rural areas of West Bengal, since the scarcity of space is less acute than in Calcutta.

11. The rural ties of the migrant work force often exert a negative influence on this exercise of authority. Workers' connections with the village and the ownership of land has allowed workers to withstand the extended general strikes in the industry. A study of social relationships within the villages from which workers migrate suggests possibilities for future research but is beyond the scope of this book.

12. Case brought before the Seventh Industrial Tribunal, West Bengal, August 6, 1983, p. 11.

13. For critical discussions of Habermas's conceptualization of the public sphere see essays in Craig Calhoun, ed., *Habermas and the Public Sphere.*

14. For a discussion of similar issues in the United States see Jacquelyn Hall et al., *Like a Family: The Making of a Southern Cotton Mill World* (Chapel Hill: University of North Carolina Press, 1987).

15. *Bhadralok,* literally, the Bengali term for "gentleman," describes the social and cultural status of members of the upper classes in West Bengal and denotes codes of "appropriate" behavior and "upbringing." Such norms have also come to define the behavior for members of the Bengali middle classes.

16. See Maria Mies, *Patriarchy and Accumulation on a World Scale* (Atlantic Highlands, NJ: Zed Books, 1986), for a discussion of the ways in which ideologies of the "natural" mystify the construction of hierarchical gendered divisions.

17. See Adrienne Rich, "Compulsory Heterosexuality," in Ann Snitow et al., *Powers of Desire: The Politics of Sexuality* (New York: Monthly Review Press, 1983).

18. Ibid.

19. Radha Kumar, *The History of Doing: An Illustrated Account of Movements for Women's Rights and Feminism in India, 1800–1990* (New York: Verso Press, 1993).

Chapter 6

1. All names used in this chapter are pseudonyms.

2. For a different view, see Jane Humphries, "The Working Class Family: A Marxist Perspective," in J. Elshtain, ed., *The Family in Political Thought* (Amherst: University of Massachusetts Press, 1982).

3. These patterns are based on my interviews with women workers in the mill and are confirmed by the results of a statistical study of one of the largest mills in the industry (whose work force consisted of more than sixteen thousand workers), conducted by Professor Sisir Mitra in 1979. See Sisir Mitra, *The Jute Workers: A Micro Profile*, Centre for Regional and Science Studies in Development Alternatives (CRESIDA), unpublished study, Calcutta, 1981.

4. For a different view see Hartsock, "Foucault on Power: A Theory for Women?" in Linda J. Nicholson, ed., Feminism/Postmodernism (New York: Routledge, 1990).

5. For a study of the role of upper-class women in the reproduction of hierarchies of social class, see Patricia Caplan, *Class and Gender in India: Women and Their Organizations in a South Indian City* (London: Tavistock Publications, 1985).

6. The conversation took place in the personnel manager's office.

7. I am thus rejecting any notion of "false consciousness" or mystification in my use of the concept of hegemony. See Scott, *Domination and the Arts of Resistance.*

Chapter 7

1. See Rudolph and Rudolph, *In Pursuit of Lakshmi.*

2. There is now a rich literature on the gendered processes and effects of economic restructuring and transnational capital movements. For a review of the literature, see Aihwa Ong, "The Gender and Labor Politics of Postmodernity," *Annual Review of Anthropology* 20 (1990): 279–309.

Glossary

aadmi	man/person
aurat	lady
budli	temporary or casual worker
bara	big
bhadralok	upper class, upper caste, educated Bengalis
brahmin	highest caste group within the caste system
bustee	squatter settlement or tenement
chatkal	jute
coolie	unskilled worker
crore	ten million
dal	lentil
dalit	untouchable caste; literal meaning: "the oppressed"
desh	country
dukh	sorrow/suffering
durwan	watchman
garib	poor
gherao	form of protest whereby workers surround and take a manager hostage
goala	buffalo herder caste
golmaal	trouble
harijan	untouchable caste, term introduced by Mahatma Gandhi
izzat	honor
janana	female
jungli	uncivilized
kaam	work
kayasth	warrior caste
katcha	temporary/makeshift
khandani	family
lakh	one hundred thousand
lohar	metal worker caste

maghikal	women's work
maidan	field/open space
majboori	problems
malik	owner/boss
marwari	migrants from Rajasthan
mazdoor	worker
mistri	mechanic/metal worker
Mohammedan	Muslim
paisa	money
prasad	sweets
pucca	permanent
puja	worship
pujipati	capitalist
pyar	love
raj	kingdom, rule
rajput	upper (warrior) caste in North India
rasta	road; way
roko	stop
roti	bread
sahib	master; reference to someone of higher status
salaam	gesture of touching one's hand to the forehead in recognition of someone of higher authority
sangh	organization
shakti	feminine power
sindoor	red mark painted by women on their foreheads to denote married status
sirdar	worker serving as shop-floor line supervisor
sukh	happiness
tamasha	show, entertainment, drama
vandana	prayer

Bibliography

Books and Articles

Abu-Lughod, Lila. 1990. "The Romance of Resistance: Tracing Transformations of Power through Bedouin Women." *American Ethnologist* 17, 1 (February): 41–55.

———. 1991. "Writing against Culture." In Richard Fox ed., *Recapturing Anthropology: Working in the Present*. Santa Fe, NM: School of American Research Press.

Acker, Joan. 1988. "Class, Gender, and the Relations of Distribution." *Signs* 13, 3 (Spring): 463–497.

———. 1989. *Doing Comparable Worth: Gender, Class, and Pay Equity*. Philadelphia: Temple University Press.

Aggarwal, Arjun. 1968. *Gheraos and Industrial Relations*. Bombay: N. M. Tripathi Private Ltd.

Agnes, Flavia. 1992. "Protecting Women against Violence? Review of a Decade of Legislation, 1980–1989." *Economic and Political Weekly* (April 25): 19–33.

Agnihotri, Vidyadhar. 1970. *Industrial Relations in India*. New Delhi: Atma, Ram and Sons.

Alcoff, Linda. 1988. "Cultural Feminism vs. Post-Structuralism: The Identity Crisis in Feminist Theory." *Signs: Journal of Women in Culture and Society* 13, 2: 405–436.

Alexander, Jacqui. 1994. "Not Just (Any) Body Can Be a Citizen: The Politics of Law, Sexuality, and Postcoloniality in Trinidad and Tobago and the Bahamas." *Feminist Review* 48 (Autumn): 5–23.

Allison, Anne. 1994. *Nightwork: Sexuality, Pleasure, and Corporate Masculinity in a Tokyo Hostess Club*. Chicago: University of Chicago Press.

Almond, Gabriel, and Sydney Verba. 1963. *The Civic Culture: Political Attitudes and Democracy in Five Nations*. Princeton, NJ: Princeton University Press.

Anderson, Benedict. 1983. *Imagined Communities: Reflections on the Origin and Spread of Nationalism*. London: Verso.

Anderson, Elijah. 1990. *Streetwise: Race, Class, and Change in an Urban Community*. Chicago: University of Chicago Press.

Appadurai, Arjun. 1992. "Putting Hierarchy in Its Place." In George Marcus, ed. *Rereading Cultural Anthropology*. Durham, NC: Duke University Press.

Apthekar, Bettina. 1989. *Tapestries of Life: Women's Work, Women's Consciousness, and the Meaning of Daily Experience*. Amherst: University of Massachusetts Press.

Baer, Judith. 1978. *The Chains of Protection: The Judicial Response to Women's Labor Legislation.* Westport, CT: Greenwood Press.

Banerjee, Nirmala. 1985a. *Women in the Unorganised Sector.* New Delhi: Sangam Books.

———. 1985b. "Modernisation and Marginalisation," *Social Scientist* 13, 10–11 (October–November): 48–71.

———. 1989. "Trends in Women's Employment, 1971–81: Some Macro-level Observations." *Economic and Political Weekly* (April 29): ws10–ws22.

———. 1991. *Indian Women in a Changing Industrial Scenario.* New Delhi: Sage Publications.

Barrett, Michele. 1988. *Women's Oppression Today: The Marxist Feminist Encounter.* London: Verso Press.

———, and Roberta Hamilton, eds. 1986. *The Politics of Diversity.* London: Verso Press.

———, and Anne Phillips, eds. 1992. *Destabilizing Theory: Contemporary Feminist Debates.* Stanford, CA: Stanford University Press.

Basu, Amrita. 1992. *Two Faces of Protest: Contrasting Modes of Women's Activism in India.* Berkeley: University of California Press.

Basu, Timir. 1978. "Cheated by Delay." *Economic and Political Weekly* (July 8): 1094–1095.

———. 1979. "Jute Workers' Struggle." *Economic and Political Weekly* (February 3): 186–187.

———. 1984. "Jute Workers' Strike." *Economic and Political Weekly* (February 18): 277–279.

Behar, Ruth, and Deborah Gordon, eds. 1995. *Women Writing Culture.* Berkeley: University of California Press.

Bell, Catherine. 1992. *Ritual Theory, Ritual Practice.* New York: Oxford University Press.

Bendix, Reinhard. 1956. *Work and Authority in Industry: Ideologies of Management in the Course of Industrialization.* New York: John Wiley and Sons.

Berger, Iris. 1989. "Gender and Working Class History: South Africa in Comparative Perspective." *Journal of Women's History* 1, 2 (Fall): 117–133.

Beteille, Andre. 1991. "Race, Caste, and Gender." In Andre Beteille, *Society and Politics in India: Essays in a Comparative Perspective.* London School of Economics Monographs on Social Anthropology No. 63. Atlantic Highlands, NJ: Athlone Press.

Boris, Eileen, and Cynthia Daniels, eds. 1989. *Homework: Historical and Contemporary Perspectives on Paid Labor at Home.* Urbana: University of Illinois Press.

Bourdieu, Pierre. 1977. *Outline of a Theory of Practice.* Translated by Richard Nice. Cambridge: Cambridge University Press.

———. 1985. "The Social Space and the Genesis of Groups." *Theory and Society* 14: 723–744.

———. 1990. "Social Space and Symbolic Power." In Pierre Bourdieu, *In Other Words: Essays towards a Reflexive Sociology.* Stanford, CA: Stanford University Press.

Breman, Jan. 1985. *Of Peasants, Migrants, and Paupers: Rural Labour Circulation and Capitalist Production in West India.* New Delhi: Oxford University Press.

Brown, Wendy. 1995. *States of Injury: Power and Freedom in Late Modernity.* Princeton, NJ: Princeton University Press.

Burawoy, Michael. 1979. *Manufacturing Consent.* Chicago: University of Chicago Press.

Butler, Judith. 1990. *Gender Trouble: Feminism and the Subversion of Identity*. New York: Routledge.

———. 1993. *Bodies that Matter: On the Discursive Limits of "Sex."* New York: Routledge.

———, and Joan Scott, eds. 1992. *Feminists Theorize the Political*. New York: Routledge.

Calhoun, Craig. 1982. *The Question of Class Struggle: Social Foundations of Popular Radicalism during the Industrial Revolution*. Chicago: University of Chicago Press.

———, ed. 1992. *Habermas and the Public Sphere*. Cambridge, MA: MIT Press.

———, ed. 1994. *Social Theory and the Politics of Identity*. Cambridge, MA: Blackwell.

Caplan, Patricia. 1985. *Class and Gender in India: Women and Their Organizations in a South Indian City*. London: Tavistock Publications.

Chakrabarty, Dipesh. 1981. "Communal Riots and Labour: Bengal's Jute Mill-Hands in the 1890s," *Past and Present* 91: 140–169.

———. 1989. *Rethinking Working Class History: Bengal 1890–1940*. New Delhi: Oxford University Press.

———. 1990. "Of 'Communal' Workers and 'Secular' Historians." *Seminar* (October): 1–4.

———. 1991. "Open Space/Public Place: Garbage, Modernity and India." *South Asia* 14, 1: 15–32.

Chandavarkar, Rajnarayan. 1981. "Workers' Politics and the Mill Districts in Bombay Between the Wars." *Modern Asian Studies* 15, 3 (July): 603–648.

———. 1994. *The Origins of Industrial Capitalism in India: Business Strategies and the Working Classes in Bombay, 1900–1940*. Cambridge South Asian Studies Series. London: Cambridge University Press.

Chandra, Bipan. 1984. *Communalism in Modern India*. New Delhi: Vikas.

Chatterji, Partha. 1984. *Bengal, 1920–1940: The Land Question*. Calcutta: K. P. Bagchi Press.

———. 1986. *Nationalist Thought and the Colonial World: A Derivative Discourse*. London: Zed Books.

———. 1991. "A Response to Taylor's 'Modes of Civil Society.'" *Public Culture*: 119–134.

———. 1993. *The Nation and Its Fragments: Colonial and Postcolonial Histories*. Princeton, NJ: Princeton University Press.

Chatterji, Rakahari. 1980. *Unions, Politics and the State: A Study of Labour Politics*. New Delhi: South Asian Publishers.

Clifford, James, and George Marcus, eds. 1986. *Writing Culture: The Poetics and Politics of Ethnography*. Berkeley: University of California Press.

Collier, David. 1976. *Squatters and Oligarchs: Authoritarian Rule and Policy Change in Peru*. Baltimore, MD: Johns Hopkins University Press.

———. 1991. "The Comparative Method: Two Decades of Change." In Dankwart Rustow and Kenneth Erikson, eds., *Comparative Political Dynamics: Global Research Perspectives*. New York: Harper Collins.

Collins, Patricia Hill. 1990. *Black Feminist Thought: Knowledge, Consciousness and the Politics of Empowerment*. Boston: Unwyn Hyman.

Collins, Patricia Hill, Lionel Maldonado, Dana Takagi, Barrie Thorne, Lynn Weber, and Howard Winant. 1995. "Symposium on West and Fenstermaker's 'Doing Difference.'" *Gender and Society* 9, 4 (August): 491–513.

Comaroff, Jean. 1985. *Body of Power Spirit of Resistance: The Culture and History of a South African People.* Chicago: University of Chicago Press.

Comaroff, John, and Jean Comaroff. 1992. *Ethnography and the Historical Imagination.* Boulder, CO: Westview Press.

Connolly, William. 1992. *Identity/Difference: Democratic Negotiations of Political Paradox.* Ithaca, NY: Cornell University Press.

Cook, Alice, Val R. Lorwin, and Arlene Kaplan Daniels. 1992. *The Most Difficult Revolution: Women and Trade Unions.* Ithaca, NY: Cornell University Press.

Crenshaw, Kimberlé. 1992. "Whose Story Is It Anyway? Feminist and Anti-racist Appropriations of Anita Hill." In Toni Morrison, ed., *Race-ing Justice, En-gendering Power: Essays on Anita Hill, Clarence Thomas, and the Construction of Social Reality.* New York: Pantheon Books.

Das Gupta, Ranajit. 1987. "Migrant Workers, Rural Connections and Capitalism: The Calcutta Jute Industrial Labor Force, 1890s to 1940s." *Working Paper Series.* Calcutta: Indian Institute of Management.

———. 1990. "The Jute General Strike of 1929." *Working Paper Series.* Calcutta: Indian Institute of Management (September).

———. 1994. *Labour and Working Class in Eastern India: Studies in Colonial History.* Calcutta: K. P. Bagchi.

Davis, Angela. 1983. *Women, Race, and Class.* New York: Vintage Books.

de Certeau, Michel. 1984. *The Practice of Everyday Life.* Translated by Steven Rendall. Berkeley: University of California Press.

de Haan, Arjan. 1994a. *Unsettled Settlers: Migrant Workers and Industrial Capitalism in Calcutta.* Hilversum: Verloren Publishers.

———. 1994b. "Towards a Single Male Earner: The Decline of Child and Female Employment in an Indian Industry." *Economic and Social History in the Netherlands* 6: 145–167.

De Lauretis, Teresa. 1987. *Technologies of Gender: Essays on Theory, Film, and Fiction.* Bloomington: Indiana University Press.

Deere, Carmen Diana. 1990. *Household and Class Relations: Peasants and Landlords in Northern Peru.* Berkeley: University of California Press.

Dirks, Nicholas. 1992. "Ritual and Resistance: Subversion as Social Fact." In Gyan Prakash and Douglas Haynes, eds., *Contesting Power: Resistance and Everyday Social Relations in South Asia.* Berkeley: University of California Press.

———, Geoff Eley, and Sherry Ortner, eds. 1994. *Culture/Power/History: A Reader in Contemporary Social Theory.* Princeton, NJ: Princeton University Press.

Doeringer, Peter, and Michael Piore. 1971. *Internal Labor Markets and Manpower Analysis.* Lexington, MA: Lexington Books.

Edwards, Richard. 1979. *Contested Terrain: The Transformation of the Workplace in the Twentieth Century.* New York: Basic Books.

Elshtain, Jean, ed. 1982. *The Family in Political Thought.* Amherst: University of Massachusetts Press.

Evans, Sara, and Harry Boyte. 1986. *Free Spaces: The Sources of Democratic Change in America.* New York: Harper and Row.

Fantasia, Rick. 1988. *Cultures of Solidarity: Consciousness, Action, and Contemporary American Workers.* Berkeley: University of California Press.

Fernandes, Leela. 1994. "The Gendered Worlds of Class and Community in India: The Politics of Organized Labor in the West Bengal Jute Mills." PhD Dissertation, University of Chicago. Ann Arbor, MI: University Microfilms International.

———. 1994. "Contesting Class: Gender, Community, and the Politics of Labor in a Calcutta Jute Mill." *Bulletin of Concerned Asian Scholars* 26 (October–December): 29–43.

Fernandez-Kelly, Maria Patricia. 1983. *For We Are Sold I and My People: Women and Industry in Mexico's Frontier.* Albany: State University of New York Press.

Fields, Karen. 1985. *Revival and Rebellion in Colonial Central Africa.* Princeton, NJ: Princeton University Press.

Folbre, Nancy. 1994. *Who Pays for the Kids? Gender and the Structures of Constraint.* New York: Routledge.

Foucault, Michel. 1972. *The Archaeology of Knowledge and the Discourse on Language.* Translated by A. M. Sheridan Smith. New York: Pantheon Books.

———. 1978. *The History of Sexuality: An Introduction.* Vol. 1. Translated by Robert Hurley. New York: Vintage Books.

———. 1979. *Discipline and Punish: The Birth of the Prison.* Translated by Alan Sheridan. New York: Vintage Books.

———. 1980. *Power/Knowledge: Selected Interviews and Other Writings 1972–1977.* Translated and edited by Colin Gordon. New York: Pantheon Books.

Frankel, Francine, and M. S. A. Rao, eds. 1990. *Dominance and State Power in Modern India: Decline of a Social Order.* Vol. 2. New Delhi: Oxford University Press.

Fraser, Nancy. 1992. "Rethinking the Public Sphere: A Contribution to the Critique of Actually Existing Democracy." In Craig Calhoun, ed., *Habermas and the Public Sphere.* Cambridge, MA: MIT Press.

Freitag, Sandria. 1989. *Collective Action and Community: Public Arenas and the Emergence of Communalism in North India.* Berkeley: University of California Press.

Gadgil, D. R. 1971. *The Industrial Evolution of India in Recent Times, 1860–1939.* Bombay: Oxford University Press.

Game, Ann, and Rosemary Pringle. 1983. *Gender at Work.* Sydney: Allen and Unwin.

Geertz, Clifford. 1973. *The Interpretation of Cultures.* New York: Basic Books.

Gerth, H. H., and C. Wright Mills, eds. 1958. *From Max Weber: Essays in Sociology.* New York: Galaxy.

Giddens, Anthony. 1981. *A Contemporary Critique of Historical Materialism. Vol. 1, Power, Property and the State.* London: Macmillan.

———, and David Held, eds. 1982. *Classes, Power, and Conflict.* Berkeley: University of California Press.

Giddings, Paula. 1984. *When and Where I Enter . . . The Impact of Black Women on Race and Sex in America.* New York: William Morrow.

Gilroy, Paul. 1987. *There Ain't No Black in the Union Jack: The Cultural Politics of Race and Nation.* London: Hutchison.

Glenn, Evelyn Nakano. 1986. *Issei, Nissei, and Warbride: Three Generations of Japanese American Women in Domestic Service.* Philadelphia, PA: Temple University Press.

———. 1992. "From Servitude to Service Work: Historical Continuities in the Racial Division of Paid Reproductive Labor." *Signs* 18, 1 (Autumn): 1–43.

Gluckman, Max. 1965. *Custom and Conflict in Africa.* Oxford: Basil Blackwell.

Gordon, David, Richard Edwards, and Michael Reich. 1982. *Segmented Work, Divided Workers: The Historical Transformation of Labor in the United States.* Cambridge: Cambridge University Press.

Goswami, Omkar. 1987. "Multiple Images: The Jute Mill Strikes of 1929 and 1937 Seen through Others' Eyes." *Modern Asian Studies* 21, 3: 547–583.

Gothoskar, Sujata, ed. 1992. *Struggles of Women at Work.* New Delhi: Vikas Publishing House.

Gramsci, Antonio. 1971. *Selections from the Prison Notebooks*. Translated and edited by Quintin Hoare and G. N. Smith. New York: International Publishers.

Guha, Ranajit. 1983. *Elementary Aspects of Peasant Insurgency in Colonial India*. New Delhi: Oxford University Press.

Guha, Ranajit, ed. 1984–1989. *Subaltern Studies*, volumes 1–6. Oxford: Oxford University Press.

Gupta, Indrajit. 1953. *Capital and Labour in the Jute Industry*. Bombay: Trade Union Publication Series, All-India Trade Union Congress.

Habermas, Jurgen. 1992. *The Structural Transformation of the Public Sphere: An Inquiry into a Category of Bourgeois Society*. Translated by Thomas Burger. Cambridge, MA: MIT Press.

Hall, Jacquelyn Dowd. 1983. "The Mind That Burns in Each Body." In Ann Snitow, Christine Stansell, and Sharon Thompson, eds., *Powers of Desire: The Politics of Sexuality*. New York: Monthly Review Press.

———, James Leloudis, Robert Korstad, Mary Murphy, Lu Ann Jones, and Christopher Daly. 1987. *Like a Family: The Making of a Southern Cotton Mill World*. Chapel Hill: University of North Carolina Press.

Hall, Stuart. 1990. "Cultural Identity and Diaspora." In Jonathan Rutherford, ed., *Identity: Community, Culture, Difference*. London: Lawrence and Wishart.

———. 1992a. "What Is This 'Black' in Black Popular Culture?" In Gina Dent, ed., *Black Popular Culture*. Seattle: Bay Press.

———. 1992b. "New Ethnicities." In James Donald and Ali Rattansi, eds., *"Race," Culture, and Difference*. London: Sage Publications.

Haraway, Donna. 1988. "Situated Knowledges: The Science Question in Feminism and the Privilege of Partial Perspective." *Feminist Studies* 14 (Fall): 575–596.

Harding, Sandra, ed. 1987. *Feminism and Methodology*. Bloomington: Indiana University Press.

Hartmann, Heidi. 1979. "Capitalism, Patriarchy and Job Segregation by Sex." In Zillah Eisenstein, ed., *Capitalist Patriarchy and the Case for Socialist Feminism*. New York: Monthly Review Press.

———. 1981. "The Family as the Locus of Gender, Class, and Political Struggle: The Example of Housework." *Signs* 6, 31: 366–394.

Hartsock, Nancy. 1983. *Money, Sex, and Power*. New York: Longman.

———. 1990. "Foucault on Power: A Theory for Women?" In Linda J. Nicholson, ed., *Feminism/Postmodernism*. New York: Routledge.

Harvey, David. 1990. *The Condition of Postmodernity*. Cambridge, MA: Blackwell.

Hattam, Victoria. 1993. *Labor Visions and State Power: The Origins of Business Unionism in the United States*. Princeton, NJ: Princeton University Press.

Hebdige, Dick. 1979. *Subculture: The Meaning of Style*. New York: Methuen.

Hennessy, Rosemary. 1994. *Materialist Feminism and the Politics of Discourse*. New York: Routledge.

Hobsbawm, Eric. 1984. *Worlds of Labour: Further Studies in the History of Labour*. London: Weidenfield and Nicolson.

———, and Terence Ranger, eds. 1983. *The Invention of Tradition*. Cambridge: Cambridge University Press.

hooks, bell. 1984. *Feminist Theory from Margin to Center*. Boston: South End Press.

Jayawardena, Kumari, and Govind Kelkar. 1989. "The Left and Feminism." *Economic and Political Weekly* (September 23): 2123–2126.

Jhabvala, Renana. 1985. "From the Mill to the Streets: A Study of Retrenchment of Women from Ahmedabad Textile Mills." *Manushi* 5, 2: 21–41.

Joshi, Chitra. 1985. "Bonds of Community, Ties of Religion: Kanpur Textile Workers in the Early Twentieth Century." *Indian Economic and Social History Review* 22, 3: 251–280.

Kapadia, Karin. 1995. *Siva and Her Sisters: Gender, Caste and Class in Rural South India.* Boulder, CO: Westview.

Karnik, V. B. 1982. *Trade Union Movement and Industrial Relations.* Bombay: Somaiya Publications.

Karpat, Kemal. 1976. *The Gecekondu: Rural Migration and Urbanization.* Cambridge: Cambridge University Press.

Katznelson, Ira. 1981. *City Trenches: Urban Politics and the Patterning of Class in the United States.* New York: Pantheon Books.

———. 1992. *Marxism and the City.* Oxford: Oxford University Press.

———, and Aristide Zolberg. 1986. *Working-Class Formation: Nineteenth-Century Patterns in Western Europe and the United States.* Princeton, NJ: Princeton University Press.

Kelly, John. 1991. *A Politics of Virtue: Hinduism, Sexuality, and Countercolonial Discourse in Fiji.* Chicago: University of Chicago Press.

Kessler-Harris, Alice. 1976. "Women, Work, and the Social Order." In Berenice A. Carroll, ed., *Liberating Women's History: Theoretical and Critical Essays.* Urbana: University of Illinois Press.

———. 1990. *A Woman's Wage: Historical Meanings and Social Consequences.* Lexington, KY: University of Kentucky Press, 1990.

———. 1993. "Treating the Male as 'Other.' " *Labor History* 34 (Spring–Summer): 190–204.

Kohli, Atul. 1987. *The State and Poverty in India: The Politics of Reform.* Cambridge: Cambridge University Press.

Kondo, Dorinne. 1990. *Crafting Selves: Power, Gender, and Discourses of Identity in a Japanese Workplace.* Chicago: University of Chicago Press.

Krishnamurty, J., ed. 1989. *Women in Colonial India.* New Delhi: Oxford University Press.

Kuhn, Annette, and Ann Marie Wolpe. 1978. *Feminism and Materialism: Women and Modes of Production.* London: Routledge and Paul.

Kumar, Nita. 1988. *The Artisans of Banaras: Popular Culture and Identity, 1880–1986.* Princeton, NJ: Princeton University Press.

Kumar, Radha. 1993. *The History of Doing: An Illustrated Account of Movements for Women's Rights and Feminism in India, 1800–1990.* New York: Verso Press.

Laitin, David. 1986. *Hegemony and Culture: Politics and Religious Change among the Yoruba.* Chicago: University of Chicago Press.

Lamphere, Louise. 1987. *From Working Mothers to Working Daughters: Immigrant Women in a New England Industrial Community.* Ithaca, NY: Cornell University Press.

———. 1992. *Structuring Diversity: Ethnographic Perspectives on the New Immigration.* Chicago: University of Chicago Press.

Leonardo, Micaela di, ed. 1991. *Gender at the Crossroads of Knowledge: Feminist Anthropology in the Postmodern Era.* Berkeley: University of California Press.

Lukacs, Georg. 1971. *History and Class Consciousness: Studies in Marxist Dialectics.* Translated by Rodney Livingstone. Cambridge, MA: MIT Press.

Mallick, Ross. 1993. *Development Policy of a Communist Government: West Bengal since 1977.* Cambridge South Asian Studies. New Delhi: Cambridge University Press.

————. 1994. *Indian Communism: Opposition, Collaboration and Institutionalization.* New Delhi: Oxford University Press.

Mamkoottam, Kuriakose. 1982. *Trade Unionism Myth and Reality: Unionism in the Tata Iron and Steel Company.* New Delhi: Oxford University Press.

————. 1984. "Trade Unions: The Sociological Dilemma." *Social Action* 34 (January–March): 36–46.

Marx, Karl. 1987. "The Eighteenth Brumaire." In David McLellan, ed., *Karl Marx: Selected Writings.* Oxford: Oxford University Press.

————. 1963 [1850]. *Capital.* New York: Vintage Books.

McClintock, Anne. 1995. *Imperial Leather: Race, Gender, and Sexuality in the Colonial Contest.* New York: Routledge.

Menon, Nivedita. 1992. "Women in Trade Unions: A Study of AITUC, INTUC and CITU." In Sujata Gothoskar, ed., *Struggles of Women at Work.* New Delhi: Vikas Publishing House.

Mies, Maria. 1986. *Patriarchy and Accumulation on a World Scale.* Atlantic Highlands, NJ: Zed Books.

Milkman, Ruth. 1987. *Gender at Work: The Dynamics of Job Segregation by Sex during World War Two.* Urbana: University of Illinois Press.

Minh-ha, Trinh T. 1989. *Woman, Native, Other.* Bloomington: Indiana University Press.

Mitchell, Timothy. 1988. *Colonizing Egypt.* Berkeley: University of California Press.

Mitra, Sisir. 1981. *The Jute Workers: A Microprofile.* Center for Regional and Science Studies in Development Alternatives (CRESIDA), unpublished study, Calcutta.

————. 1985. "The Jute Workers: A Microprofile." *Transactions* 2, 1–2: 123–157.

Mohanty, Chandra. 1991. "Under Western Eyes." In Ann Russo, Chandra Mohanty, and Lourdes Torres, eds., *Third World Women and the Politics of Feminism.* Bloomington: Indiana University Press.

Molund, Stefan. 1988. *First We Are People: The Koris of Kanpur between Caste and Class.* Stockholm: Stockholm Studies in Social Anthropology.

Morrison, Toni, ed. 1992. *Race-ing Justice, En-gendering Power: Essays on Anita Hill, Clarence Thomas, and the Construction of Social Reality.* New York: Pantheon Books.

Narayan, Kirin. 1993. "How Native Is a Native Anthropologist?" *American Anthropologist* 95: 671–686.

Nelson, Cary, and Lawrence Grosberg, eds. 1988. *Marxism and the Interpretation of Culture.* Urbana: University of Illinois Press.

Ong, Aihwa. 1988. *Spirits of Resistance and Capitalist Discipline: Factory Women in Malaysia.* Albany: State University of New York Press.

————. 1990. "The Gender and Labor Politics of Postmodernity." *Annual Review of Anthropology* 20: 279–309.

Pandey, Gyanendra. 1990. *The Construction of Communalism in Colonial North India.* New Delhi: Oxford University Press.

Parker, Andrew, Mary Russo, Doris Sommer, and Patricia Yaeger, eds. 1992. *Nationalisms and Sexualities.* New York: Routledge.

Pateman, Carole. 1989. *The Disorder of Women: Democracy, Feminism and Political Theory.* Stanford, CA: Stanford University Press.

Peiss, Kathy. 1986. *Cheap Amusements: Working Women and Leisure in Turn-of-the-Century New York.* Philadelphia, PA: Temple University Press.

Prakash, Gyan. 1990. *Bonded Histories: Genealogies of Labor Servitude in Colonial*

India. Cambridge South Asian Studies, no. 44. New York: Cambridge University Press.

———. 1990. "Writing Post-Orientalist Histories of the Third World: Perspectives from Indian Historiographies." *Comparative Studies in Society and History* 32, 2 (April): 383–408.

———, and Douglas Haynes, eds. 1992. *Contesting Power: Resistance and Everyday Social Relations in South Asia.* Berkeley: University of California Press.

Pye, Lucien, and Sydney Verba. 1965. *Political Culture and Political Development.* Princeton, NJ: Princeton University Press.

Raj, Maithrayi Krishna. 1987. "Women and Industrial Working Class Movement." *Mainstream* 25 (March 7): 24–26.

Rajan, Rajeswari Sunder. 1993. *Real and Imagined Women: Gender, Culture and Postmodernism.* New York: Routledge.

Ramaswamy, E. A. 1984. *Power and Justice: The State in Industrial Relations.* New Delhi: Oxford University Press.

Ramaswamy, Uma. 1983. *Work, Union, Community: Industrial Man in South India.* New Delhi: Oxford University Press.

Ranadive, Vimal. 1976. *Women Workers of India.* Calcutta: National Book Agency.

Rao, Raman. 1965. *Essays on Indian Labour.* Bombay: Popular Prakashan.

Roediger, David. 1991. *The Wages of Whiteness: Race and the Making of the American Working Class.* New York: Verso.

Rose, Kalima. 1992. *Where Women Are Leaders: The SEWA Movement in India.* Atlantic Highlands, NJ: Zed Books.

Roy, Ajit. 1989. "West Bengal: CPI(M)–CPI Relations, The Basic Issues." *Economic and Political Weekly* (May): 1081–1082.

Roy, Biren. 1985. "CITU—A Critical Review." *Marxist Review* 207–214.

———. 1992a. "Left Front Lukewarm to Workers' Cooperatives." *Economic and Political Weekly* (June 27): 1303–1304.

———. 1992b. "Jute Mill Owners' Offensive against Workers." *Economic and Political Weekly* (September 5): 1893–1894.

Rudolph, Lloyd, and Susanne Rudolph. 1967. *The Modernity of Tradition: Political Development in India.* Chicago: University of Chicago Press.

———. 1987. *In Pursuit of Lakshmi: The Political Economy of the Indian State.* Chicago: University of Chicago Press.

Sacks, Karen. 1988. *Caring by the Hour: Women, Work, and Organizing at Duke Medical Center.* Urbana: University of Illinois Press.

———. 1990. "Towards a Unified Theory of Race, Class, and Gender." *American Ethnologist* 17: 534–550.

Sacks, Karen, and Dorothy Remy, eds. 1984. *My Troubles Are Going to Have Trouble with Me: Everyday Trials and Triumphs of Women Workers.* New Brunswick, NJ: Rutgers University Press.

Said, Edward. 1978. *Orientalism.* New York: Pantheon Books.

Sangari, Kum kum, and Sudesh Vaid, eds. 1989. *Recasting Women: Essays in Colonial History.* New Delhi: Kali for Women Press.

Sanjek, Roger, ed. 1990. *Fieldnotes: The Makings of Anthropology.* Ithaca, NY: Cornell University Press.

Sarkar, Kamal. 1977. "Toiling for the Jute Barons." *Social Scientist* 5, 12 (July): 62–75.

Sarkar, Tanika, and Urvashi Butalia, eds. 1995. *Women and the Hindu Right: A Collection of Essays.* New Delhi: Kali for Women Press.

Schmitter, Philippe. 1974. "Still the Century of Corporatism?" *Review of Politics* 36, 1 (January): 85–131.

Scott, James. 1985. *Weapons of the Weak: Everyday Forms of Peasant Resistance.* New Haven, CT: Yale University Press.

———. 1990. *Domination and the Arts of Resistance: Hidden Transcripts.* New Haven, CT: Yale University Press.

Scott, Joan. 1988. *Gender and the Politics of History.* New York: Columbia University Press.

———. 1992. "Experience." In Judith Butler and Joan Scott, eds., *Feminists Theorize the Political.* New York: Routledge.

Sen, Samita. 1992. "Women Workers in the Bengal Jute Industry, 1890–1940: Migration, Motherhood and Militancy." PhD thesis, University of Cambridge.

Sen, Sunil. 1985. *Women and Popular Movements in West Bengal: From the Gandhi Era to the Present Day.* Calcutta: K. P. Bagchi.

Sen, Ilina. 1989. "Feminists, Women's Movement and the Working Class." *Economic and Political Weekly* (July 22): 1639–1641.

Sengupta, Padmini. 1965. *Women Workers of India.* Bombay: Asia Publishing House.

Sewell, William. 1980. *Work and Revolution in France: The Language of Labor from the Old Regime to 1848.* Cambridge: Cambridge University Press.

———. 1992. "A Theory of Structure: Duality, Agency, and Transformation." *American Journal of Sociology* 98, 1 (July): 1–29.

Sheth, N. R. 1979. "The Current Scene of Industrial Relations: Some Reflections." *Social Action* 29 (April–June): 185–197.

———. 1984. "Sociology for Industrial Relations," *Social Action* 34 (January–March): 1–19.

Simeon, Dilip. 1995. *The Politics of Labour under Late Colonialism: Workers, Unions, and the State in Chota Nagpur 1928–1939.* New Delhi: Manohar Press.

Sinha, G. P., and P. R. N. Sinha. 1977. *Industrial Relations and Labour Legislation.* New Delhi: Oxford and IBH Publishing Company.

Smith, Adam. 1937 [1776]. *The Wealth of Nations.* New York: Modern Library.

Smith, Dorothy. 1987. *The Everyday World as Problematic.* Boston: Northeastern University Press.

Snitow, Ann, Christine Stansell, and Sharon Thompson, eds. 1983. *Powers of Desire: The Politics of Sexuality.* New York: Monthly Review Press.

Sombart, Werner. 1976. *Why Is There No Socialism in the United States?* Translated by Patricia M. Hocking and C. T. Husbands. New York: M. E. Sharpe.

Somers, Margaret. 1994. "Where Is Sociology after the Historic Turn? Knowledge Cultures and Historical Epistemologies." In Terence J. McDonald, ed., *The Historic Turn in the Human Sciences.* Ann Arbor: University of Michigan Press.

———, and Gloria Gibson. 1994. "Reclaiming the Epistemological 'Other': Narrative and the Social Constitution of Identity." In Craig Calhoun, ed., *Social Theory and the Politics of Identity.* Cambridge, MA: Blackwell Press.

Spivak, Gayatri Chakravorty. 1988. *In Other Worlds: Essays in Cultural Politics.* New York: Routledge.

Stacey, Judith. 1988. "Can There Be a Feminist Ethnography?" *Women's Studies International Forum* 11, 1: 21–27.

Stansell, Christine. 1986. *City of Women: Sex and Class in New York, 1789–1860.* New York: Random House.

Stark, David. 1982. "Class Struggle and the Transformation of the Labour Process: A Relational Approach." In Anthony Giddens and David Held, eds., *Classes, Power, and Conflict.* Berkeley: University of California Press.

Stedman Jones, Gareth. 1983. *Languages of Class: Studies in English Working Class History, 1832–1982.* Cambridge: Cambridge University Press.

Stepan, Nancy Leys. 1993. "Race and Gender: The Role of Analogy in Science." In Sandra Harding, ed., *The Racial Economy of Science: Toward a Democratic Future.* Bloomington: Indiana University Press.

Tanden, Rajesh. 1984. "A Theory of Trade Union Organisation in India." *Social Action* 34 (January–March): 20–35.

Taussig, Michael. 1980. *The Devil and Commodity Fetishism in South America.* Chapel Hill: University of North Carolina Press.

Taylor, Charles. 1992. *Multiculturalism and the Politics of Recognition.* Princeton, NJ: Princeton University Press.

Thapar, Romila. 1989. "Imagined Religious Communities?" *Modern Asian Studies* 23 (May): 209–231.

Thengadi, D. B. 1959. *Why Bharatiya Mazdoor Sangh?* Bharatiya Mazdoor Sangh Publications.

Thomas, K. I. 1988. *Labour in Indian Planning.* New Delhi: National Labour Institute.

Thompson, Edward P. 1966. *The Making of the English Working Class.* New York: Vintage Books.

———. 1978. "Class Struggle without Class?" *Social History* 3, 2 (May): 133–178.

———. 1982. "Time, Work Discipline, and Industrial Capitalism." In Anthony Giddens and David Held, eds., *Classes, Power, and Conflict.* Berkeley: University of California Press.

Tilly, Louise, and Joan Scott. 1978. *Women, Work, and Family.* New York: Holt, Rinehart, and Winston.

Tonnies, Ferdinand. 1988. *Gemeinschaft und Gesellschaft.* New Brunswick, NJ: Transaction Books.

Touraine, Alain, Michel Wieviorka, and Francois Dubet. 1984. *The Workers' Movement.* Translated by Ian Patterson. Cambridge: Cambridge University Press.

Touraine, Alain. 1986. "Unionism as a Social Movement." In Martin Seymour Lipset, ed. *Unions in Transition: Entering the Second Century.* San Francisco: Institute for Contemporary Studies Press.

Tucker, Robert, ed. 1978. *The Marx-Engels Reader.* 2d ed. New York: Norton.

Tulpule, Bagaram. 1979. "Trends in Industrial Relations." *Social Action* 29 (January–March): 14–24.

Upadhyay, Shashi Bhushan. 1989. "Communalism and Working Class Riot of 1893 in Bombay City." *Economic and Political Weekly* (July 29): PE69–PE75.

Vaid, K. N. *Gheraos and Labour Unrest in West Bengal.* 1972. New Delhi: Center for Industrial Relations and Human Resources.

van der Veer, Peter. 1994. *Religious Nationalism: Hindus and Muslims in India.* Berkeley: University of California Press.

Viswanathan, Aparna. 1992. "Sex Discrimination in Employment: No Legal Protection." *Economic and Political Weekly* (May 2): 935–936.

Visweswaran, Kamala. 1994. *Fictions of Feminist Ethnography.* Minneapolis: University of Minnesota Press.

Weber, Max. *Economy and Society.* Vol. 2. 1979. Edited by Guenther Roth and Claus Wittich. Berkeley: University of California Press.

West, Candace, and Sarah Fenstermaker. 1995. "Doing Difference." *Gender and Society* 9, 1 (February): 8–37.

Wilentz, Sean. 1984. "Against Exceptionalism: Class Consciousness and the Labour Movement, 1790–1928." *International Labor and Working Class History* 26 (Fall): 1–24.

Williams, Patricia. 1991. *The Alchemy of Race and Rights.* Cambridge, MA: Harvard University Press.

Willis, Paul. 1977. *Learning to Labour: How Working Class Kids Get Working Class Jobs.* Farnborough, England: Saxon House.

Wolf, Diane. 1992. *Factory Daughters: Gender, Household Dynamics, and Rural Industrialization in Java.* Berkeley: University of California Press.

———, ed. 1994. *Feminist Dilemmas in Fieldwork.* Boulder, CO: Westview.

Zavella, Patricia. 1987. *Women's Work and Chicano Families: Cannery Workers of the Santa Clara Valley.* Ithaca, NY: Cornell University Press.

Government Documents

Government of India. *Seventh Industrial Tribune.* West Bengal, August 6, 1983.

———. Labour Bureau. *Indian Labour Yearbook.* Simla, 1950–1987.

———. Tripartite Committee. *Industrial Committee on Jute: Report on Women Workers.* 1959.

———. *Women in Industry.* 1975.

———. Department of Textiles. *Report of the Task Force on Jute Textiles.* 1981.

———. Labour Bureau. *Socioeconomic Conditions of Women Workers in Textiles, Khandsari and Sugar Products Industries.* Simla, 1984.

———. Ministry of Social and Women's Welfare. *Women in India.* April 1985.

———. Labour Bureau. Statistical Profile on Women Labour, Third Issue, Chandigarh, 1990.

West Bengal Government, Department of Labour. *Labour in West Bengal.* 1970–1990.

———. Labour Directorate. *A Report on Employment Attendance, Absenteeism and Earnings in Jute Textile Industry,* 1970.

Reports of Organizations

Bengal Chatkal Mazdoor Union, Annual Conference General Secretary's Reports.

Centre for Indian Trade Unions, *The Working Class.*

Indian Jute Mills Association, Annual Reports, 1947–1992.

Indian Jute Mills Association, Weekly Labour Reports, Internal Circulars, 1950–1990.

Indian Trade Union Congress, *Constitution.*

Newspapers

Economic Times, Calcutta, India.

Financial Express, Calcutta, India.

Frontier, Calcutta, India.

Statesman, Calcutta, India.

Index